OSTEO SCHOOL PROFILES

Osteopathic Medical School Admissions Data and Analysis

Rachel A. Winston, Ph.D.

Lizard Publishing is not sponsored by any college. While data was derived by school, state, or nationally published sources, some statistics may be out of date as published sources vary widely based upon the date of submission and currency of numbers. Attempts were made to obtain the best information during the writing of this book from American Osteopathic Association, American Association of Colleges of Osteopathic Medicine, Commission on Osteopathic College Accreditation, Student Osteopathic Medical Association, American Association of Colleges of Osteopathic Medicine Application Service, The Student Doctor Network, NCES, U.S. Census Bureau, U.S. Department of Education, Common Data Set, College Board, U.S. News & World Report, college, and organizational sites. Descriptions of colleges are a compilation of college website information as well as student, faculty, and staff interviews with individuals and often from unique experiences and impressions. Attempts were made to triangulate multiple points of light. If you would like to share program information, data, or an impression of a specific college, please write to Lizard Publishing at the address below or at the e-mail address: *info@ mylizard.org.*

ISBN 978-1946432445 (hardback); 978-1946432421 (paperback); 978-1946432438 (e-book)

LCCN: 2021923443

Lizard Publishing* 7700 Irvine Center Drive, Suite 800, Irvine, CA 92618 *www.lizard-publishing.com*

Lizard Publishing creates, designs, produces, and distributes books and resources to provide academic, admissions, and career information. Our mental process is fueled by three tenets:

- Ignite the hunger to learn and the passion to make a difference
- Illuminate the expanse of knowledge by sharing cutting edge thinking
- Innovate to create a world that makes the transition from dreams to reality

We work with academic leaders who transform the educational landscape to publish relevant content and advise students of their educational and professional options, with the aim of developing 21st-century learners and leaders. We also work with students to publish their books and present widely diverse ideas to the college/graduate school-bound community. With headquarters in Irvine, California, Lizard Publishing works virtually with authors to edit, publish, and distribute both hard copy and paperback books.

This book was published in the U.S.A. Lizard Publishing is a premium quality provider of educational reference, career guidance, and motivational publications/merchandise for global learners, educators, and stakeholders in education.

Book design by Michelle Tahan *www.michelletahan.com*

Book formatting by Obinna Chinemerem Ozuo

Book website: *www.medschoolexpert.com*

LIZARD PUBLISHING

This book is dedicated to students who seek to become patient-centered physicians and are passionately devoted to their pursuit of compassionate, ethical, and service-oriented medicine. This book was inspired by Zenobia Miro, Harrison White, Ida Ramezani, Nadia Aluzri, and Sean Wong.

Working at hospitals and conducting research in neurobiochemistry at Upstate Medical School and genetics at Syracuse University, I was surrounded by pre-med hopeful students eagerly pursuing their medical career. Subsequently, I spent most of my life helping students gain admission to medical school and working with authors who wrote books on medical school admission and MCAT prep.

Surrounded by students and teaching college for thirty-five years provided a keen insight into the student pursuit. I have also completed more than a dozen degrees and certificates and know the challenge and rigor of meshing rigorous coursework with a full complement of activities. Supporting students in their quest to attend medical school further inspired me to continuously adapt to changes in medical school admissions as well as investigate the broader picture of cutting-edge medical research.

ACKNOWLEDGMENTS

There is never enough room to acknowledge every person. Many people contributed to my perspective about medicine, assisted in the development of my knowledge base, or taught me indelible lessons. In a lifetime of experiences working with students, I am wiser and more worldly.

I gratefully acknowledge Michelle Tahan, Jasmine Jhunjhnuwala, and E. Liz Kim, as well as my family, friends, colleagues, and professors. It is with profound gratitude that I mention and acknowledge the many physicians I have known.

As a faculty member in the UCLA College Counseling Certificate Program, I met numerous dedicated counselors who spend their life serving and supporting students. Meaningful contributions to the book have been made indirectly by admissions representatives, college counselors, faculty members who took a special interest in this book's success.

I would also like to thank the thousands of students I have taught, counseled, or supported in my nearly four decades of service.

Isaac Newton once said, "If I see so far, it is because I stand on the shoulders of giants."

"If I see so far, it is because I stand on the shoulders of giants."
— Isaac Newton

A few of those giants whose broad shoulders lifted me higher and helped teach invaluable lessons include: David Waugh, John E. Roueche, Zenobia Miro, Harrison White, Sandra Savage, Arpi Kapuria, Monette Tarvaran, Sophia Tazerouni, Shauna Bahri, Sean Wong, Jennifer Pearson, Vianney Tames, Matthew Robledo, Lynne Foose, Cliff Sobel, Candice Katayama, Batzi Heger, Ray Adler, and Dave Sanford.

Finally, there would be no book on osteopathic medical school and no career college admissions counseling, without the support of Robert Helmer whose tireless efforts support me every single day.

ABOUT THE AUTHOR

Dr. Rachel A. Winston is a tireless student advocate. She has served the educational community as a university professor, college advisor, statistician, researcher, author, cryptanalyst, motivational speaker, publishing executive, and lifelong student. As one of the leading experts in college counseling and an award-winning faculty member, Dr. Winston has spent her lifetime learning, teaching, mentoring, and coaching students. Much of her counseling practice is focused on admissions to medical, dental, vet, and engineering schools.

She started college at thirteen and graduated from college programs in such widely ranging disciplines as chemistry, mathematics, computers, liberal arts, international relations, negotiation, conflict resolution, peacebuilding, business administration, higher education leadership, interpreting, college counseling, and publishing. Throughout her education, she attended and graduated from Harvard, University of Chicago, GWU, UCLA, Syracuse, CSUF, CSUDH, Pepperdine, Claremont Graduate University, and Gallaudet University.

Her position working in Washington, D.C. on Capitol Hill and with the White House in the 1980s took her to approximately a hundred universities training campaign managers at colleges from Colorado to California, thoroughly dotting the western states. Later, she led college tours with students and their families on road trips throughout the United States. She has taught or counseled thousands of students over her career and speaks at conferences and academic programs throughout the world.

As a professor and avid writer for numerous publications, she won the 2012 McFarland Literary Achievement Award, Bletchley Park Cryptanalyst Award, and numerous other awards, including Faculty Member of the Year, Leadership Tomorrow Leader of the Year, and college service and leadership awards. While studying Human Capital at Claremont Graduate University, she was a scholarship recipient at the Drucker School of Management. She was also elected to the statewide Board of Governors for the Faculty Association for California Community Colleges, where she served on their executive committee.

She served as a faculty member for the UCLA College Counselor Certificate Program, the Director of Mathematics at Brandman University, and Embry Riddle Aeronautical University, Chapman University, Cal State Fullerton, and a handful of California Community Colleges, including Cerro Coso College where she also served as the Academic Senate President and retired in 2016. Over her career, she taught mathematics online, on television, live interactive satellite, telecourses, and in large and small lecture halls.

AUTHORS' NOTE

You are reading this book because you are considering admission to osteopathic medical school. Whatever route you took to get to this point, you are in the right place. Right now, you need to gather information to make informed decisions.

While many people offer advice, suggestions differ. Friends will tell you the 'right' way or the way their neighbor was accepted. Graciously accept this anecdotal information while you commit to learning more. This opportunity to pursue medicine is your future.

Dig deeper to consider both expert and current information from counselors who have worked with hundreds of students. Changes in programs, curricula, requirements, and links happen each year.

Double-check each program's specifics yourself. This guide is current as of September 2021, with each school's profile information. However, since researching this book, changes may have taken place. There are other osteopathic medical school books written by talented and experienced counselors. We admire and cheer on their efforts.

> *"We are what we think. All that we are arises with our thoughts. With our thoughts, we make the world."*
> — *Buddha*

This set of profiles and lists is different in that it also provides and unique tidbits. We hope you find this information valuable. Your job is to begin early by assembling information for the schools you are considering. Create a road map and set yourself on a clear path.

If you see an error in this book or even a suggestion for a future edition, please write to Rachel Winston at collegeguide@yahoo.com. We will fix the entry with the next printed version. All of that said, this book was written for you in mind.

There is a wealth of information on the Internet with free downloads, FAQs, testimonials, and offers to help you with your applications. Some of these advisors are knowledgeable and could help you. Students and parents hunt around the web, searching for a tremendous number of hours to seek the information they need.

This book of profiles was designed to make your search easier. For now, though, we will assume that you are reasonably confident that you want to attend medical school and are exploring this avenue as a possible way to take advantage of a program that will get you on your way toward your goal.

We assume that you are a highly academic candidate who is willing to work very hard. You may be fascinated with the human body, human physiology, or holistic health. Selflessly serving others is virtually a prerequisite for medical programs. This book will help you get to your goal. Applying to osteopathic medical schools and writing essays for each program will require a persistent effort. Research the schools that are the best fit for your future goals.

While you might believe that osteopathic medical school programs are relatively similar, each program's nuances make them very different. These small differences may seem confusing. My goal with this book is to demystify this information and your application process.

CONTENTS

CHAPTER 1

THE PURSUIT OF OSTEOPATHIC MEDICINE

Few students know they want to pursue osteopathic medical school early in life. However, as they gain clinical experiences in college, they become more aware of the opportunities in osteopathic medicine and the need for primary care physicians. Recently, though, more DO graduates are also gaining acceptance into specialty residencies as well.

According to the American Osteopathic Association, in 2021, "the number of osteopathic physicians in the U.S. climbed to nearly 135,000," representing an 80% increase over the past ten years. Surprisingly, one in every four physicians graduating from medical school is a DO. With the tremendous physician shortage, this increase in osteopathic medical doctors will help alleviate healthcare access in many communities.

In the past, there was a stigma against DOs. Any hesitancy with respect to DO programs is slowly disappearing.

First, DOs and MDs are both physicians with the ability to practice in clinical settings like hospitals and healthcare centers. Quite possibly, you have been to a medical facility where the attending physician was a DO. Second, osteopathic medical school is not easier. DO programs frequently spend more time in classes and clinical than most medical schools due to the additional training. Third, the number of osteopathic medical schools is growing due to the need for training and medical care in rural communities. Finally, more MD schools now include a few of the approaches to healthcare traditionally practiced by DOs. Thus, the types of medicine practiced by MDs and DOs are decidedly different but moving closer to similar training.

The challenge is that few people understand the practices of a DO. On a very basic level, DOs focus less on prescribing drugs and performing surgery and more on lifelong, comprehensive healthcare. Although many MDs espouse a proactive, comprehensive care model, this practice is not routinely executed in physician's offices. DOs typically spend more time with their patients in OMM (osteopathic manipulative medicine), which basically means that they use hand-body techniques to locate and feel anomalies that are not necessarily seen in a blood test.

For example, by feeling the clavicle, the DO physician can determine whether an irregularity is causing a problem in fluid flow, or by walking the fingers down a tibia, they can tell an alignment problem causing a problem with joints or movement. In short, OMM consists of hands-on techniques that apply pressure to a person's anatomy to more clearly understand a problem that may be better resolved by less invasive self-healing methods other than prescription drugs and surgery.

Osteopathic medical doctors also prescribe medicines and perform surgery. DOs are also called doctors or physicians. The only difference is the treatment methods and the prevention-first philosophy that lays the foundation for how they approach their medical practice. With specialized training in the musculoskeletal system, the way DOs approach medicine differs, offering a more natural approach to human health and healing.

ATTENDING OSTEOPATHIC MEDICAL SCHOOL

In one precipitating moment, students know they want to attend medical school. That could be the tragic illness, pain, or death of a friend or family member. On the other hand, the decision to pursue medicine could be due to the onset of a disease, disorder, or pain. Occasionally, this event happens in childhood, though often the journey begins in high school or college. While it is never too late to begin this journey, the number of prerequisites required and the foundation needed favors those who know when they begin college.

Nevertheless, while medical school is challenging and the time requirement is daunting, the profession is rewarding. You will directly impact a person's present and future, making a significant impact on a family and community. From bringing a newborn into the world as he or she takes its first breaths to surgery that will save a life, you will contribute to the world and become a colleague to those with similar goals and aspirations.

NUMEROUS AREAS TO EXPLORE

Whether you want to pursue primary care, cardiology, dermatology, oncology, neurology, or psychiatry, you are on the right path. Often medical school applicants have an idea of the direction they want to pursue. However, medical school offers numerous opportunities to explore new areas. Furthermore, after medical school, you can choose from many paths. For example, students may head into private practice, community clinic, or pursue other areas such as public health, research, teaching, or community-based service.

APPLYING TO OSTEOPATHIC MEDICAL SCHOOL

Applying to osteopathic medical school is a process that requires more work than you may expect. Students spend more than a year in the application process. Students start with developing an organized method to approach the application process and a timeline to follow. This effort is typically followed by research on MD and DO programs and prerequisite requirements yet to be completed. Every school is different. There are no two schools with precisely the exact same course requirements, admissions dates, GPA/MCAT profiles, interview schedules, and essays. Next, students need to determine who will serve as their recommenders, make formal requests to professors/practitioners, and secure the recommendations. Some schools have formal committee letters.

ORGANIZE YOUR EFFORT

I typically make charts of medical schools for those students I counsel, though you can do this on your own. Here is one of the charts I create. You do not need to hire an advisor to create solid materials that make your work organized and efficient. You can create your own charts. Choose the schools you are interested in attending and fill in the data from various online sources.

Condense the data. There are numerous variables for you to consider. You can get lost in the volumes of information available. For example, each school has a range of GPAs and MCAT scores. This effort may seem overwhelming, but I use simple, colorful charts/tables in Microsoft Word that I can color-code. Some people like Excel, though I find it clunky and uninviting. Remember applying to osteopathic medical school is a long process. It is helpful if you can see and code the information for your own purposes.

The AACOM and AACOMAS websites are very helpful. Note that statistical information and cost of attendance change from year to year. Thus, when you begin to make your chart, you may find that the data from last month is not the same. Don't worry. For now you just need to get a general idea of where you stand, what you need to do, how you need to do it, and track what you need to remember.

Osteopathic Medical Schools	USNWR Primary Care	USNWR Rank Research	GPA	MCAT	Attendance Rate Class Size/ Applications	Percent In-State Matriculants	# Inter-viewed	# Accept	# In Class	Accept Rate	Other Imp Info

Another chart I make for my students is also very helpful for your planning purposes. Again, you can construct this from scratch using information from this book and other sources. Planning, organization, and one-stop informational charts will save you a ton of time. Every time you contact a med school (student, faculty, admissions, or alumnus) or learn details about the school, input the information into the chart. Small fonts are okay so you can fit more information.

Osteopathic Medical Schools	Prerequisite Requirements	Recommended Classes	Key Dates, Logins, Interview Type	Contact w/ Med School, Follow Up Rules

While students are quick to start working on their essays, this endeavor may not be prudent. There is much to learn before you know what to tell a medical school about yourself. The best way to start is by constructing a chart using the data from this book. This data is current for the 2021-2022 admissions cycle. However, there are rarely significant changes from one year to the next, though dates, costs, and statistics will change. The pandemic has altered admissions, but requirements are likely to remain. However, the grace colleges allowed at a few schools with pass/fail classes, community college courses, delays, waivers etc., are unlikely to continue a few years from now.

WHAT MAJOR SHOULD I CHOOSE?

One question students always ask is whether or not the choice of a major is more important than GPA and MCAT scores. Actually, students can major in anything and attend medical school provided they complete the required courses for entrance. GPA and MCAT scores are most important. I have had students get accepted to medical school in anthropology, political science, music, Spanish, and philosophy, while others major in chemistry, biology, engineering, and public health. Either way, they are in medical school now.

The point is that if you are genuinely interested in the subject you are studying, you will be motivated to persist in the most demanding classes. When you are passionate about your classes, you dive into the material with true appreciation for the subject. Additionally, you will have numerous experiences that allow you to reflect on the world and solidify your decision to serve communities, help patients, and live your life as a physician. Otherwise, you can get lost in the checklist approach to medical school admissions. If you only go through the motions, you will not enjoy the journey along the way. Instead, know your why; take action on your how; invent your future.

Especially if you are majoring in a non-science subject, make sure that you have medical service, clinical experience, and community health experiences. You can shadow physicians. However, this passive experience, while illuminating, has little involvement. Serving as a scribe is more active while working as a medical assistant or EMT is immersive and invaluable in your preparation. International medical experiences also provide a valuable foundation.

Research aids in gaining awareness for medicine and its advances on the whole. The fine detail and continuous repetition of scientific work provide an appreciation for the field and the outcomes of science. Besides, furthering science by taking innovations one step further is beneficial to all of society. Getting published, presenting at conferences, and expanding the field are all noble goals.

One of the reasons why some students who major in a non-traditional subject have difficulties is that, with fewer science courses, a different mindset is needed to be re-oriented toward science as opposed to the orientation of, let's say, the analysis of literature. Note that your Science GPA is a key component in the admissions process. Medical schools use the BCPM (Biology, Chemistry, Physics, and Math) GPA. However, AACOMAS uses a set of GPA with guidelines given at this website: https://help.liaisonedu.com/AACOMAS_Applicant_Help_Center/ Submitting_and_Monitoring_Your_AACOMAS_Application/Verification_and_GPA_ Calculations_for_AACOMAS/3_Calculating_Your_GPAs

With the ability to go back and forth between science and societal issues, medical schools get a student who can access more of the humanistic side of academia as well. Having a broader background and deeper connections to the world is invaluable for medicine. Besides, more well-rounded students with varied backgrounds add a different type of diversity to the school and contribute an engaging intellectual exchange between students.

Nearly all medical schools require a year of each of the following: Biology, General Chemistry, Organic Chemistry, Physics, Mathematics (Calculus, Statistics), English, Humanities, and Social Science. Most also require Biochemistry and two other semesters of Biology. Review the chart you create and work with your academic advisor to determine what classes you need and how they will fit into your college experience. In the end, your academic performance matters the most.

INTERVIEWS

If you are invited to interview, you will most likely have the Multiple Mini Interview or MMI for short. You can think of it as many shorter interviews with different people who evaluate your quick thinking, attitude, judgments, behaviors, ethical decision-making, and overall answers. The interview is your 'win it or blow it' chance.

- What ethical dilemma was most impactful to you?
- How would you handle a situation where you knew a person was unvaccinated and not wearing a mandated mask?
- What would you do if you knew that insurance would not allow a patient to get the medicine they need and forced you to prescribe one or two others first?
- If you were Anthony Fauci, what would you have done regarding vaccinations at the beginning and during the pandemic?

The challenge in these interviews is that multiple people will assess you on your strengths and weaknesses and give you scores. For most people, interviews of any type are uncomfortable, although there are advantages to the MMI. For example, you can prepare with scenarios and determine how to respond in general and what not to say. Longer explanations and preparation are found in my book, *Osteopathic Medical School: Preparation, Application, Admission*.

Nonetheless, in short, the MMI includes multiple stations that have various formats, from pre-reading and writing to situational activities followed by an interview. These are short, and each has a rubric from which the evaluator gives you a ranking or score. The rubric is standardized and formatted, so that much of the intrinsic bias is removed. Interviewers objectively provide an evaluation that is combined with the rest of the results to earn a composite score. Some of the areas that may be considered include:

Communication	Empathy
Relationship	Compassion
Connection	Awareness
Critical Thinking	Self-description
Problem Solving	Maturity
Reaction to Setbacks	

DEMAND FOR PHYSICIANS

No matter what specialty you pursue, the demand for physicians will continue to outweigh the supply. At this point in time, data show a shortage of physicians. This situation will only worsen. First, there are more people with healthcare needs, which was exacerbated by the pandemic. Second, the population of older people will increase demand. Third, many physicians will retire in the upcoming years and new physicians will be needed. Finally, global demand for healthcare professionals is increasing, particularly in areas like Africa, where the population is expected to double by 2050.

PRIMARY CARE NEEDS

New MD and DO programs have opened in the last five years due to the increasing shortage of primary care physicians. Especially in rural and other underserved areas, comprehensive healthcare is essential. The concern is so great that the federal government provides scholarships to encourage medical school students to serve this need. Investigate possibilities with the National Health Service Corps for programs which have been created in conjunction with the U.S. Department of Health and Human Services. With the high costs of medical school education, these scholarships are extremely helpful.

A FINAL NOTE

This profile book provides a handy resource for your research and understanding of osteopathic medical schools and does not cover MD schools. I wrote a separate book on medical school admission along with one that profiles medical schools. Additionally, this book is the companion guide to *Osteopathic Medical School: Preparation, Application, Admission.* In that book, you will find hints and information on the entire application process, as well as detailed information on alternative medical programs, what happens after the interview, and how to strengthen your application.

Few books cover DO schools, though this path is an avenue that offers unique opportunities for comprehensive, holistic healthcare. I have written books on medical school, dental school, PharmD, PA, and veterinary medicine as well.

Best wishes in your pursuit of an amazing career and your commitment to serving the healthcare needs of our society.

4
Regions

37
Programs

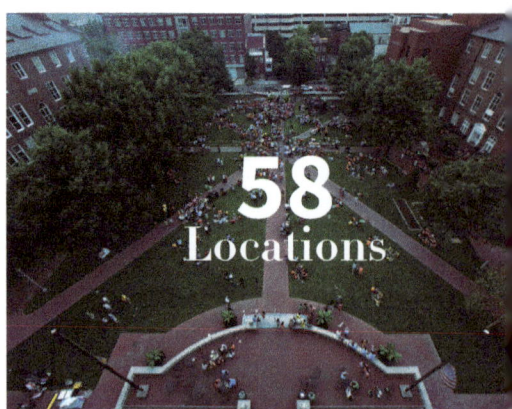

58
Locations

COLLEGE
PROFILES AND
REQUIREMENTS

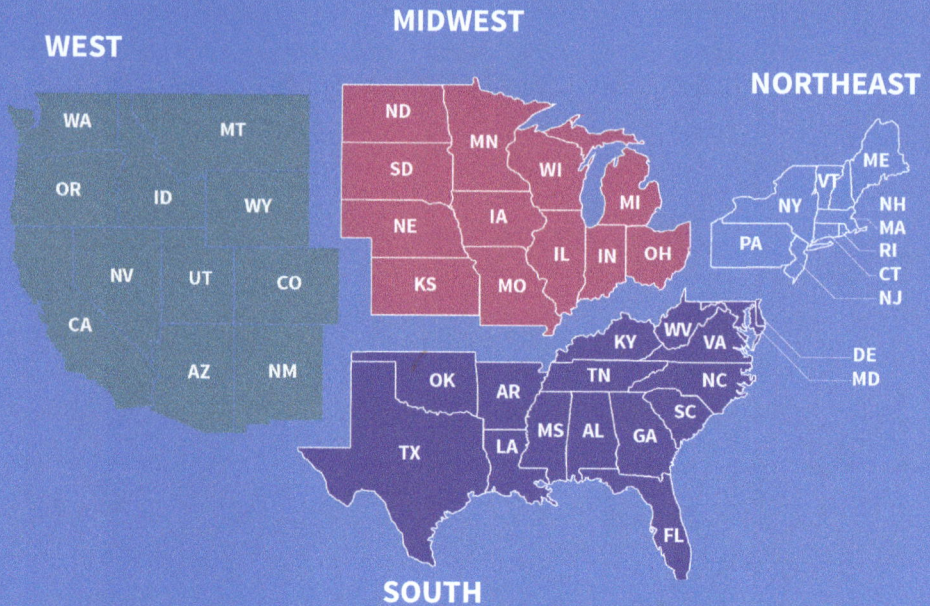

WEST

MIDWEST

NORTHEAST

SOUTH

DO PROGRAMS BY REGION
U.S. CENSUS BUREAU CLASSIFICATIONS

REGION 1 – NORTHEAST

Connecticut, Maine, Massachusetts, New Hampshire, New Jersey, New York, Pennsylvania, Rhode Island, and Vermont

REGION 2 – MIDWEST

Illinois, Indiana, Iowa, Kansas, Michigan, Minnesota, Missouri, Nebraska, North Dakota, Ohio, South Dakota, and Wisconsin

REGION 3 – SOUTH

Alabama, Arkansas, Delaware, District of Columbia, Florida, Georgia, Kentucky, Louisiana, Maryland, Mississippi, North Carolina, Oklahoma, South Carolina, Tennessee, Texas, Virginia, and West Virginia

REGION 4 – WEST

Alaska, Arizona, California, Colorado, Hawaii, Idaho, Montana, Nevada, New Mexico, Oregon, Utah, Washington, and Wyoming

LIST OF DO PROGRAMS

T he programs listed in the following pages include DO programs. This book also provides lists of MD, dental, PharmD, physician assistant, and vet schools, since many students interested in medical school are also interested in healthcare. There are many facets of the healthcare world. One of these other areas might be a good option for you.

Osteopathic medical school is not for everyone.

Thus, this book aims to provide you with a more comprehensive set of lists so that you can explore your options. Keep the book handy. You may find that even after you begin college, if you choose a traditional pre-med path, you may find the additional programs in the back a good option for you.

Creating lists is often tedious and cumbersome. These lists were gathered to help you with this task.

These descriptions of the college programs, tuition, requirements, and deadlines are accurate as of April 2021. Requirements may have changed somewhat due to the pandemic, but all of this information is a great place to start!

Note: To simplify the text and fit information into the charts and descriptions, abbreviations were used as well as shortened sentences and acronyms.

CONNECTICUT

MAINE

MASSACHUSETTS

NEW HAMPSHIRE

NEW JERSEY

NEW YORK

PENNSYLVANIA

RHODE ISLAND

VERMONT

CHAPTER 2

REGION ONE

NORTHEAST

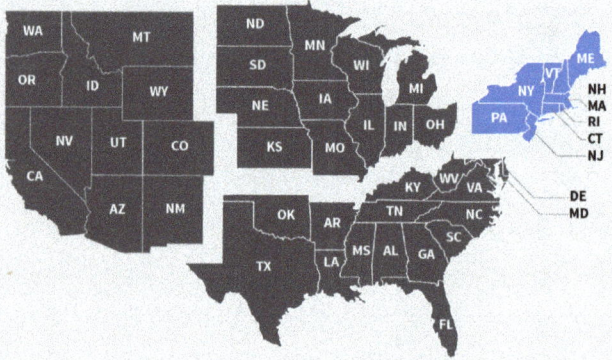

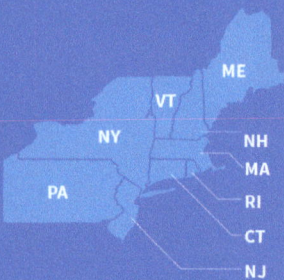

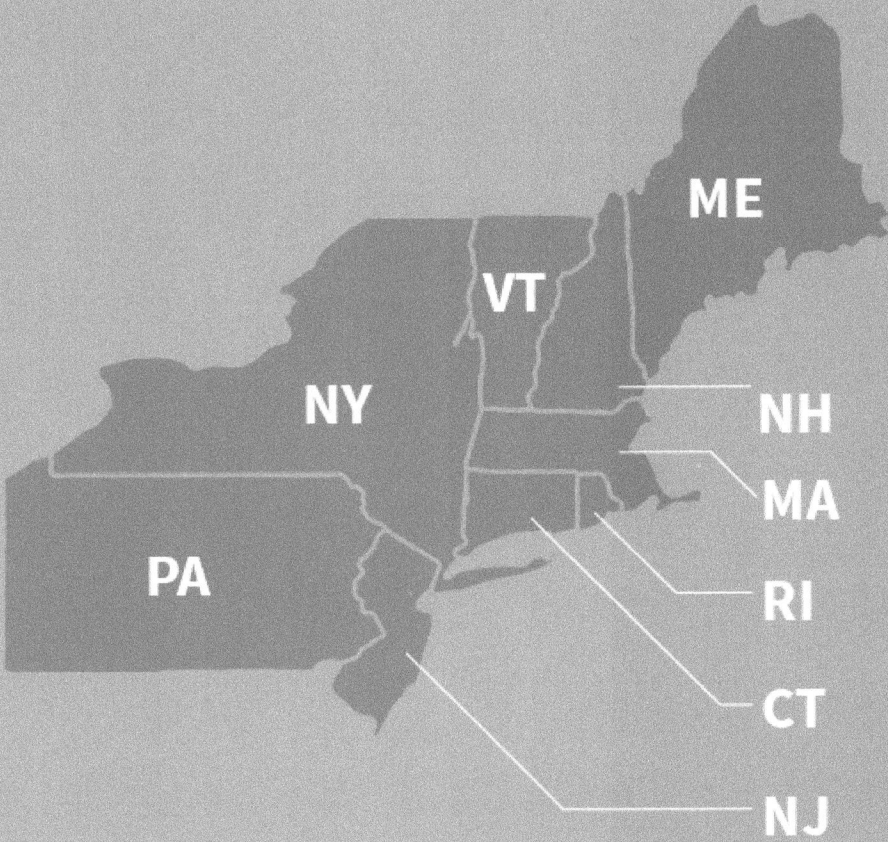

9 *Programs* | **9** *States*

1. ME – University of New England College of Osteopathic Medicine (UNECOM)
2. NJ - Rowan University School of Osteopathic Medicine (RowanSOM)
3. NY - Lake Erie College of Osteopathic Medicine - Elmira (LECOM-Elmira)
4. NY - New York Institute of Technology College of Osteopathic Medicine (NYITCOM)
5. NY - Touro College of Osteopathic Medicine TouroCOM
6. NY - Touro College of Osteopathic Medicine (TouroCOM-Middletown)
7. PA - Lake Erie College of Osteopathic Medicine - Seton Hill (LECOM-Seton Hill)
8. PA - Lake Erie College of Osteopathic Medicine (LECOM)
9. PA - Philadelphia College of Osteopathic Medicine (PCOM)

Osteo School	Ave. GPA & MCAT / Early Decision (ED): Yes/No / Int'l Students: Yes/No / Reapps: Yes/No	Admissions Statistics	Science Req. Other than Gen Chem, OChem, Physics, Bio
Univ. of New England 11 Hills Beach Road, Biddeford, ME 04005	3.57 (overall) 3.51 (science) MCAT: 504 ED: No Int'l Student: Yes Reapps: N/A	**(2019)** Apps Received: 3,000 Interview Received: N/A Number Enrolled: 178 Admitted Rate: 5.9% **(2020)** Apps Received: 4,045 Interview Received: N/A Number Enrolled: 178 Admitted Rate: 4.4%	Biochemistry Upper-level courses w/ Lab Behavioral Science
Rowan University One Medical Center Drive Stratford, NJ 08084	3.65 (overall) 3.6 (science) MCAT: 505 ED: Yes Int'l Student: Yes Reapps: Yes	**(2019)** Apps Received: 5.434 Interview Received: N/A Number Enrolled: 202 Admitted Rate: 3.7% **(2020)** Apps Received: 6,933 Interview Received: N/A Number Enrolled: 219 Admitted Rate: 3.2%	College level Math Behavioral Science Additional Science Courses
LECOM-Elmira* 1 LECOM Place, Elmira, NY 14901	N/A MCAT: N/A ED: No Int'l Student: Yes Reapps: N/A	**(2019)** Apps Received: N/A Interview Received: N/A Number Enrolled: N/A Admitted Rate: N/A **(2020)** Apps Received: N/A Interview Received: N/A Number Enrolled: N/A Admitted Rate: N/A	N/A

Osteo School	Ave. GPA & MCAT Early Decision (ED): Yes/No Int'l Students: Yes/No Reapps: Yes/No	Admissions Statistics	Science Req. Other than Gen Chem, OChem, Physics, Bio
NYITCOM** Serota Academic Center, Northern Boulevard, P.O. Box 8000, Old Westbury, NY 11568	3.6 (overall) N/A (science) MCAT: 505 ED: No Int'l Student: Yes Reapps: N/A	**(2019)** Apps Received: 6,092 Interview Received: 1,100 Number Enrolled: 435 Admitted Rate: 7.14% **(2020)** Apps Received: 9,927 Interview Received: N/A Number Enrolled: 438 Admitted Rate: 4.4%	OChem 2 (Biochem. can substitute)
TouroCOM - Harlem 230 West 125th Street, New York, NY	3.4 (overall) 3.4 (science) MCAT: 505 ED: No Int'l Student: Yes Reapps: N/A	**(2019)** Apps Received: 6,444 Interview Received: 500 (per campus) Number Enrolled: 271 Admitted Rate: 4.5% **(2020)** Apps Received: 7,943 Interview Received: N/A Number Enrolled: 270 Admitted Rate: 3.4%	Math and/or Comp. Sci Behavioral Sciences
TouroCOM – Middletown 60 Prospect Avenue, Middletown, NY 10940	3.4 (overall) 3.4 (science) MCAT: 505 ED: No Int'l Student: Yes Reapps: N/A	**(2019)** Apps Received: 6,444 Interview Received: 500 (per campus) Number Enrolled: 271 Admitted Rate: 4.5% **(2020)** Apps Received: 7,943 Interview Received: N/A Number Enrolled: 270 Admitted Rate: 3.4%	Math and/or Comp. Sci Behavioral Sciences

NORTHEAST

OSTEO PROGRAMS

Osteo School	Ave. GPA & MCAT Early Decision (ED): Yes/No Int'l Students: Yes/No Reapps: Yes/No	Admissions Statistics	Science Req. Other than Gen Chem, OChem, Physics, Bio
LECOM – Seton Hill* 20 Seton Hill Drive, Greensburg, PA 15601	3.5 (overall) 3.4 (science) MCAT: 503 ED: No Int'l Student: Yes Reapps: Yes	**(2019)** Apps Received: 8,827 Interview Received: N/A Number Enrolled: 389 Admitted Rate: 4.45% **(2020)** Apps Received: 11,822 Interview Received: N/A Number Enrolled: 381 Admitted Rate: 3.2%	Behavioral Sciences Adv. Coursework rec.
LECOM* 1858 W. Grandview Blvd., Erie, PA 16509	3.5 (overall) 3.4 (science) MCAT: 503 ED: No Int'l Student: Yes Reapps: Yes	**(2019)** Apps Received: 8,827 Interview Received: N/A Number Enrolled: 389 Admitted Rate: 4.45% **(2020)** Apps Received: 11,822 Interview Received: N/A Number Enrolled: 381 Admitted Rate: 3.2%	Behavioral Sciences Adv. Coursework rec.
Philadelphia College of Osteopathic Medicine (PCOM) 4170 City Avenue, Philadelphia, PA 19131	3.5 (overall) 3.4 (science) MCAT: 504 ED: No Int'l Student: No Reapps: N/A	**(2019)** Apps Received: 6.984 Interview Received: N/A Number Enrolled: 268 Admitted Rate: 3.8% 6,984 N/A 268 6.3%* **(2020)** Apps Received: 9,962 Interview Received: N/A Number Enrolled: 270	Biochemistry

*LECOM – Elmira's first class will matriculate in Fall 2020. No admissions data has been updated yet.
**NYITCOM table data reflects total enrolled at both NYIT campuses and Émigré Physicians Program (EPP) students.
***LECOM table data reflects totals from Erie and Seton Hill Campuses.

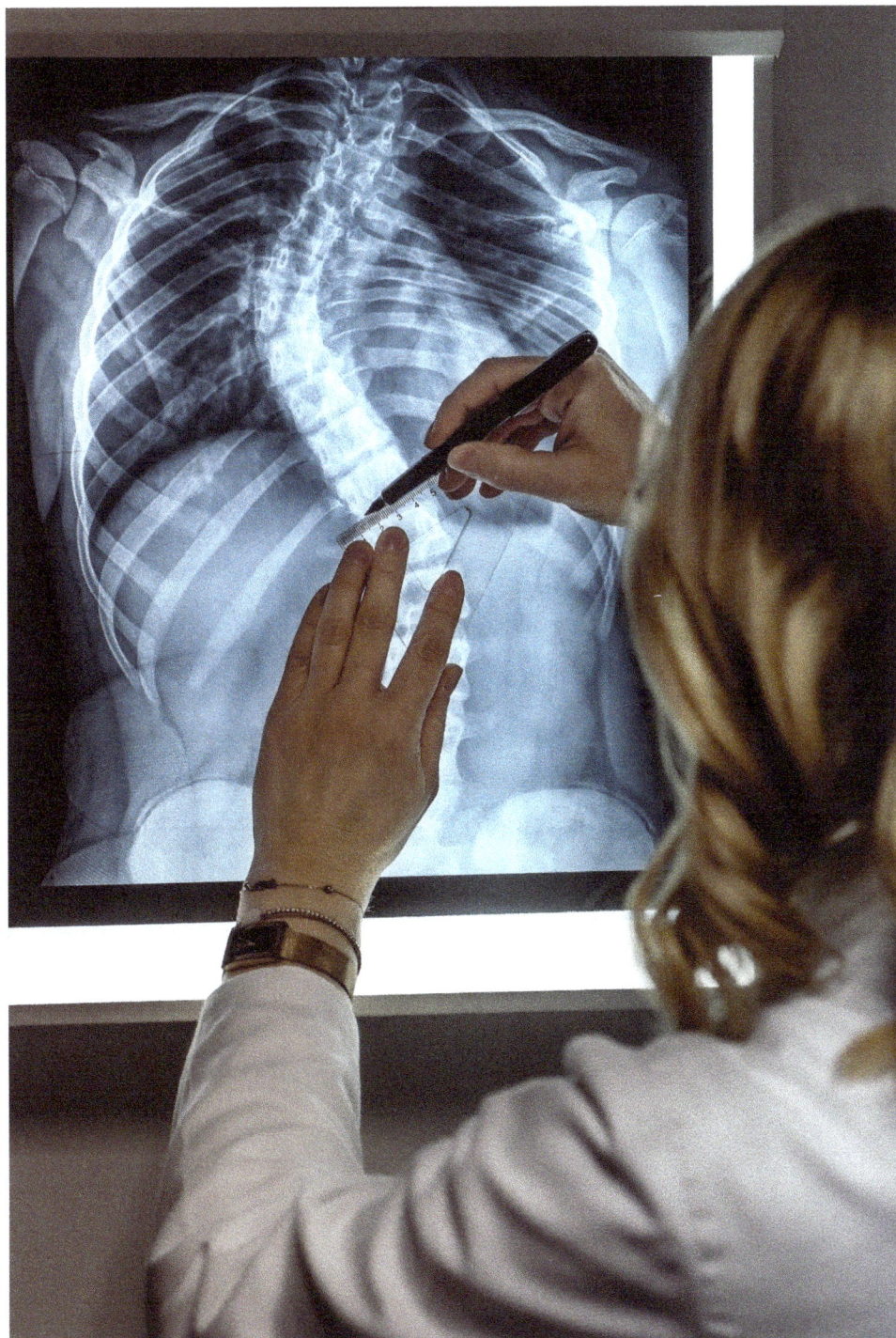

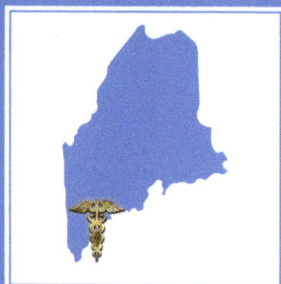

CONNECTICUT

MAINE

MASSACHUSETTS

NEW HAMPSHIRE

NEW JERSEY

NEW YORK

PENNSYLVANIA

RHODE ISLAND

VERMONT

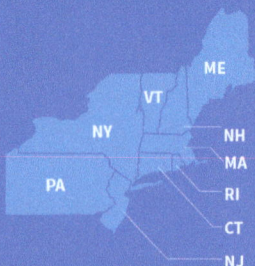

UNIVERSITY OF NEW ENGLAND COLLEGE OF OSTEOPATHIC MEDICINE (UNECOM)

Address: 11 Hills Beach Road, Biddeford, ME 04005
Website: *https://www.une.edu/com*
Contact: *https://www.une.edu/com/contact-us*
Phone: (207) 283-0171

Other campus locations: N/A

COST OF ATTENDANCE

Tuition: $61,040
Fees & Expenses: $26,838
Total: $87,878

Financial Aid: https://www.une.edu/sfs/graduate

Percent Receiving Aid: 77%

ADDITIONAL INFORMATION

Interesting tidbit: The creation of UNE COM was based on regionalism - one osteopathic medical school to serve the six New England states.

What international experiences are available? Medical Service Trip

What dual degree options exist? No dual degree options listed.

Percent of graduates receiving residency matches: 94% (2021)

What service learning opportunities exist? Public Health Fair, Blood Pressure and Vaccination Clinics, Maine Marathon, and more. For more information, visit: https://www.une.edu/com/student-life/get-involved/volunteer-opportunities

Important Updates due to COVID-19: Pass/Fail courses are acceptable for prerequisite courses taken in spring 2020 only. Online courses offered through UNE's Online science prerequisites as well as online courses from other regionally accredited U.S. colleges or universities are acceptable.

Were tests required? MCAT required.

Are tests expected next year? Yes.

COMLEX First-Time Pass Rate (Level 1, Level 2 Cognitive Evaluation, Level 2 Performance Evaluation, Level 3) (2018-2019)

Level 1: 98.8%

Level 2 CE: 98.9%

Level 2 PE: 92.8%

Level 3: 99.1%

ROWAN UNIVERSITY SCHOOL OF OSTEOPATHIC MEDICINE (ROWANSOM)

Address: One Medical Center Drive Stratford, NJ 08084
Website: *https://som.rowan.edu/*
Contact: *https://som.rowan.edu/education/admissions/contact.html*
Phone: (856) 566-7050

Other campus locations: Rowan College of South Jersey (expansion for this campus in 2021)

COST OF ATTENDANCE

In-State Tuition: 41,339
Fees & Expenses: $51,358
Total: $92,697

Out-of-State Tuition: $66,324
Fees & Expenses: $51,358
Total: $117,682

Financial Aid: https://som.rowan.edu/education/financialaid/financial-planning/index.html

Percent Receiving Aid: 76%

ADDITIONAL INFORMATION

Interesting tidbit: Rowan SOM has implemented new curriculum, Tenegrity Curriculum. The Tensegrity Curriculum is an integrated, balanced program that trains future physicians to treat the whole patient and promote health by addressing their mental, physical and spiritual well-being.

What international experiences are available? N/A

What dual degree options exist? Dual degree programs available. For more information, visit: https://som.rowan.edu/education/learntodo/combined.html

Percent of graduates receiving residency matches: 100% (2020)

What service learning opportunities exist? Rowan Community Health Center and OMM Free Clinic. For more information, visit: https://som.rowan.edu/education/studentlife/volunteer.html

Important Updates due to COVID-19: Physician Letter strongly recommended, but not required. Accept either Virtual or In-Person shadowing. Accept online coursework to fulfill prerequisite requirements. Accept prerequisite coursework Pass/Fail grades on a case-by-case basis. Accept online lab coursework on a case-by-case basis.

Were tests required? MCAT required.

Are tests expected next year? Yes.

COMLEX First-Time Pass Rate (Level 1, Level 2 Cognitive Evaluation, Level 2 Performance Evaluation, Level 3) (2019/20)

Level 1: 97%

Level 2 CE: 94%

Level 2 PE: 95%

Level 3: 95% (2018-2019)

CONNECTICUT

MAINE

MASSACHUSETTS

NEW HAMPSHIRE

NEW JERSEY

NEW YORK

PENNSYLVANIA

RHODE ISLAND

VERMONT

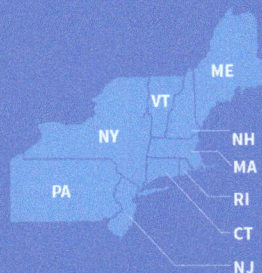

NORTHEAST

CONNECTICUT

MAINE

MASSACHUSETTS

NEW HAMPSHIRE

NEW JERSEY

NEW YORK

PENNSYLVANIA

RHODE ISLAND

VERMONT

ME

VT

NY

NH

MA

PA

RI

CT

NJ

LAKE ERIE COLLEGE OF OSTEOPATHIC MEDICINE (LECOM) – ELMIRA

Address: 1 LECOM Place, Elmira, NY 14901
Website: *https://lecom.edu/academics/the-college-of-medicine/*
Contact: *https://lecom.edu/contact-us/*
Phone: (607) 795-8158

Other campus locations: Erie, PA; Seton Hill at Greensburg, PA; Bradenton, FL

COST OF ATTENDANCE

Tuition: 39,700
Fees & Expenses: $29,728
Total: $69,428

Financial Aid: https://lecom.edu/admissions/tuition-and-financial-aid/

Percent Receiving Aid: N/A

ADDITIONAL INFORMATION

Interesting tidbit: LECOM at Elmira welcomed its inaugural class, consisting of 120 osteopathic students, in July 2020. Their arrival signified the official opening of LECOM's fourth campus, the first and only medical college in the region.

What international experiences are available? N/A

What dual degree options exist? No dual degree options listed.

Percent of graduates receiving residency matches: 99.3% (2020) (assuming aggregate for four campuses)

What service learning opportunities exist? N/A

Important Updates due to COVID-19: N/A

Were tests required? MCAT required.

Are tests expected next year? Yes.

COMLEX First-Time Pass Rate (Level 1, Level 2 Cognitive Evaluation, Level 2 Performance Evaluation, Level 3) - N/A*

Other: LECOM has partnerships with several undergraduate institutions for the Early Acceptance Program. This program is intended for high school applicants to receive conditional acceptance to LECOM. For more information, visit: https://lecom.edu/admissions/entrance-requirements/early-acceptance-programs/

*No Match or COMLEX data for this campus, since it will matriculate its first class in Fall 2020.

Note: One application for all LECOM campuses: Bradenton, Elmira, Erie, and Seton Hill.

NEW YORK INSTITUTE OF TECHNOLOGY COLLEGE OF OSTEOPATHIC MEDICINE (NYITCOM)

Address: Serota Academic Center, Northern Boulevard, P.O. Box 8000, Old Westbury, NY 11568
Website: *https://www.nyit.edu/medicine*
Contact: *https://www.nyit.edu/admissions/request_information?degree=osteopathic_medicine_do*
Phone: (516) 686-3997

Other campus locations: Jonesboro, AR

COST OF ATTENDANCE
Tuition: 60,450
Fees & Expenses: $35,333
Total: $95,783

Financial Aid: https://www.nyit.edu/medicine/financial_aid

Percent Receiving Aid: 83%

ADDITIONAL INFORMATION

Interesting tidbit: Dr. W. Kenneth Riland, who was the personal physician to former President Nixon, Vice President Nelson Rockefeller, and Secretary of State Henry Kissinger, and and his colleagues saw the establishment of the medical school as a way to promote and strengthen the credibility of osteopathic medicine and leveraged the support of Rockefeller and other political leaders to establish the New York College of Osteopathic Medicine in 1977. The college changed its name to the NYIT College of Osteopathic Medicine in 2012.

What international experiences are available? Global Health Center and opportunity to obtain Global Health Certificate. For more information, visit: https://www.nyit.edu/medicine/center_for_global_health

What dual degree options exist? dual degree program available. For more information, visit: https://www.nyit.edu/degrees/medical_and_biological_sciences_do_phd

Percent of graduates receiving residency matches: 98%* (2020)
*Combined statistics for Long Island and Arkansas campuses.

What service learning opportunities exist? Community Free Clinic. For more information, visit: https://www.nyit.edu/medicine/community_free_clinic

Important Updates due to COVID-19: Accept pass/fail grading for spring/summer 2020 coursework.

Were tests required? MCAT required.

Are tests expected next year? Yes.

COMLEX First-Time Pass Rate (Level 1, Level 2 Cognitive Evaluation, Level 2 Performance Evaluation, Level 3)

Level 1: 94.42% (2019/20)
Level 2 CE: 95.07% (2019/20)
Level 2 PE: 92.6% (2018/19)
Level 3: 98% (2019/20)

Other: NYITCOM offers the only program in the U.S. to retrain "émigré physicians born and educated outside the United States." This program is only available at the Long Island campus. For more information, visit: https://www.nyit.edu/medicine/osteopathic_medicine_do_emigre_admissions

CONNECTICUT

MAINE

MASSACHUSETTS

NEW HAMPSHIRE

NEW JERSEY

NEW YORK

PENNSYLVANIA

RHODE ISLAND

VERMONT

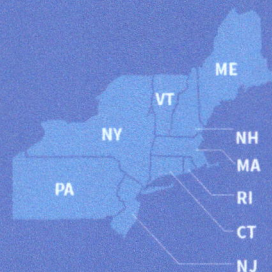

NORTHEAST

TOURO COLLEGE OF OSTEOPATHIC MEDICINE (TOUROCOM) – HARLEM

Address: 230 West 125th Street, New York, NY
Website: *https://tourocom.touro.edu/*
Contact: *https://tourocom.touro.edu/about-us/contact/*
Phone: (212) 851-1199

Other campus locations: Middletown, NY

COST OF ATTENDANCE

Tuition: $59,780
Fees & Expenses: $46,672
Total: $106,452

Financial Aid: https://tourocom.touro.edu/admissions--aid/financial-aid/

Percent Receiving Aid: 83.6% (assuming same percentage for both Harlem and Middletown campuses)

ADDITIONAL INFORMATION

Interesting tidbit: The mission and goal at TouroCOM is to help the underserved and underrepresented so they are no longer underserved or underrepresented. TouroCOM has a strong focus on encouraging our graduates to practice medicine in underserved areas geographically, like many rural areas, and in underserved areas of medicine, like primary care.

What international experiences are available? Medical Mission trips

What dual degree options exist? No dual degree options listed.

Percent of graduates receiving residency matches: 98.60% (2020)

What service learning opportunities exist? Community Programs available. For more information, visit: https://tourocom.touro.edu/in-the-community/community-programs/

Important Updates due to COVID-19: Accept "pass/satisfactory" grading for coursework, including pre-requisite coursework fulfillment, for the Spring 2020 semester and onward. Accept all online coursework for the Spring 2020 semester and onward. Review your application without all required laboratory coursework if interrupted by Covid-19 but proof of completion is required prior to matriculation. Physician LOR can be substituted.

Were tests required? MCAT & CASPer required.

Are tests expected next year? Yes.

COMLEX First-Time Pass Rate (Level 1, Level 2 Cognitive Evaluation, Level 2 Performance Evaluation, Level 3) (2019/20)

Level 1: 96.35%

Level 2 CE: 98.62%

Level 2 PE: 86.60%

Level 3: 92.11%

Other: TouroCOM offers pre-med pathways for K-12 students. For more information, visit: https://tourocom.touro.edu/admissions--aid/pre-med-pathways/

CONNECTICUT

MAINE

MASSACHUSETTS

NEW HAMPSHIRE

NEW JERSEY

NEW YORK

PENNSYLVANIA

RHODE ISLAND

VERMONT

TOURO COLLEGE OF OSTEOPATHIC MEDICINE (TOUROCOM) – MIDDLETOWN

Address: 60 Prospect Avenue, Middletown, NY 10940
Website: *https://tourocom.touro.edu/*
Contact: *https://tourocom.touro.edu/about-us/contact/*
Phone: (845) 648-1000

Other campus locations: Harlem – New York, NY

COST OF ATTENDANCE

Tuition: $59,780
Fees & Expenses: $43,798
Total: $103,578*

*The given estimate is for on-campus living. Off-campus COA is $91,424.

Financial Aid: https://tourocom.touro.edu/admissions--aid/financial-aid/

Percent Receiving Aid: 83.6% (assume the same percentage for both Harlem and Middletown campuses)

ADDITIONAL INFORMATION

Interesting tidbit: The Middletown Campus opened its doors on July 21, 2014. It's housed in the former Horton Hospital building. It also has support and clinical training facilities on site, like our OSCE and Sim Labs, where students can begin applying and honing their practical skills.

What international experiences are available? Medical Mission trips

What dual degree options exist? No dual degree options listed.

Percent of graduates receiving residency matches: 97% (2020)

What service learning opportunities exist? Community Programs available. For more information, visit: https://tourocom.touro.edu/in-the-community/

Important Updates due to COVID-19: Accept "pass/satisfactory" grading for coursework, including pre-requisite coursework fulfillment, for the Spring 2020 semester and onward. Accept all online coursework for the Spring 2020 semester and onward. Review your application without all required laboratory coursework if interrupted by Covid-19 but proof of completion will be required prior to matriculation. Physician LOR can be substituted.

Were tests required? MCAT & CASPer required.

Are tests expected next year? Yes.

COMLEX First-Time Pass Rate (Level 1, Level 2 Cognitive Evaluation, Level 2 Performance Evaluation, Level 3) (2019/20)

Level 1: 98.47%

Level 2 CE: 97.01%

Level 2 PE: 88.80%

Level 3: 98.88%

Other: TouroCOM offers pre-med pathways for K-12 students. For more information, visit: https://tourocom.touro.edu/admissions--aid/pre-med-pathways/

CONNECTICUT

MAINE

MASSACHUSETTS

NEW HAMPSHIRE

NEW JERSEY

NEW YORK

PENNSYLVANIA

RHODE ISLAND

VERMONT

NORTHEAST

LAKE ERIE COLLEGE OF OSTEOPATHIC MEDICINE (LECOM) – SETON HILL

Address: 20 Seton Hill Drive, Greensburg, PA 15601
Website: *https://lecom.edu/academics/the-college-of-medicine/*
Contact: *https://lecom.edu/contact-us/*
Phone: (724) 552-2880
Other campus locations: Erie, PA; Bradenton, FL; Elmira, NY

COST OF ATTENDANCE

Tuition: $37,000
Fees & Expenses: $29,653
Total: $66,653

Financial Aid: https://lecom.edu/admissions/tuition-and-financial-aid/

Percent Receiving Aid: N/A

ADDITIONAL INFORMATION

Interesting tidbit: LECOM at Seton Hill offer Problem-Based Learning exclusively. The Problem-Based Learning Pathway (PBL) is a nationally recognized innovative approach to medical education, offering students the opportunity to study the biomedical and clinical sciences by utilizing medical case studies in a small-group environment.

What international experiences are available? N/A

What dual degree options exist? No dual degree options listed.

Percent of graduates receiving residency matches: 99.3% (2020) (assuming aggregate for four campuses)

What service learning opportunities exist? N/A

Important Updates due to COVID-19: N/A

Were tests required? MCAT required.

Are tests expected next year? Yes.

COMLEX First-Time Pass Rate (Level 1, Level 2 Cognitive Evaluation, Level 2 Performance Evaluation, Level 3)

Level 1: N/A

Level 2 CE: N/A

Level 2 PE: N/A

Level 3: N/A

Other: LECOM has partnerships with several undergraduate institutions for the Early Acceptance Program. This program is intended for high school applicants to receive conditional acceptance to LECOM. For more information, visit: https://lecom.edu/admissions/entrance-requirements/early-acceptance-programs/

Note: One application for four LECOM campuses: Elmira, Erie, Bradenton, and Seton Hill.

CONNECTICUT

MAINE

MASSACHUSETTS

NEW HAMPSHIRE

NEW JERSEY

NEW YORK

PENNSYLVANIA

RHODE ISLAND

VERMONT

LAKE ERIE COLLEGE OF OSTEOPATHIC MEDICINE (LECOM) – ERIE

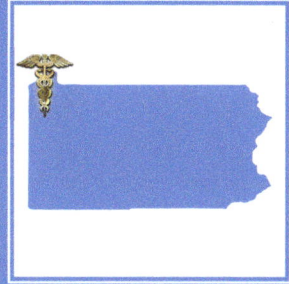

Address: 1858 W. Grandview Blvd., Erie, PA 16509
Website: *https://lecom.edu/academics/the-college-of-medicine/*
Contact: *https://lecom.edu/contact-us/*
Phone: (814) 866-6641
Other campus locations: Seton Hill at Greensburg, PA; Bradenton, FL; Elmira, NY

COST OF ATTENDANCE

Tuition: $37,000
Fees & Expenses: $34,048
Total: $71,048

Financial Aid: https://lecom.edu/admissions/tuition-and-financial-aid/

Percent Receiving Aid: 83%

ADDITIONAL INFORMATION

Interesting tidbit: The Lake Erie College of Osteopathic Medicine (LECOM) is the nation's largest medical college and is the only Academic Health Center in the osteopathic profession. Also, the LECOM Erie Campus is the only medical school in the country with five student-centered learning pathways for the first two years of education in osteopathic medicine.

What international experiences are available? N/A

What dual degree options exist? No dual degree options listed.

Percent of graduates receiving residency matches: 99.3% (2020) (assuming aggregate for four campuses)

What service learning opportunities exist? N/A

Important Updates due to COVID-19: Physician LOR not required but recommended. Accept online coursework to fulfill prerequisite requirements. Accept Pass/Fail coursework to fulfill prerequisite requirements on a case-by-case basis. Accept online lab coursework.

Were tests required? MCAT required.

Are tests expected next year? Yes.

COMLEX First-Time Pass Rate (Level 1, Level 2 Cognitive Evaluation, Level 2 Performance Evaluation, Level 3) (2019/20)

Level 1: 98.1%

Level 2 CE: 98.6%

Level 2 PE: 92.2%

Level 3: 98.1%

Other: LECOM has partnerships with several undergraduate institutions for the Early Acceptance Program. This program is intended for high school applicants to receive conditional acceptance to LECOM. For more information, visit: https://lecom.edu/admissions/entrance-requirements/early-acceptance-programs/

Note: One application for four LECOM campuses: Elmira, Erie, Bradenton, and Seton Hill

CONNECTICUT

MAINE

MASSACHUSETTS

NEW HAMPSHIRE

NEW JERSEY

NEW YORK

PENNSYLVANIA

RHODE ISLAND

VERMONT

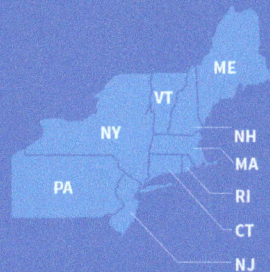

NORTHEAST

CONNECTICUT

MAINE

MASSACHUSETTS

NEW HAMPSHIRE

NEW JERSEY

NEW YORK

PENNSYLVANIA

RHODE ISLAND

VERMONT

PHILADELPHIA COLLEGE OF OSTEOPATHIC MEDICINE (PCOM) – PHILADELPHIA

Address: 4170 City Avenue, Philadelphia, PA 19131
Website: *https://www.pcom.edu/*
Contact: *https://discover.pcom.edu/inquiryform*
Phone: (215) 871-6100

Other campus locations: Suwanee, GA (Georgia Campus) and Moultrie, GA (South Georgia Campus)

COST OF ATTENDANCE

Tuition: $54,336
Fees & Expenses: $25,302
Total: $79,638

Financial Aid: https://www.pcom.edu/about/departments/financial-aid/

Percent Receiving Aid: 85.1%

ADDITIONAL INFORMATION

Interesting tidbit: Applicants may apply to any of PCOM's three locations: PCOM (Philadelphia, PA), PCOM South Georgia (Moultrie, GA), PCOM Georgia (Suwanee, GA). Each application is evaluated for that particular location by the individual Faculty Committee on Admissions for each location.

What international experiences are available? Medical Missions available.

What dual degree options exist? Dual degree programs available. For more information, visit: https://www.pcom.edu/academics/programs-and-degrees/doctor-of-osteopathic-medicine-philadelphia-campus/related-programs/

Percent of graduates receiving residency matches: 99.6% (2021)

What service learning opportunities exist? Community Outreach opportunities available at all three campuses. For more information, visit: https://www.pcom.edu/admissions/community-minority-outreach.html

Important Updates due to COVID-19: Physician LOR not required. Accept online coursework to fulfill prerequisite requirements if taken for credit at a regionally accredited college or university. Accept prerequisite coursework Pass/Fail grades. Accept online lab coursework.

Were tests required? MCAT required.

Are tests expected next year? Yes.

COMLEX First-Time Pass Rate (Level 1, Level 2 Cognitive Evaluation, Level 2 Performance Evaluation, Level 3) (2019/20)

Level 1: 93.8%

Level 2 CE: 94.5%

Level 2 PE: 91.5%

Level 3: N/A

ILLINOIS

INDIANA

IOWA

KANSAS

MICHIGAN

MINNESOTA

MISSOURI

NEBRASKA

NORTH DAKOTA

OHIO

SOUTH DAKOTA

WISCONSIN

CHAPTER 3

REGION TWO
MIDWEST

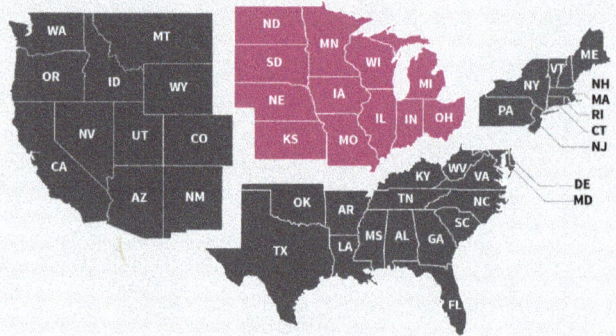

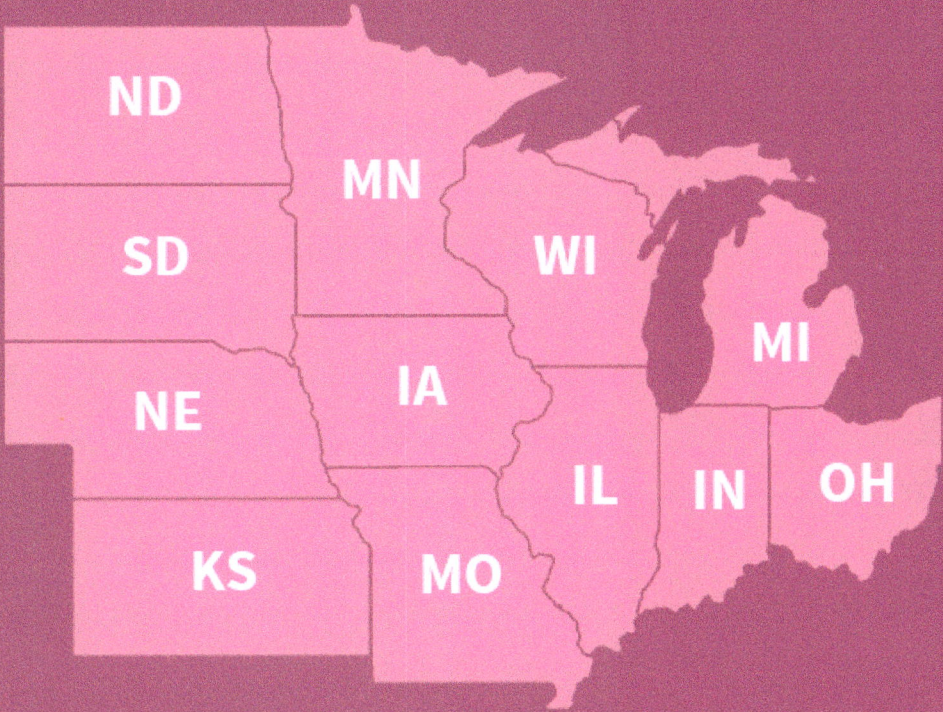

12 *Programs* | **12** *States*

1. IL - Midwestern University Chicago College of Osteopathic Medicine (MWU/CCOM)
2. IN - Marian University College of Osteopathic Medicine (MU-COM)
3. IA – Des Moines University College of Osteopathic Medicine (DMU-COM)
4. MI - Michigan State University College of Osteopathic Medicine (MSUCOM)
5. MI - Michigan State University College of Osteopathic Medicine (MSUCOM-DMC)
6. MI - Michigan State University College of Osteopathic Medicine (MSUCOM-MUC)
7. MO - A. T. Still University Kirksville College of Osteopathic Medicine (ATSU-KCOM)
8. MO - Kansas City University of Medicine and Biosciences College of Osteopathic Medicine (KCU-COM-Joplin)
9. MO - Kansas City University of Medicine and Biosciences College of Osteopathic Medicine (KCU-COM)
10. OH - Ohio University Heritage College of Osteopathic Medicine (OU-HCOM)
11. OH - Ohio University Heritage College of Osteopathic Medicine in Cleveland (OU-HCOM-Cleveland)
12. OH - Ohio University Heritage College of Osteopathic Medicine in Dublin (OU-HCOM-Dublin)

OSTEO PROGRAMS

Osteo School	Ave. GPA & MCAT Early Decision (ED): Yes/No Int'l Students: Yes/No Reapps: Yes/No	Admissions Statistics	Science Req. Other than Gen Chem, OChem, Physics, Bio
Midwestern University Chicago (MWU/CCOM) 555 31st Street, Downers Grove, IL 60515	3.6 (overall) 3.5 (science) MCAT: 508 ED: No Int'l Student: Yes* Reapps: Yes	**(2019)** Apps Received: 3,000 Interview Received: N/A Number Enrolled: 178 Admitted Rate: 5.9% **(2020)** Apps Received: 8,570 Interview Received: N/A Number Enrolled: 205 Admitted Rate: 2.4%	Anatomy, Physio., and Biochem. recommended
Marian University (MU-COM) 3200 Cold Spring Rd, Indianapolis, IN 46222	3.72 (overall) 3.58 (science) MCAT: 504 ED: Yes Int'l Student: Yes Reapps: N/A	**(2019)** Apps Received: 4,577 Interview Received: 523 Number Enrolled: 168 Admitted Rate: 3.6% **(2020)** Apps Received: 5,701 Interview Received: N/A Number Enrolled: 158 Admitted Rate: 2.8%	Biochemistry
Des Moines University College of Osteopathic Medicine (DMU-COM) 3200 Grand Avenue, Des Moines, IA 50312	3.65 (overall) 3.58 (science) MCAT: 507 ED: No Int'l Student: No Reapps: N/A	**(2019)** Apps Received: 4,000 Interview Received: 800 Number Enrolled: 218 Admitted Rate: 5.45% **(2020)** Apps Received: 4,696 Interview Received: N/A Number Enrolled: 221 Admitted Rate:4.7%	Biochemistry
Michigan State University College of Osteopathic Medicine (MSUCOM)** 965 Wilson Rd, East Lansing, MI 48824	3.6 (overall) 3.6 (science) MCAT: 506 ED: No Int'l Student: Yes Reapps: Yes	**(2019)** Apps Received: 5,764 Interview Received: N/A Number Enrolled: 300 Admitted Rate: 5.2% **(2020)** Apps Received: 8,162 Interview Received: N/A Number Enrolled: 294 Admitted Rate: 3.6%	Biochemistry

Osteo School	Ave. GPA & MCAT / Early Decision (ED): Yes/No / Int'l Students: Yes/No / Reapps: Yes/No	Admissions Statistics	Science Req. Other than Gen Chem, OChem, Physics, Bio
Michigan State University College of Osteopathic Medicine at Detroit Medical Center (MSUCOM-DMC)** 4707 Saint Antoine St., Detroit, MI 48201	3.6 (overall) 3.6 (science) MCAT: 506 ED: No Int'l Student: Yes Reapps: Yes	**(2019)** Apps Received: 5,764 Interview Received: N/A Number Enrolled: 300 Admitted Rate: 5.2% **(2020)** Apps Received: 8,162 Interview Received: N/A Number Enrolled: 294 Admitted Rate: 3.6%	Biochemistry
Michigan State University College of Osteopathic Medicine at Macomb University Center (MSUCOM-MUC)** 44575 Garfield Rd., Clinton Twp, MI 48038	3.6 (overall) 3.6 (science) MCAT: 506 ED: No Int'l Student: Yes Reapps: Yes	**(2019)** Apps Received: 5,764 Interview Received: N/A Number Enrolled: 300 Admitted Rate: 5.2% **(2020)** Apps Received: 8,162 Interview Received: N/A Number Enrolled: 294 Admitted Rate: 3.6%	Biochemistry
A. T. Still University Kirksville (ATSU-KCOM) 800 W. Jefferson Street, Kirksville, MO 63501	3.66 (overall) 3.6 (science) MCAT: 504 ED: Yes Int'l Student: No Reapps: N/A	**(2019)** Apps Received: 4,358 Interview Received: 509 Number Enrolled: 170 Admitted Rate: 3.9% **(2020)** Apps Received: 5,323 Interview Received: N/A Number Enrolled: 168 Admitted Rate: 3.2%	N/A

MIDWEST

OSTEO PROGRAMS

Osteo School	Ave. GPA & MCAT Early Decision (ED): Yes/No Int'l Students: Yes/No Reapps: Yes/No	Admissions Statistics	Science Req. Other than Gen Chem, OChem, Physics, Bio
Kansas City University of Medicine and Biosciences College of Osteopathic Medicine (KCU-COM) 1750 Independence Ave., Kansas City, MO 64106	3.58 (overall) 3.63 (science) MCAT: 507 ED: No Int'l Student: Yes Reapps: N/A	**(2019)** Apps Received: N/A Interview Received: N/A Number Enrolled: 270 Admitted Rate: N/A **(2020)*** Apps Received: 5,982 Interview Received: N/A Number Enrolled: 432 Admitted Rate: 7.2%	Biochemistry
Kansas City University of Medicine and Biosciences College of Osteopathic Medicine in Joplin (KCU-COM-Joplin) 2901 St. John's Boulevard, Joplin, MO 64804	3.62 (overall) 3.55 (science) MCAT: 506 ED: No Int'l Student: Yes Reapps: N/A	**(2019)** Apps Received: N/A Interview Received: N/A Number Enrolled: 162 Admitted Rate: N/A **(2020)*** Apps Received: 5,982 Interview Received: N/A Number Enrolled: 432 Admitted Rate: 7.2%	Biochemistry
Ohio University Heritage College of Osteopathic Medicine (OU-HCOM)** 204 Grosvenor Hall, Athens, OH 45701	3.74 (overall) 3.59 (science) MCAT: 504 ED: No Int'l Student: No Reapps: N/A	**(2019)** Apps Received: 4,820 Interview Received: N/A Number Enrolled: 249 Admitted Rate: 5.2% **(2020)** Apps Received: 5,692 Interview Received: N/A Number Enrolled: 252 Admitted Rate: 4.4%	Behavioral Science

Osteo School	Ave. GPA & MCAT Early Decision (ED): Yes/No Int'l Students: Yes/No Reapps: Yes/No	Admissions Statistics	Science Req. Other than Gen Chem, OChem, Physics, Bio
Ohio University Heritage College of Osteopathic Medicine in Cleveland (OU-HCOM-Cleveland)** 4180 Warrensville Center Road, Warrensville Heights, OH 44122	3.6 (overall) 3.74 (overall) 3.59 (science) MCAT: 504 ED: No Int'l Student: No Reapps: N/A	**(2019)** Apps Received: 4,820 Interview Received: N/A Number Enrolled: 249 Admitted Rate: 5.2% **(2020)** Apps Received: 5,692 Interview Received: N/A Number Enrolled: 252 Admitted Rate: 4.4%	Behavioral Science

*Intl. students must complete 30+ semester hours of coursework from college or university in the U.S.
**MSUCOM table data reflects totals from all campuses.
***KCU-COM admissions statistics for 2020 reflect totals from all campuses.
****OU-HCOM table data reflects totals from both campuses.

MIDWEST

MIDWESTERN UNIVERSITY CHICAGO COLLEGE OF OSTEOPATHIC MEDICINE (MWU/CCOM)

Address: 555 31st Street, Downers Grove, IL 60515
Website: *https://www.midwestern.edu/academics/degrees-and-programs/doctor-of-osteopathic-medicine-il.xml*
Contact: *https://online.midwestern.edu/public/reqinfo.cgi*
Phone: (630) 515-6171

Other campus locations: Glendale, AZ

COST OF ATTENDANCE

Tuition: $73,348
Fees & Expenses: $32,547
Total: $105,895

Financial Aid: https://www.midwestern.edu/admissions/tuition-and-financial-aid/scholarships.xml

Percent Receiving Aid: 94%

ADDITIONAL INFORMATION

Interesting tidbit: The origin of Midwestern University is one of osteopathic medicine. It was founded in 1900 as the American College of Osteopathic Medicine. MWU is organized primarily to provide graduate and postgraduate education in the health sciences; Healthcare education is what it does.

What international experiences are available? N/A

What dual degree options exist? DO/MS in Biomedical Sciences available.

Percent of graduates receiving residency matches: 98.5% (2021)

What service learning opportunities exist? Clinical rotations throughout Chicago area, Northwest Indiana, Midwest, and throughout the U.S.

Important Updates due to COVID-19: Accept online coursework to fulfill prerequisite requirements. Accept prerequisite coursework Pass/Fail grades. Accept online lab coursework.

Were tests required? MCAT required.

Are tests expected next year? Yes.

COMLEX First-Time Pass Rate (Level 1, Level 2 Cognitive Evaluation, Level 2 Performance Evaluation, Level 3)*

Level 1: 96% (2019)

Level 2 CE: 97% (2019)

Level 2 PE: 96% (2019)

Level 3: 98.1% (2018)

ILLINOIS

INDIANA

IOWA

KANSAS

MICHIGAN

MINNESOTA

MISSOURI

NEBRASKA

NORTH DAKOTA

OHIO

SOUTH DAKOTA

WISCONSIN

MARIAN UNIVERSITY COLLEGE OF OSTEOPATHIC MEDICINE (MU-COM)

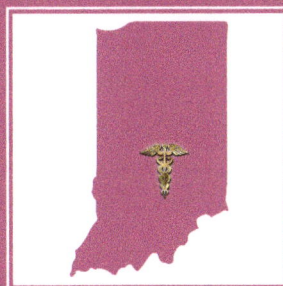

Address: 3200 Cold Spring Rd, Indianapolis, IN 46222
Website: *https://www.marian.edu/osteopathic-medical-school*
Contact: *https://www.marian.edu/osteopathic-medical-school/contact-us*
Phone: (317) 955-6297

Other campus locations: N/A

COST OF ATTENDANCE

Tuition: $55,300
Fees & Expenses: $21,681
Total: $76,981

Financial Aid: https://www.marian.edu/osteopathic-medical-school/financial-aid/Scholarships

Percent Receiving Aid: 76%

ADDITIONAL INFORMATION

Interesting tidbit: Opening in 2013, the Marian University College of Osteopathic Medicine (MU-COM) became Indiana's first medical school in 110 years. With the provisional accreditation in July 2012 from the American Osteopathic Association Commission on Osteopathic College Accreditation (COCA), MU-COM enrolled the first class of osteopathic medical students in the state's history in August 2013.

What international experiences are available? N/A

What dual degree options exist? No dual degree options listed.

Percent of graduates receiving residency matches: 96% (2021)

What service learning opportunities exist? Clinical rotations include treating patients in rural, suburban, and urban environments.

Important Updates due to COVID-19: Accept online coursework to fulfill prerequisite requirements. Accept prerequisite coursework Pass/Fail grades. Accept online lab coursework.

Were tests required? MCAT required.

Are tests expected next year? Yes.

COMLEX First-Time Pass Rate (Level 1, Level 2 Cognitive Evaluation, Level 2 Performance Evaluation, Level 3)

Level 1: 94.19% (2019/20)

Level 2 CE: 99.36% (2019/20)

Level 2 PE: 91.8% (2019/20)

Level 3: 99.40% (2018/19)

Other: Fast Track Program for undergraduates at partnering institutions. Early admission or guaranteed interview given to these students. For more information, visit: https://www.marian.edu/osteopathic-medical-school/admissions/special-programs

ILLINOIS

INDIANA

IOWA

KANSAS

MICHIGAN

MINNESOTA

MISSOURI

NEBRASKA

NORTH DAKOTA

OHIO

SOUTH DAKOTA

WISCONSIN

MIDWEST

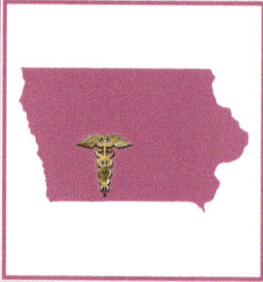

ILLINOIS

INDIANA

IOWA

KANSAS

MICHIGAN

MINNESOTA

MISSOURI

NEBRASKA

NORTH DAKOTA

OHIO

SOUTH DAKOTA

WISCONSIN

DES MOINES UNIVERSITY COLLEGE OF OSTEOPATHIC MEDICINE (DMU-COM)

Address: 3200 Grand Avenue, Des Moines, IA 50312
Website: *https://www.dmu.edu/do/*
Contact: *https://www.dmu.edu/admission/request-information/*
Phone: (515) 271-1400

Other campus locations: N/A

COST OF ATTENDANCE

Tuition: $53,720
Fees & Expenses: $25,373
Total: $79,093

Financial Aid: https://www.dmu.edu/financial-aid/scholarships/

Percent Receiving Aid: 83%

ADDITIONAL INFORMATION

Interesting tidbit: DMU is the largest medical school in Iowa–and among the top 25 largest accredited schools in the nation (for D.O.s or M.D.s). Hence, it is one of the institutions producing most of the primary care physicians in the nation.

What international experiences are available? Global service trips, rotations, and internships available. For more information, visit: https://www.dmu.edu/globalhealth/

What dual degree options exist? Dual degree programs available. For more information, visit: https://www.dmu.edu/do/dual-degree/

Percent of graduates receiving residency matches: 99% (2021)

What service learning opportunities exist? See "International Experiences".

Important Updates due to COVID-19: Physician LOR not required. Accept online coursework to fulfill prerequisite requirements. Accept prerequisite coursework Pass/Fail grades on a case-by-case basis. Accept online lab coursework.

Were tests required? MCAT required and SJT by AAMC strongly encouraged.

Are tests expected next year? Yes.

COMLEX First-Time Pass Rate (Level 1, Level 2 Cognitive Evaluation, Level 2 Performance Evaluation, Level 3) (2019/20)

Level 1: 95.8%

Level 2 CE: 98.6%

Level 2 PE: 96.2%

Level 3: N/A

MICHIGAN STATE UNIVERSITY COLLEGE OF OSTEOPATHIC MEDICINE (MSUCOM)

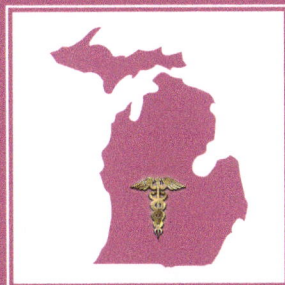

Address: 965 Wilson Rd, East Lansing, MI 48824
Website: *https://com.msu.edu/*
Contact: *https://com.msu.edu/about-us/contact-information*
Phone: (517) 353-7740

Other campus locations: Clinton Township (Macomb University Center); Detroit, MI

COST OF ATTENDANCE

In-State Tuition: $46,968
Fees & Expenses: $34,784
Total: $81,752

Out-of-State Tuition: $65,323
Fees & Expenses: $34,784
Total: $100,107

Financial Aid: https://com.msu.edu/future-students/applying/financial-aid-and-scholarships

Percent Receiving Aid: 83%

ADDITIONAL INFORMATION

Interesting tidbit: Since 2009, the college has operated under a model of "One College, Three Sites." Each campus is home to roughly one-third of each enrolled class. The college also receives more research funding from the National Institutes of Health than any other osteopathic college in the nation.

What international experiences are available? Various elective international experiences and clerkships offered in Guatemala, Peru, Cuba, South Korea, etc. For more information, visit: https://com.msu.edu/about-us/international-opportunities

What percent of students take an extra year for research or a dual degree? 47 students enrolled in DO/PhD program across three campuses. For more information on dual degree options, visit: https://com.msu.edu/future-students/dual-degree-programs

Percent of graduates receiving residency matches: 94% (2021)

What service learning opportunities exist? Community Integrated Medicine and other clinical outreach opportunities available. For more information, visit: https://com.msu.edu/about-us/clinical-outreach

Important Updates due to COVID-19: Accept pass/fail coursework for any courses impacted by this situation. This holds both in cases where pass/fail is mandated by your institution and also in cases of individual choice.

Were tests required? MCAT required.

Are tests expected next year? Yes.

COMLEX First-Time Pass Rate (Level 1, Level 2 Cognitive Evaluation, Level 2 Performance Evaluation, Level 3) (2019/20)

Level 1: 94.46%

Level 2 CE: 97.96%

Level 2 PE: N/A

Level 3: N/A

ILLINOIS

INDIANA

IOWA

KANSAS

MICHIGAN

MINNESOTA

MISSOURI

NEBRASKA

NORTH DAKOTA

OHIO

SOUTH DAKOTA

WISCONSIN

MIDWEST

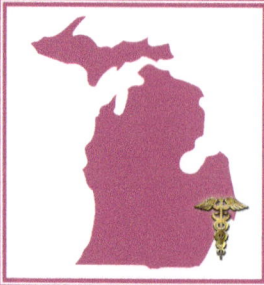

ILLINOIS

INDIANA

IOWA

KANSAS

MICHIGAN

MINNESOTA

MISSOURI

NEBRASKA

NORTH DAKOTA

OHIO

SOUTH DAKOTA

WISCONSIN

MICHIGAN STATE UNIVERSITY COLLEGE OF OSTEOPATHIC MEDICINE (MSUCOM-DMC)

Address: 4707 Saint Antoine St., Detroit, MI 48201
Website: *https://com.msu.edu/*
Contact: *https://com.msu.edu/about-us/contact-information*

Phone: (517) 884-9600

Other campus locations: Clinton Township (Macomb University Center); East Lansing, MI

COST OF ATTENDANCE

In-State Tuition: $46,968
Fees & Expenses: $34,784
Total: $81,752

Out-of-State Tuition: $65,323
Fees & Expenses: $34,784
Total: $100,107

Financial Aid: https://com.msu.edu/future-students/applying/financial-aid-and-scholarships

Percent Receiving Aid: 83%

ADDITIONAL INFORMATION

Interesting tidbit: MSU College of Osteopathic Medicine students have three great options for completing their first two years of medical school. Whether you decide to study at the Detroit Medical Center site, on the MSU campus in East Lansing or at the Macomb University Center in Clinton Township, you'll get the same exceptional preclinical experience.

What international experiences are available? Various elective international experiences and clerkships offered in Guatemala, Peru, Cuba, South Korea, etc. For more information, visit: https://com.msu.edu/about-us/international-opportunities

What percent of students take an extra year for research or a dual degree? 47 students enrolled in DO/PhD program across three campuses. For more information on dual degree options, visit: https://com.msu.edu/future-students/dual-degree-programs

Percent of graduates receiving residency matches: 94% (2021)

What service learning opportunities exist? Community Integrated Medicine and other clinical outreach opportunities available. For more information, visit: https://com.msu.edu/about-us/clinical-outreach

Important Updates due to COVID-19: Accept pass/fail coursework for any courses impacted by this situation. This holds both in cases where pass/fail is mandated by your institution and also in cases of individual choice.

Were tests required? MCAT required.

Are tests expected next year? Yes.

COMLEX First-Time Pass Rate (Level 1, Level 2 Cognitive Evaluation, Level 2 Performance Evaluation, Level 3)

Level 1: 94.46%

Level 2 CE: 97.96%

Level 2 PE: N/A

Level 3: N/A

MICHIGAN STATE UNIVERSITY COLLEGE OF OSTEOPATHIC MEDICINE (MSUCOM-MUC)

Address: 44575 Garfield Rd., Clinton Twp, MI 48038
Website: *https://com.msu.edu/*
Contact: *https://com.msu.edu/about-us/contact-information*
Phone: (586) 263-6731

Other campus locations: Detroit, MI; East Lansing, MI

COST OF ATTENDANCE

In-State Tuition: $46,968
Fees & Expenses: $34,784
Total: $81,752

Out-of-State Tuition: $65,323
Fees & Expenses: $34,784
Total: $100,107

Financial Aid: https://com.msu.edu/future-students/applying/financial-aid-and-scholarships

Percent Receiving Aid: 83%

ADDITIONAL INFORMATION

Interesting tidbit: Located within a 20-mile radius of seven hospitals with over 600 osteopathic graduate medical education positions, this site is housed within the Macomb University Center at Macomb Community College.

What international experiences are available? Various elective international experiences and clerkships offered in Guatemala, Peru, Cuba, South Korea, etc. For more information, visit: https://com.msu.edu/about-us/international-opportunities

What percent of students take an extra year for research or a dual degree? 47 students enrolled in DO/PhD program across three campuses. For more information on dual degree options, visit: https://com.msu.edu/future-students/dual-degree-programs

Percent of graduates receiving residency matches: 94% (2021)

What service learning opportunities exist? Community Integrated Medicine and other clinical outreach opportunities available. For more information, visit: https://com.msu.edu/about-us/clinical-outreach

Important Updates due to COVID-19: Accept pass/fail coursework for any courses impacted by this situation. This holds both in cases where pass/fail is mandated by your institution and also in cases of individual choice.

Were tests required? MCAT required.

Are tests expected next year? Yes.

COMLEX First-Time Pass Rate (Level 1, Level 2 Cognitive Evaluation, Level 2 Performance Evaluation, Level 3)

Level 1: 94.46%

Level 2 CE: 97.96%

Level 2 PE: N/A

Level 3: N/A

ILLINOIS

INDIANA

IOWA

KANSAS

MICHIGAN

MINNESOTA

MISSOURI

NEBRASKA

NORTH DAKOTA

OHIO

SOUTH DAKOTA

WISCONSIN

MIDWEST

ILLINOIS

INDIANA

IOWA

KANSAS

MICHIGAN

MINNESOTA

MISSOURI

NEBRASKA

NORTH DAKOTA

OHIO

SOUTH DAKOTA

WISCONSIN

A. T. STILL UNIVERSITY KIRKSVILLE COLLEGE OF OSTEOPATHIC MEDICINE (ATSU-KCOM)

Address: 800 W. Jefferson Street, Kirksville, MO 63501
Website: *https://www.atsu.edu/kirksville-college-of-osteopathic-medicine*
Contact: *https://www.atsu.edu/connect/contact-atsu*
Phone: (660) 626-2121

Other campus locations: Mesa, AZ

COST OF ATTENDANCE

Tuition: $59,368
Fees & Expenses: $27,839
Total: $87,207

Financial Aid: https://www.atsu.edu/department-of-student-affairs/enrollment-services/types-of-aid

Percent Receiving Aid: 90%

ADDITIONAL INFORMATION

Interesting tidbit: ATSU-KCOM is the first institution of osteopathic education in the world. As the founding college of osteopathic medicine, ATSU-KCOM has a 125-year history of upholding healthcare with a holistic approach.

What international experiences are available? Students may spend their fourth year at an approved international rotation.

What dual degree options exist? DO/MPH and DO/MHA available.

Percent of graduates receiving residency matches: 99.6% (three year average)

What service learning opportunities exist? Clinical rotations in rural/underserved family medicine

Important Updates due to COVID-19: Accept online coursework to fulfill prerequisite requirements and lab coursework. Accept prerequisite coursework Pass/Fail grades.

Were tests required? MCAT required.

Are tests expected next year? Yes.

COMLEX First-Time Pass Rate (Level 1, Level 2 Cognitive Evaluation, Level 2 Performance Evaluation, Level 3)

Level 1: 98.17% (2019/20)

Level 2 CE: 97.09% (2019/20)

Level 2 PE: 94% (2019/20)

Level 3: 96.7% (2019/19)

Other: ATSU-KCOM has the Museum of Osteopathic Medicine, which details the history of the field. For more information: https://www.atsu.edu/museum-of-osteopathic-medicine/

Still Scholars Early Acceptance Program available to U.S. citizens. This program provides conditional admission and an academic scholarship for selected students to attend ATSU-KCOM. Open to students with 2 years of undergraduate coursework complete. For more information, visit: https://www.atsu.edu/kirksville-college-of-osteopathic-medicine/admissions/still-scholars-admission-requirements

KANSAS CITY UNIVERSITY OF MEDICINE AND BIOSCIENCES COLLEGE OF OSTEOPATHIC MEDICINE (KCU-COM)

Address: 1750 Independence Ave., Kansas City, MO 64106
Website: *http://www.kcumb.edu/programs/college-of-osteopathic-medicine*
Contact: *http://www.kcumb.edu/contact-us*
Phone: (816) 654-7000

Other campus locations: Joplin, MO

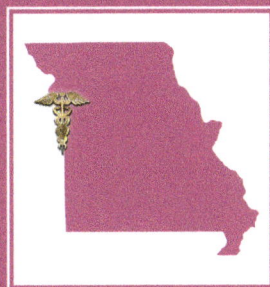

COST OF ATTENDANCE

Tuition: $49,888
Fees & Expenses: $26,307
Total: $76,195

Financial Aid: http://www.kcumb.edu/admissions/financial-aid/scholarships

Percent Receiving Aid: 75%

ADDITIONAL INFORMATION

Interesting tidbit: As one of the five original schools of osteopathic medicine, KCU-COM has been a leader in osteopathic medicine for more than a century.

What international experiences are available? Medical Mission trips. For more information, visit: http://www.kcumb.edu/programs/clinical-experience/medical-mission

What dual degree options exist? Dual degree programs available. For more information, visit: http://www.kcumb.edu/programs/dual-degrees

Percent of graduates receiving residency matches: 100% (2020)

What service learning opportunities exist? Medical Mission. See "International Experiences". In addition, they offer rural clerkship opportunities.

Important Updates due to COVID-19: Accept online coursework to fulfill prerequisite requirements. Accept prerequisite coursework Pass/Fail grades if from a regionally accredited university/college. Accept online lab coursework.

Were tests required? MCAT required.

Are tests expected next year? Yes.

COMLEX First-Time Pass Rate (Level 1, Level 2 Cognitive Evaluation, Level 2 Performance Evaluation, Level 3)

Level 1: 96.8% (2019/20)

Level 2 CE: 98.9% (2019/20)

Level 2 PE: 93.7% (2019/20)

Level 3: 98.2% (2018/19)

Other: KCU-COM offers a Military Honors Track for DO students. For more information, visit: https://www.kcumb.edu/programs/college-of-osteopathic-medicine/curriculum/military-medicine

ILLINOIS

INDIANA

IOWA

KANSAS

MICHIGAN

MINNESOTA

MISSOURI

NEBRASKA

NORTH DAKOTA

OHIO

SOUTH DAKOTA

WISCONSIN

MIDWEST

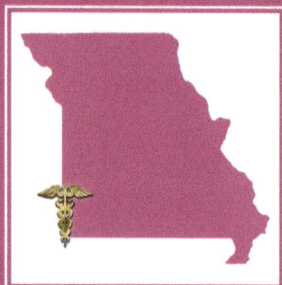

ILLINOIS

INDIANA

IOWA

KANSAS

MICHIGAN

MINNESOTA

MISSOURI

NEBRASKA

NORTH DAKOTA

OHIO

SOUTH DAKOTA

WISCONSIN

KANSAS CITY UNIVERSITY OF MEDICINE AND BIOSCIENCES COLLEGE OF OSTEOPATHIC MEDICINE (KCU-COM-JOPLIN)

Address: 2901 St. John's Boulevard, Joplin, MO 64804
Website: *http://www.kcumb.edu/programs/college-of-osteopathic-medicine*
Contact: *http://www.kcumb.edu/contact-us*
Phone: (417) 208-0630

Other campus locations: Kansas City, MO

COST OF ATTENDANCE

Tuition: $49,888
Fees & Expenses: $26,307
Total: $76,195

Financial Aid: http://www.kcumb.edu/admissions/financial-aid/scholarships

Percent Receiving Aid: 75%

ADDITIONAL INFORMATION

Interesting tidbit: KCU-COM found a second home in Joplin to address issues of providing adequate health care to a growing, aging and rural population.

What international experiences are available? Medical Mission trips. For more information, visit: http://www.kcumb.edu/programs/clinical-experience/medical-mission

What dual degree options exist? Dual degree programs not currently available. However, a dual degree for an MBA or Bioethics may be available in the future.

Percent of graduates receiving residency matches: 100% (2020)

What service learning opportunities exist? Rural clerkship opportunities and international medical mission trips.

Important Updates due to COVID-19: Accept online coursework to fulfill prerequisite requirements. Accept prerequisite coursework Pass/Fail grades if from a regionally accredited university/college. Accept online lab coursework.

Were tests required? MCAT required.

Are tests expected next year? Yes.

COMLEX First-Time Pass Rate (Level 1, Level 2 Cognitive Evaluation, Level 2 Performance Evaluation, Level 3)

Level 1: 96.8% (2019/20)

Level 2 CE: 98.9% (2019/20)

Level 2 PE: 93.7% (2019/20)

Level 3: 98.2% (2018/19)

Other: KCU-COM at Joplin offers a Military Honors Track for DO students. For more information, visit: https://www.kcumb.edu/programs/college-of-osteopathic-medicine/curriculum/military-medicine

OHIO UNIVERSITY HERITAGE COLLEGE OF OSTEOPATHIC MEDICINE (OU-HCOM)

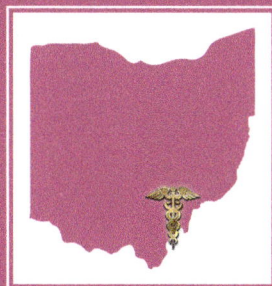

Address: 204 Grosvenor Hall, Athens, OH 45701
Website: *https://www.ohio.edu/medicine/*
Contact: *https://www.ohio.edu/medicine/about/offices/admissions/directory*
Phone: (800) 345-1560

Other campus locations: Cleveland, OH; Dublin, OH

COST OF ATTENDANCE

In-State Tuition: $37,068
Fees & Expenses: $32,795
Total: $69,863

Out-of-State Tuition: $52,864
Fees & Expenses: $32,795
Total: $85,659

Financial Aid: https://www.ohio.edu/medicine/med-admissions/financing

Percent Receiving Aid: 89%

ADDITIONAL INFORMATION

Interesting tidbit: The Heritage College is working with Ohio University to plan a new $65 million academic home for its Athens campus.

What international experiences are available? N/A

What dual degree options exist? Dual degree programs available. For more information, visit: https://www.ohio.edu/medicine/med-education/dual-degree

Percent of graduates receiving residency matches: 99% (2020)

What service learning opportunities exist? Diabetes Community Partners, Community Health Programs, and Diabetes Free Clinic. For more information, visit: https://www.ohio.edu/medicine/di/community-outreach

Rural and Urban Scholars Pathways (RUSP) available. For more information, visit: https://www.ohio.edu/medicine/about/offices/rural-underserved-programs/programs/pathways-programs

Important Updates due to COVID-19: Accept Pass/Fail grading.

Were tests required? MCAT required.

Are tests expected next year? Yes.

COMLEX First-Time Pass Rate (Level 1, Level 2 Cognitive Evaluation, Level 2 Performance Evaluation, Level 3)
Level 1: 90%
Level 2 CE: 95%
Level 2 PE: 92%
Level 3: 97%

Other: Early Assurance Program available for high school applicants. MCAT not required. For more information, visit: https://www.ohio.edu/medicine/med-admissions/apply/eap

Note: One application for all three OU-HCOM campuses. Rank campus of choice in the secondary application and submit a separate essay for each campus ranked.

ILLINOIS

INDIANA

IOWA

KANSAS

MICHIGAN

MINNESOTA

MISSOURI

NEBRASKA

NORTH DAKOTA

OHIO

SOUTH DAKOTA

WISCONSIN

MIDWEST

ILLINOIS

INDIANA

IOWA

KANSAS

MICHIGAN

MINNESOTA

MISSOURI

NEBRASKA

NORTH DAKOTA

OHIO

SOUTH DAKOTA

WISCONSIN

OHIO UNIVERSITY HERITAGE COLLEGE OF OSTEOPATHIC MED. IN CLEVELAND (OU-HCOM-CLEVELAND)

Address: 4180 Warrensville Center Road, Warrensville Heights, OH 44122
Website: *https://www.ohio.edu/medicine/*
Contact: *https://www.ohio.edu/medicine/about/offices/admissions/ directory*
Phone: (800) 345-1560
Other campus locations: Athens, OH; Dublin, OH

COST OF ATTENDANCE

In-State Tuition: $37,068
Fees & Expenses: $32,795
Total: $69,863

Out-of-State Tuition: $52,864
Fees & Expenses: $32,795
Total: $85,659

Financial Aid: https://www.ohio.edu/medicine/med-admissions/financing
Percent Receiving Aid: 89%

ADDITIONAL INFORMATION

Interesting tidbit: OU-HCOM-Cleveland is the newest campus to OU-HCOM. With the interactive videoconferencing system, students can study with world-renowned physicians, participate in lectures across the state, access the resources of affiliate health care systems, and connect to fellow students in Athens and Dublin.

What international experiences are available? N/A

What dual degree options exist? Dual degree programs available. For more information, visit: https://www.ohio.edu/medicine/med-education/dual-degree

Percent of graduates receiving residency matches: 99% (2020)

What service learning opportunities exist? Diabetes Community Partners, Community Health Programs, and Diabetes Free Clinic. For more information, visit: https://www.ohio.edu/medicine/di/community-outreach

Rural and Urban Scholars Pathways (RUSP) available. For more information, visit: https://www.ohio.edu/medicine/about/offices/rural-underserved-programs/programs/pathways-programs

Important Updates due to COVID-19: Accept Pass/Fail grading.

Were tests required? MCAT required.

Are tests expected next year? Yes.

COMLEX First-Time Pass Rate (Level 1, Level 2 Cognitive Evaluation, Level 2 Performance Evaluation, Level 3)

Level 1: 90%

Level 2 CE: 95%

Level 2 PE: 92%

Level 3: 97%

Other: Early Assurance Program available for high school applicants. MCAT not required. For more information, visit: https://www.ohio.edu/medicine/med-admissions/apply/eap

Note: One application for all three OU-HCOM campuses. Rank campus of choice in the secondary application and submit a separate essay for each campus ranked.

OHIO UNIVERSITY HERITAGE COLLEGE OF OSTEOPATHIC MED. IN DUBLIN (OU-HCOM-DUBLIN)

Address: 6775 Bobcat Way, Dublin, OH 43016
Website: *https://www.ohio.edu/medicine/*
Contact: *https://www.ohio.edu/medicine/about/offices/admissions/ directory*
Phone: (800) 345-1560
Other campus locations: Athens, OH; Cleveland, OH

COST OF ATTENDANCE

In-State Tuition: $37,068
Fees & Expenses: $32,795
Total: $69,863

Out-of-State Tuition: $52,864
Fees & Expenses: $32,795
Total: $85,659

Financial Aid: https://www.ohio.edu/medicine/med-admissions/ financing

Percent Receiving Aid: 89%

ADDITIONAL INFORMATION

Interesting tidbit: As with students on Athens and Cleveland campuses, students at Dublin campus have the opportunity to participate in the T.O.U.C.H Program, a national volunteer initiative organized through the Council of Osteopathic Student Government Presidents. All Heritage College students must enroll in the program and can earn their volunteer hours through services offered through the college's Community Health Programs and community partners in Athens, Columbus and Cleveland.
What international experiences are available? N/A
What dual degree options exist? Dual degree programs available. For more information, visit: https://www.ohio.edu/medicine/med-education/dual-degree
Percent of graduates receiving residency matches: 99% (2020)
What service learning opportunities exist? Diabetes Community Partners, Community Health Programs, and Diabetes Free Clinic. For more information, visit: https://www.ohio.edu/medicine/di/ community-outreach
Rural and Urban Scholars Pathways (RUSP) available. For more information, visit: https://www.ohio.edu/medicine/about/offices/ rural-underserved-programs/programs/pathways-programs
Important Updates due to COVID-19: Accept Pass/Fail grading.
Were tests required? MCAT required.
Are tests expected next year? Yes.
COMLEX First-Time Pass Rate (Level 1, Level 2 Cognitive Evaluation, Level 2 Performance Evaluation, Level 3)
Level 1: 90%
Level 2 CE: 95%
Level 2 PE: 92%
Level 3: 97%
Other: Early Assurance Program available for high school applicants. MCAT not required. For more information, visit: https://www.ohio.edu/medicine/med-admissions/apply/eap
Note: One application for all three OU-HCOM campuses. Rank campus of choice in secondary application and submit separate essay for each campus ranked.

ILLINOIS

INDIANA

IOWA

KANSAS

MICHIGAN

MINNESOTA

MISSOURI

NEBRASKA

NORTH DAKOTA

OHIO

SOUTH DAKOTA

WISCONSIN

MIDWEST

CHAPTER 4
REGION THREE
SOUTH

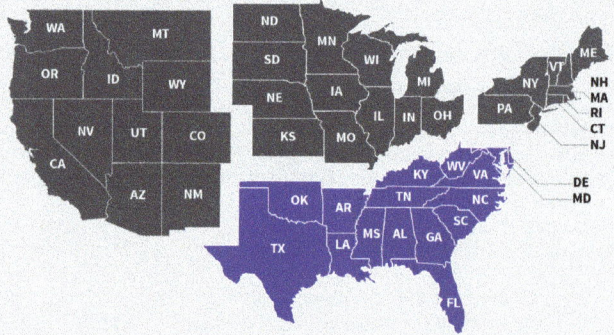

ALABAMA

ARKANSAS

DELAWARE

DISTRICT OF
COLUMBIA

FLORIDA

GEORGIA

KENTUCKY

LOUISIANA

MARYLAND

MISSISSIPPI

NORTH CAROLINA

OKLAHOMA

SOUTH CAROLINA

TENNESSEE

TEXAS

VIRGINIA

WEST VIRGINIA

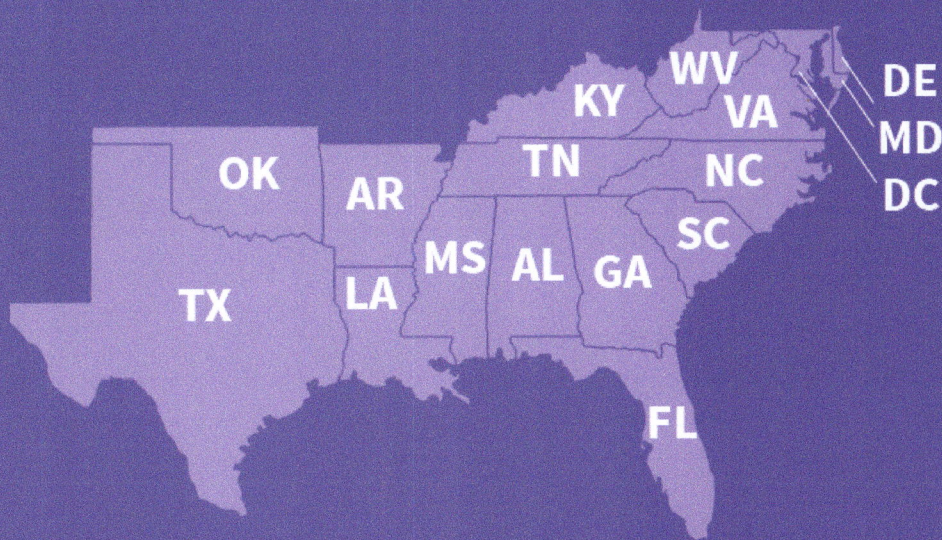

24 *Programs* | **16** *States*

1. AL – Alabama College of Osteopathic Medicine (ACOM)
2. AL - Edward Via College of Osteopathic Medicine (VCOM - Auburn Campus)
3. AR - Arkansas College of Osteopathic Medicine (ARCOM)
4. AR - New York Institute of Technology College of Osteopathic Medicine at Arkansas State (NYITCOM)
5. FL - Lake Erie College of Osteopathic Medicine-Bradenton (LECOM-Bradenton)
6. FL - Nova Southeastern University Dr. Kiran C. Patel College of Osteopathic Medicine (NSU-KPCOM)
7. FL - Nova Southeastern University Dr. Kiran C. Patel College of Osteopathic Medicine (NSU-KPCOM-Clearwater)
8. GA - Philadelphia College of Osteopathic Medicine Georgia (PCOM Georgia)
9. GA - Philadelphia College of Osteopathic Medicine South Georgia (PCOM South Georgia)
10. KY - University of Pikeville Kentucky College of Osteopathic Medicine (UP-KYCOM)
11. LA - Edward Via College of Osteopathic Medicine-Monroe Campus (VCOM - Monroe Campus)
12. MS - William Carey University College of Osteopathic Medicine (WCUCOM)
13. NC - Campbell University Jerry M. Wallace School of Osteopathic Medicine (CUSOM)
14. OK - Oklahoma State University Center for Health Sciences College of Osteopathic Medicine (OSU-COM)
15. OK - Oklahoma State University Center for Health Sciences College of Osteopathic Medicine - Tahlequah (OSU-COM Tahlequah)
16. SC - Edward Via College of Osteopathic Medicine-Carolinas Campus (VCOM - Carolinas Campus)
17. TN - Lincoln Memorial University DeBusk College of Osteopathic Medicine - Knoxville (LMU-DCOM)
18. TN - Lincoln Memorial University DeBusk College of Osteopathic Medicine (LMU-DCOM Knoxville)
19. TX - Sam Houston State University College of Osteopathic Medicine
20. TX - University of North Texas Health Science Center Texas College of Osteopathic Medicine (UNTHSC/ TCOM)
21. TX - University of the Incarnate Word School of Osteopathic Medicine (UIWSOM)
22. VA - Edward Via College of Osteopathic Medicine (VCOM-Virginia Campus)
23. VA - Liberty University College of Osteopathic Medicine (LUCOM)
24. WV - West Virginia School of Osteopathic Medicine (WVSOM)

OSTEO PROGRAMS

Osteo School	Ave. GPA & DAT / Early Decision (ED) : Yes/No / Int'l Students: Yes/No / Reapps: Yes/No	Admissions Statistics	Science Req. Other than Gen Chem, OChem, Physics, Bio
Alabama College of Osteopathic Medicine (ACOM) 445 Health Sciences Blvd, Dothan, AL 36303	3.45 (overall) 3.35 (science) MCAT: 504 ED: No Int'l Student: Yes Reapps: N/A	**(2019)** Apps Received: 3,000 Interview Received: N/A Number Enrolled: 178 Admitted Rate: 5.9% **(2020)** Apps Received: 5,871 Interview Received: N/A Number Enrolled: 206 Admitted Rate: 3.5%	N/A
VCOM - Auburn Campus 910 South Donahue Dr., Auburn, AL 36832	3.65 (overall) 3.59 (science) MCAT: 501 ED: Yes Int'l Student: No Reapps: Yes	**(2019)** Apps Received: 3,335 Interview Received: N/A Number Enrolled: 162 Admitted Rate: 4.85% **(2020)** Apps Received: 3,962 Interview Received: N/A Number Enrolled: 162 Admitted Rate: 4.15	6+ Biomedical Sci. Credit Hours: Anatomy, Physio., Biochem., Immunology, Microbio., virology, or genetics
Arkansas College of Osteopathic Medicine (ARCOM) 7000 Chad Colley Blvd., Fort Smith, AR 72916	3.6 (overall) N/A (science) MCAT: 502 ED: No Int'l Student: No Reapps: N/A	**(2019)** Apps Received: N/A Interview Received: N/A Number Enrolled: 150 Admitted Rate: N/A **(2020)** Apps Received: 3,463 Interview Received: N/A Number Enrolled: 162 Admitted Rate: 4.7%	Biochemistry Science Electives

OSTEO PROGRAMS

Osteo School	Ave. GPA & DAT Early Decision (ED) : Yes/No Int'l Students: Yes/No Reapps: Yes/No	Admissions Statistics	Science Req. Other than Gen Chem, OChem, Physics, Bio
NYITCOM at Arkansas State* 2405 Aggie Rd, Jonesboro, AR 72401	3.6 (overall) N/A (science) MCAT: 505 ED: No Int'l Student: Yes Reapps: N/A	6,092 1100 435 7.14% **(2019)** Apps Received: 6,092 Interview Received: 1,100 Number Enrolled: 435 Admitted Rate: 7.14% **(2020)** Apps Received: 7,700 Interview Received: N/A Number Enrolled: 438 Admitted Rate: 5.7%	OChem 2 (Biochem. can substitute)
LECOM-Bradenton 5000 Lakewood Ranch Boulevard, Bradenton, FL 34211	3.5 (overall) 3.4 (science) MCAT: 503 ED: No Int'l Student: Yes Reapps: Yes	**(2019)** Apps Received: 6,853 Interview Received: N/A Number Enrolled: 200 Admitted Rate: 2.9% **(2020)** Apps Received: 9,052 Interview Received: N/A Number Enrolled: 196 Admitted Rate: 2.2%	Behavioral Sciences Adv. Coursework rec.
NSU-KPCOM** 3301 College Avenue, Fort Lauderdale, FL 33314	3.5 (overall) 3.5 (science) MCAT: 505 ED: No Int'l Student: Yes Reapps: Yes	**(2019)** Apps Received: 7,500 Interview Received: 1,000 Number Enrolled: 410 Admitted Rate: 5.5% **(2020)** Apps Received: 8,212 Interview Received: N/A Number Enrolled: 410 Admitted Rate: 5.5%	Biochemistry

SOUTH

OSTEO PROGRAMS

Osteo School	Ave. GPA & DAT Early Decision (ED) : Yes/No Int'l Students: Yes/No Reapps: Yes/No	Admissions Statistics	Science Req. Other than Gen Chem, OChem, Physics, Bio
NSU-KPCOM-Clearwater** 3400 Gulf to Bay Blvd., Clearwater, FL 33759	3.5 (overall) 3.5 (science) MCAT: 505 ED: No Int'l Student: Yes Reapps: Yes	(2019) Apps Received: 7,500 Interview Received: 1,000 Number Enrolled: 410 Admitted Rate: 5.5% (2020) Apps Received: 8,212 Interview Received: N/A Number Enrolled: 410 Admitted Rate: 5.5%	Biochemistry
PCOM Georgia 625 Old Peachtree Road NW, Suwanee, GA 30024	N/A (overall) N/A (science) MCAT: 503 ED: No Int'l Student: No Reapps: N/A	(2019) Apps Received: 3,527 Interview Received: N/A Number Enrolled: 132 Admitted Rate: 3.7% (2020) Apps Received: 4,410 Interview Received: N/A Number Enrolled: 135 Admitted Rate: 3.15	Biochemistry
PCOM S. Georgia 2050 Tallokas Road, Moultrie, GA 31768	N/A (overall) N/A (science) MCAT: 500 ED: No Int'l Student: NO Reapps: N/A	(2019) Apps Received: 2,108 Interview Received: N/A Number Enrolled: 59 Admitted Rate: 2.8% (2020) Apps Received: Interview Received: Number Enrolled: Admitted Rate:	Biochemistry
Univ. of Pikeville Kentucky (UP-KYCOM) 147 Sycamore Street, Pikeville, KY 41501	3.5 (overall) 3.4 (science) MCAT: 500 ED: No Int'l Student: No Reapps: N/A	(2019) Apps Received: 3,800 Interview Received: 800 Number Enrolled: 140 Admitted Rate: 3.7% (2020) Apps Received: 4,513 Interview Received: N/A Number Enrolled: 132 Admitted Rate: 2.9%	8 sem. hours of OChem (4 may be Biochem.)

OSTEO PROGRAMS

Osteo School	Ave. GPA & DAT / Early Decision (ED) : Yes/No / Int'l Students: Yes/No / Reapps: Yes/No	Admissions Statistics	Science Req. Other than Gen Chem, OChem, Physics, Bio
VCOM - Monroe Campus 4408 Bon Aire Dr., Monroe, LA 71203	3.65 (overall) 3.59 (science) MCAT: 501 ED: Yes Int'l Student: No Reapps: Yes	**(2019)*** Apps Received: N/A Interview Received: N/A Number Enrolled: 162 Admitted Rate: N/A **(2020)** Apps Received: 1,673 Interview Received: N/A Number Enrolled: 154 Admitted Rate: 9.2%	6+ Biomedical Sci. Credit Hours: Anatomy, Physio., Biochem., Immunology, Microbio., virology, or genetics
William Carey University (WCUCOM) 710 William Carey Parkway, Hattiesburg, MS 39401	N/A (overall) 3.4 (science) MCAT: 500 ED: No Int'l Student: Yes Reapps: N/A	**(2019)** Apps Received: 3,500 Interview Received: 450 Number Enrolled: 150 Admitted Rate: 4.29% **(2020)** Apps Received: 3,836 Interview Received: N/A Number Enrolled: 158 Admitted Rate: 4.1%	N/A
Campbell University Jerry M. Wallace (CUSOM) 4350 US 421 South, Lillington, NC 27546	3.6 (overall) 3.54 (science) MCAT: 507 ED: Yes Int'l Student: Yes Reapps: N/A	**(2019)** Apps Received: 4,500 Interview Received: 700 Number Enrolled: 162 Admitted Rate: 3.6% **(2020)** Apps Received: 4,823 Interview Received: N/A Number Enrolled: 162 Admitted Rate: 3.4%	N/A

SOUTH

OSTEO PROGRAMS

Osteo School	Ave. GPA & DAT Early Decision (ED) : Yes/No Int'l Students: Yes/No Reapps: Yes/No	Admissions Statistics	Science Req. Other than Gen Chem, OChem, Physics, Bio
OSU-COM**** 1111 W. 17 Street, Tulsa, OK 74107	3.6 (overall) 3.6 (science) MCAT: 500 ED: No Int'l Student: No Reapps: N/A	**(2019)** Apps Received: 3,500 Interview Received: 300 Number Enrolled: 165 Admitted Rate: 4.7% **(2020)** Apps Received: 4,.707 Interview Received: N/A Number Enrolled: 171 Admitted Rate: 3.6%	At least 1 upper div. science course (e.g., Human Anatomy, Biochem., Microbio., etc.) See chart for more details.
OSU-COM Tahlequah**** 19500 E. Ross Street, Tahlequah, OK 74464	3.6 (overall) 3.6 (science) MCAT: 500 ED: No Int'l Student: No Reapps: N/A	**(2019)** Apps Received: 3,500 Interview Received: 300 Number Enrolled: 165 Admitted Rate: 4.7% **(2020)** Apps Received: 4,.707 Interview Received: N/A Number Enrolled: 171 Admitted Rate: 3.6%	At least 1 upper div. science course (e.g., Human Anatomy, Biochem., Microbio., etc.) See chart for more details.
VCOM - Carolinas Campus 350 Howard Street, Spartanburg, SC 29303	3.65 (overall) 3.59 (science) MCAT: 501 ED: Yes Int'l Student: No Reapps: Yes	**(2019)** Apps Received: 4,171 Interview Received: N/A Number Enrolled: 162 Admitted Rate: 3.9% **(2020)** Apps Received: 5,093 Interview Received: N/A Number Enrolled: 162 Admitted Rate: 3.2%	6+ Biomedical Sci. Credit Hours: Anatomy, Physio., Biochem., Immunology, Microbio., virology, or genetics
LMU-DCOM 6965 Cumberland Gap Parkway, Harrogate, TN 37752	N/A (overall) 3.4 (science) MCAT: 501 ED: N/A Int'l Student: Yes Reapps: Yes	**(2019)** Apps Received: 5,547 Interview Received: 900 Number Enrolled: 243 Admitted Rate: 4.4% **(2020)**** Apps Received: 7,068 Interview Received: N/A Number Enrolled: 393 Admitted Rate: 5.6%	Biochem. may be substituted

OSTEO PROGRAMS

Osteo School	Ave. GPA & DAT Early Decision (ED) : Yes/No Int'l Students: Yes/No Reapps: Yes/No	Admissions Statistics	Science Req. Other than Gen Chem, OChem, Physics, Bio
LMU-DCOM Knoxville 9737 Cogdill Road, Knoxville, TN 37932	3.71 (overall) 3.63 (science) MCAT: 507 ED: N/A Int'l Student: No Reapps: Yes	**(2019)** Apps Received: N/A Interview Received: N/A Number Enrolled: 125 Admitted Rate: N/A **(2020)******* Apps Received: 7,068 Interview Received: N/A Number Enrolled: 393 Admitted Rate: 5.6%	Biochem. may be substituted
Sam Houston State University College of Osteopathic Medicine****** 1905 University Avenue, Huntsville, TX 77341	3.62 (overall) N/A (science) MCAT: 504 ED: No Int'l Student: N/A Reapps: Yes	**(2019)** N/A **(2020)** Apps Received: N/A Interview Received: N/A Number Enrolled: 75 Admitted Rate: N/A	Biochem. may be substituted for OChem 2 Math (6 credit hrs.), with 3 being Stats.
UNTHSC/TCOM 3500 Camp Bowie Blvd., Fort Worth, TX 76107	3.71 (overall) 3.63 (science) MCAT: 507 ED: Yes Int'l Student: Yes Reapps: Yes	**(2019)** Apps Received: 3,942 Interview Received: 755 Number Enrolled: 230 Admitted Rate: 5.8% **(2020)** Apps Received: N/A******* Interview Received: N/A Number Enrolled: 237 Admitted Rate: N/A	Statistics

SOUTH

OSTEO PROGRAMS

Osteo School	Ave. GPA & DAT Early Decision (ED) : Yes/No Int'l Students: Yes/No Reapps: Yes/No	Admissions Statistics	Science Req. Other than Gen Chem, OChem, Physics, Bio
Univ. of the Incarnate Word (UIWSOM) 4301 Broadway, San Antonio, TX 78209	3.57 (overall) 3.46 (science) MCAT: 503 ED: No Int'l Student: No Reapps: Yes	**(2019)** Apps Received: 3,980 Interview Received: 680 Number Enrolled: 160 Admitted Rate: 4% **(2020)** Apps Received: 5,323 Interview Received: N/A Number Enrolled: 162 Admitted Rate: 3%	N/A
VCOM-Virginia Campus 2265 Kraft Dr. SW, Blacksburg, VA 24060	3.65 (overall) 3.59 (science) MCAT: 501 ED: Yes Int'l Student: No Reapps: Yes	**(2019)** Apps Received: 5,183 Interview Received: 400 Number Enrolled: 185 Admitted Rate: 3.6% **(2020)** Apps Received: 6,518 Interview Received: N/A Number Enrolled: 185 Admitted Rate: 2.8%	6+ Biomedical Sci. Credit Hours: Anatomy, Physio., Biochem., Immunology, Microbio., virology, or genetics
Liberty University (LUCOM) 1971 University Boulevard, Lynchburg, VA 24502	3.4 (overall) 3.4 (science) MCAT: 504 ED: No Int'l Student: Yes Reapps: N/A	**(2019)** Apps Received: 3,500 Interview Received: 450 Number Enrolled: 170 Admitted Rate: 4.9% **(2020)** Apps Received: 4,363 Interview Received: N/A Number Enrolled: 159 Admitted Rate: 3.6%	Biochem. or Cellular Bio. 4 additional hrs. of science: Genetics, Human Anatomy, Immunology, or Epidemiology

OSTEO PROGRAMS

Osteo School	Ave. GPA & DAT Early Decision (ED) : Yes/No Int'l Students: Yes/No Reapps: Yes/No	Admissions Statistics	Science Req. Other than Gen Chem, OChem, Physics, Bio
West Virginia School of Osteopathic Medicine (WVSOM) 400 Lee Street North, Lewisburg, WV 24901	N/A (overall) 3.54 (science) MCAT: 501 ED: No Int'l Student: No Reapps: Yes	**(2019)** Apps Received: 5,298 Interview Received: 549 Number Enrolled: 200 Admitted Rate: 3.77% **(2020)** Apps Received: 5,258 Interview Received: N/A Number Enrolled: 207 Admitted Rate: 3.9%	Biochemistry

*NYITCOM table data reflects total enrolled at both NYIT campuses and Émigré Physicians Program (EPP) students.
** VCOM – Monroe opened in 2020. No admissions data for 2019 listed.
***NSU-KPCOM table data reflects totals from all campuses.
****OSU-COM table data reflects totals from all campuses. OSU-COM Tahlequah's entering class of 54 first year medical students began class in Fall 2020.
*****LMU-DCOM Knoxville 2020 admissions statistics reflect totals from both campuses.
******Sam Houston State COM matriculated its first class in fall 2020. No admissions data has been updated yet.
*******The University of North Texas Health Sciences Center at Fort Worth/Texas College of Osteopathic Medicine and NYIT-COM's émigré program applicants are not included because the data is not available through the AACOMAS database. UNTHSC/TCOM receives its applications through the Texas Medical and Dental School Application Service (TMDSAS).

SOUTH

ALABAMA

ARKANSAS

DELAWARE

DISTRICT OF
COLUMBIA

FLORIDA

GEORGIA

KENTUCKY

LOUISIANA

MARYLAND

MISSISSIPPI

NORTH CAROLINA

OKLAHOMA

SOUTH CAROLINA

TENNESSEE

TEXAS

VIRGINIA

WEST VIRGINIA

ALABAMA COLLEGE OF OSTEOPATHIC MEDICINE (ACOM)

Address: 445 Health Sciences Blvd, Dothan, AL 36303
Website: *https://www.acom.edu/*
Contact: *https://discover.acom.edu/inquiryform*
Phone: (334) 699-2266

Other campus locations: N/A

COST OF ATTENDANCE

Tuition: $55,440
Fees & Expenses: $27,680
Total: $83,120

Financial Aid: https://www.acom.edu/financial-aid/

Percent Receiving Aid: 83%

ADDITIONAL INFORMATION

Interesting tidbit: At ACOM, career development is integrated into preclinical curriculum. During the clinical years, students benefit from a dedicated student credentialing team for clerkship training and mock interview and COMLEX-USA Level 2 PE preparation.

What international experiences are available? N/A

What dual degree options exist? Dual degree programs available. For more information, visit: https://www.acom.edu/dual-degrees/

Important Updates due to COVID-19: Accept online coursework to fulfill prerequisite requirements. Accept prerequisite coursework Pass/Fail grades.

Were tests required? MCAT and CASPer required.

Are tests expected next year? Yes.

Percent of graduates receiving residency matches: 99% (2021)

What service learning opportunities exist? Translating Osteopathic Understanding into Community Health (TOUCH). For more information, visit: https://www.acom.edu/touch-program/

COMLEX First-Time Pass Rate (Level 1, Level 2 Cognitive Evaluation, Level 2 Performance Evaluation, Level 3)

Level 1: 96.2% (2019/20)

Level 2 CE: N/A

Level 2 PE: N/A

Level 3: N/A

EDWARD VIA COLLEGE OF OSTEOPATHIC MEDICINE (VCOM - AUBURN CAMPUS)

Address: 910 South Donahue Dr., Auburn, AL 36832
Website: *https://www.vcom.edu/*
Contact: *https://www.vcom.edu/admissions/admissions-contact-information*
Phone: (334) 442-4000

Other campus locations: Blacksburg, VA; Monroe, LA; Spartanburg, SC

COST OF ATTENDANCE

Tuition: $46,900
Fees & Expenses: $28,282
Total: $75,182

Financial Aid: https://www.vcom.edu/virginia/current-students/tuition-and-financial-aid

Percent Receiving Aid: 91.5%

ADDITIONAL INFORMATION

Interesting tidbit: VCOM has four campuses - Auburn (AL), Blacksburg (VA), Monroe (LA), and Spartanburg (SC). All VCOM campuses have the same academic program, but students' experience will be shaped by which location they choose.

What international experiences are available? N/A

What dual degree options exist? Dual degree programs available. For more information, visit: https://www.vcom.edu/admissions/parallel-degree

Important Updates due to COVID-19: LOR from a physician not required but encouraged.

Were tests required? MCAT required.

Are tests expected next year? Yes.

Percent of graduates receiving residency matches: 96% (2020)

What service learning opportunities exist? Student organizations focused on community outreach.

COMLEX First-Time Pass Rate (Level 1, Level 2 Cognitive Evaluation, Level 2 Performance Evaluation, Level 3)

Level 1: 95% (2019/20)

Level 2 CE: 98% (2019/20)

Level 2 PE: 94% (2019/20)

Level 3: 93% (2018/19)

Note: An applicant sends one application to VCOM's central admissions department through AACOMAS, and then the applicant has the option of specifying which campus he prefers later on in the process. Each applicant is only considered at one campus; he cannot interview at more than one.

ALABAMA
ARKANSAS
DELAWARE
DISTRICT OF COLUMBIA
FLORIDA
GEORGIA
KENTUCKY
LOUISIANA
MARYLAND
MISSISSIPPI
NORTH CAROLINA
OKLAHOMA
SOUTH CAROLINA
TENNESSEE
TEXAS
VIRGINIA
WEST VIRGINIA

SOUTH

ALABAMA

ARKANSAS

DELAWARE

DISTRICT OF
COLUMBIA

FLORIDA

GEORGIA

KENTUCKY

LOUISIANA

MARYLAND

MISSISSIPPI

NORTH CAROLINA

OKLAHOMA

SOUTH CAROLINA

TENNESSEE

TEXAS

VIRGINIA

WEST VIRGINIA

ARKANSAS COLLEGE OF OSTEOPATHIC MEDICINE (ARCOM)

Address: 7000 Chad Colley Blvd., Fort Smith, AR 72916
Website: *https://acheedu.org/arcom/*
Contact: *https://explore.acheedu.org/inquiryform*
Phone: (479) 308-2243

Other campus locations: N/A

COST OF ATTENDANCE

Tuition: $43,000
Fees & Expenses: $33,326
Total: $76,326*

*Indicated total is for living on-campus. COA for off-campus is $76,108.

Financial Aid: https://acheedu.org/apply-for-scholarships/

Percent Receiving Aid: 85%

ADDITIONAL INFORMATION

Interesting tidbit: The Arkansas College of Osteopathic Medicine welcomed its inaugural class of 150 aspiring physicians in August of 2017. The emphasis is placed on preparing students to become primary care physicians.

What international experiences are available? N/A

What dual degree options exist? No dual degree options listed.

Important Updates due to COVID-19: Accept online coursework to fulfill prerequisite requirements and lab coursework. Accept prerequisite coursework Pass/Fail grades.

Were tests required? MCAT and CASPer required.

Are tests expected next year? Yes.

Percent of graduates receiving residency matches: 95% (2021)

What service learning opportunities exist? N/A

COMLEX First-Time Pass Rate (Level 1, Level 2 Cognitive Evaluation, Level 2 Performance Evaluation, Level 3)

Level 1: 85.71% (2019/20)

Level 2 CE: 100% (2019/20)

Level 2 PE: N/A

Level 3: N/A

NEW YORK INSTITUTE OF TECHNOLOGY COLLEGE OF OSTEO. MED. (NYITCOM) - ARKANSAS

Address: 2405 Aggie Rd, Jonesboro, AR 72401
Website: *https://www.nyit.edu/arkansas*
Contact: *https://www.nyit.edu/admissions/request_information?degree=osteopathic_medicine_do*
Phone: (870) 972-2786

Other campus locations: Old Westbury, NY

COST OF ATTENDANCE

Tuition: $60,450
Fees & Expenses: $35,333*
Total: $95,783

*Figure based on NY expenses.

Financial Aid: https://www.nyit.edu/medicine/financial_aid

Percent Receiving Aid: 83%

ADDITIONAL INFORMATION

Interesting tidbit: NYITCOM at A-State is dedicated to improving access to healthcare for the underserved and rural populations in Arkansas and the Mississippi Delta Region. Arkansas ranks 48th in overall population health status, 46th in the number of active physicians per capita, and 39th in the number of primary care physicians.

What international experiences are available? Opportunity to obtain Global Health Certificate. For more information, visit: https://www.nyit.edu/medicine/center_for_global_health

What dual degree options exist? Dual degree DO/MBA under development.

Important Updates due to COVID-19: accept pass/fail grading for spring/summer 2020 coursework.

Were tests required? MCAT required.

Are tests expected next year? Yes.

Percent of graduates receiving residency matches: 98% (2020)**

What service learning opportunities exist? NYITCOM at A-State students are required to complete a four-week rotation in a rural area. Additionally, plans are in motion for students to gain further clinical training in the mobile medical clinic to treat underserved and rural populations.

COMLEX First-Time Pass Rate (Level 1, Level 2 Cognitive Evaluation, Level 2 Performance Evaluation, Level 3)**

Level 1: 94.42% (2019/20)

Level 2 CE: 95.07% (2019/20)

Level 2 PE: N/A (2019/20)

Level 3: 98% (2019/20)

** Combined statistics for Long Island and Arkansas campuses.

ALABAMA

ARKANSAS

DELAWARE

DISTRICT OF COLUMBIA

FLORIDA

GEORGIA

KENTUCKY

LOUISIANA

MARYLAND

MISSISSIPPI

NORTH CAROLINA

OKLAHOMA

SOUTH CAROLINA

TENNESSEE

TEXAS

VIRGINIA

WEST VIRGINIA

SOUTH

ALABAMA

ARKANSAS

DELAWARE

DISTRICT OF
COLUMBIA

FLORIDA

GEORGIA

KENTUCKY

LOUISIANA

MARYLAND

MISSISSIPPI

NORTH CAROLINA

OKLAHOMA

SOUTH CAROLINA

TENNESSEE

TEXAS

VIRGINIA

WEST VIRGINIA

LAKE ERIE COLLEGE OF OSTEOPATHIC MEDICINE (LECOM) – BRADENTON

Address: 5000 Lakewood Ranch Boulevard, Bradenton, FL 34211
Website: *https://lecom.edu/academics/the-college-of-medicine/*
Contact: *https://lecom.edu/contact-us/*
Phone: (941) 756-0690

Other campus locations: Erie, PA; Seton Hill at Greensburg, PA; Elmira, NY

COST OF ATTENDANCE

In-State Tuition: $35,830
Fees & Expenses: $33,958
Total: $69,788

Out-of-State Tuition: $37,640
Fees & Expenses: $33,958
Total: $71,598

Financial Aid: https://lecom.edu/admissions/tuition-and-financial-aid/

Percent Receiving Aid: 83%

ADDITIONAL INFORMATION

Interesting tidbit: The Bradenton campus requires a separate application. The Bradenton campus offers only the Problem-Based Learning Pathway (PBL) curriculum.

What international experiences are available? N/A

What dual degree options exist? No dual degree options listed.

Important Updates due to COVID-19: Physician LOR not required. Accept online coursework to fulfill prerequisite requirements. Accept prerequisite coursework Pass/Fail grades only if the student is not provided an option by the college. Students would need to provide documentation from school regarding P/F policies. Accept online lab coursework.

Were tests required? MCAT required.

Are tests expected next year? Yes.

Percent of graduates receiving residency matches: 99.3% (2020)

What service learning opportunities exist? N/A

COMLEX First-Time Pass Rate (Level 1, Level 2 Cognitive Evaluation, Level 2 Performance Evaluation, Level 3)

Level 1: 96.2% (2019/20)

Level 2 CE: 96% (2019/20)

Level 2 PE: 92.6% (2019/20)

Level 3: 99.6% (2018/19)

Other: LECOM has partnerships with several undergraduate institutions for the Early Acceptance Program. This program is intended for high school applicants to receive conditional acceptance to LECOM. For more information, visit: https://lecom.edu/admissions/entrance-requirements/early-acceptance-programs/

NOVA SOUTHEASTERN UNIVERSITY DR. KIRAN C. PATEL COLLEGE OF OSTEOPATHIC MEDICINE (NSU-KPCOM)

Address: 3301 College Avenue, Fort Lauderdale, FL 33314
Website: *https://osteopathic.nova.edu/index.html*
Contact: *https://osteopathic.nova.edu/request-info/*
Phone: (800) 541-6682

Other campus locations: Clearwater, FL

COST OF ATTENDANCE

In-State Tuition: $55,784
Fees & Expenses: $46,212
Total: $101,996

Out-of-State Tuition: $63,638
Fees & Expenses: $46,212
Total: $109,850

Financial Aid: https://www.nova.edu/financialaid/scholarships/index.html

Percent Receiving Aid: 77%

ADDITIONAL INFORMATION

Interesting tidbit: A notable aspect of NSU-KPCOM clinical training program is a three-month clinical rotation in a rural setting where many residents have little access to health care. Students will learn to treat various cultural and ethnic groups whose lifestyles and attitudes toward health care differ from those they will see in more traditional training sites.

What international experiences are available? International medical rotations. For more information, visit: https://osteopathic.nova.edu/community/international-programs/index.html

What dual degree options exist? Dual degree program available. For more information, visit: https://osteopathic.nova.edu/dodmd/index.html

Important Updates due to COVID-19: Accept online coursework to fulfill prerequisite requirements taken from a regionally accredited institution. Accept prerequisite coursework Pass/Fail grades. Accept online lab coursework. Accept applications without lab coursework.

Were tests required? MCAT required.

Are tests expected next year? Yes.

Percent of graduates receiving residency matches: 99.9% (2020)

What service learning opportunities exist? Community Outreach opportunities. For more information, visit: https://www.nova.edu/community-outreach/index.html

COMLEX First-Time Pass Rate (Level 1, Level 2 Cognitive Evaluation, Level 2 Performance Evaluation, Level 3)

Level 1: 89.58% (2019/20)

Level 2 CE: 92.08% (2019/20)

Level 2 PE: 89% (2019/20)

Level 3: 97.2% (2018/19)

Other: NSU-KPCOM offers a Dual Admission program where undergraduate students may apply early for a seat in the DO program. For more information, visit: https://www.nova.edu/undergraduate/academics/dual-admission/index.html

ALABAMA
ARKANSAS
DELAWARE
DISTRICT OF COLUMBIA
FLORIDA
GEORGIA
KENTUCKY
LOUISIANA
MARYLAND
MISSISSIPPI
NORTH CAROLINA
OKLAHOMA
SOUTH CAROLINA
TENNESSEE
TEXAS
VIRGINIA
WEST VIRGINIA

SOUTH

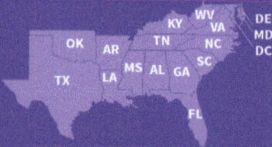

NOVA SOUTHEASTERN UNIVERSITY DR. KIRAN C. PATEL COLLEGE OF OSTEOPATHIC MEDICINE (NSU-KPCOM – CLEARWATER)

Address: 3400 Gulf to Bay Blvd., Clearwater, FL 33759
Website: *https://osteopathic.nova.edu/index.html*
Contact: *https://osteopathic.nova.edu/request-info/*
Phone: (813) 574-5200

Other campus locations: Fort Lauderdale, FL

COST OF ATTENDANCE

In-State Tuition: $55,784
Fees & Expenses: $46,212
Total: $101,996

Out-of-State Tuition: $63,638
Fees & Expenses: $46,212
Total: $109,850

Financial Aid: https://www.nova.edu/financialaid/scholarships/index.html

Percent Receiving Aid: 77%

ADDITIONAL INFORMATION

Interesting tidbit: NSU-KPCOM-Clearwater campus held a ribbon cutting on September 14, 2019.

What international experiences are available? International medical rotations. For more information, visit: https://osteopathic.nova.edu/community/international-programs/index.html

What dual degree options exist? No dual degree options listed.

Important Updates due to COVID-19: Accept online coursework to fulfill prerequisite requirements taken from a regionally accredited institution. Accept prerequisite coursework Pass/Fail grades. Accept online lab coursework. Accept applications without lab coursework.

Were tests required? MCAT required.

Are tests expected next year? Yes.

Percent of graduates receiving residency matches: N/A*

What service learning opportunities exist? Community Outreach opportunities. For more information, visit: https://www.nova.edu/community-outreach/index.html

COMLEX First-Time Pass Rate (Level 1, Level 2 Cognitive Evaluation, Level 2 Performance Evaluation, Level 3) - N/A*

*Note: This campus opened in 2019. No COMLEX or Match data yet.

ALABAMA

ARKANSAS

DELAWARE

DISTRICT OF COLUMBIA

FLORIDA

GEORGIA

KENTUCKY

LOUISIANA

MARYLAND

MISSISSIPPI

NORTH CAROLINA

OKLAHOMA

SOUTH CAROLINA

TENNESSEE

TEXAS

VIRGINIA

WEST VIRGINIA

PHILADELPHIA COLLEGE OF OSTEOPATHIC MEDICINE (PCOM) – GEORGIA

Address: 625 Old Peachtree Road NW, Suwanee, GA 30024
Website: *https://www.pcom.edu/academics/programs-and-degrees/doctor-of-osteopathic-medicine-georgia-campus/*
Contact: *https://discover.pcom.edu/inquiryform*
Phone: (678) 225-7500

Other campus locations: Philadelphia, PA; Moultrie, GA (South Georgia Campus)

COST OF ATTENDANCE

Tuition: $54,336
Fees & Expenses: $25,302
Total: $79,638

Financial Aid: https://www.pcom.edu/about/departments/financial-aid/

Percent Receiving Aid: 85.1%

ADDITIONAL INFORMATION

Interesting tidbit: Responding to a growing need for healthcare providers in the South, PCOM established a new campus in Suwanee, Georgia in 2005. PCOM Georgia is a branch campus of Philadelphia College of Osteopathic Medicine.

What international experiences are available? Medical Missions available.

What dual degree options exist? Dual degree programs available. For more information, visit: https://www.pcom.edu/academics/programs-and-degrees/doctor-of-osteopathic-medicine-georgia-campus/joint-degree-programs.html

Important Updates due to COVID-19: Accept online prerequisite coursework and lab coursework. Accept pass/fail for prerequisite coursework.

Were tests required? MCAT required.

Are tests expected next year? Yes.

Percent of graduates receiving residency matches: 99.6% (2021)

What service learning opportunities exist? Community Outreach opportunities available at all three campuses. For more information, visit: https://www.pcom.edu/admissions/community-minority-outreach.html

COMLEX First-Time Pass Rate (Level 1, Level 2 Cognitive Evaluation, Level 2 Performance Evaluation, Level 3)

Level 1: 88.46% (2019/20)

Level 2 CE: 92.86% (2019/20)

Level 2 PE: 75.2% (2019/20)

Level 3: 94.7% (2018/19)

ALABAMA

ARKANSAS

DELAWARE

DISTRICT OF COLUMBIA

FLORIDA

GEORGIA

KENTUCKY

LOUISIANA

MARYLAND

MISSISSIPPI

NORTH CAROLINA

OKLAHOMA

SOUTH CAROLINA

TENNESSEE

TEXAS

VIRGINIA

WEST VIRGINIA

SOUTH

ALABAMA

ARKANSAS

DELAWARE

DISTRICT OF
COLUMBIA

FLORIDA

GEORGIA

KENTUCKY

LOUISIANA

MARYLAND

MISSISSIPPI

NORTH CAROLINA

OKLAHOMA

SOUTH CAROLINA

TENNESSEE

TEXAS

VIRGINIA

WEST VIRGINIA

PHILADELPHIA COLLEGE OF OSTEOPATHIC MEDICINE (PCOM) – SOUTH GEORGIA

Address: 2050 Tallokas Road, Moultrie, GA 31768
Website: *https://www.pcom.edu/academics/programs-and-degrees/doctor-of-osteopathic-medicine-south-georgia/*
Contact: *https://discover.pcom.edu/inquiryform*
Phone: (229) 668-3110

Other campus locations: Philadelphia, PA; Suwanee, GA (Georgia Campus)

COST OF ATTENDANCE

Tuition: $54,336
Fees & Expenses: $25,302
Total: $79,638

Financial Aid: https://www.pcom.edu/about/departments/financial-aid/

Percent Receiving Aid: 85.1%

ADDITIONAL INFORMATION

Interesting tidbit: PCOM South Georgia welcomed its inaugural class of doctor of osteopathic medicine (DO) students on Aug. 12, 2019.

What international experiences are available? Medical Missions available.

What dual degree options exist? Dual degree programs available. For more information, visit:

Important Updates due to COVID-19: Accept online coursework to fulfill prerequisite requirements. Accept prerequisite coursework Pass/Fail grades. Accept online lab coursework.

Were tests required? MCAT required.

Are tests expected next year? Yes.

Percent of graduates receiving residency matches: N/A*

What service learning opportunities exist? Community Outreach opportunities available at all three campuses. For more information, visit: https://www.pcom.edu/admissions/community-minority-outreach.html

COMLEX First-Time Pass Rate (Level 1, Level 2 Cognitive Evaluation, Level 2 Performance Evaluation, Level 3) - N/A*

*PCOM South Georgia opened in 2019. No Match or COMLEX data yet.

UNIVERSITY OF PIKEVILLE KENTUCKY COLLEGE OF OSTEOPATHIC MEDICINE (UP-KYCOM)

Address: 147 Sycamore Street, Pikeville, KY 41501
Website: *https://www.upike.edu/osteopathic-medicine/*
Contact: *https://www.upike.edu/department-list/*
Phone: (606) 218-5250

Other campus locations: N/A

COST OF ATTENDANCE

Tuition: $50,000
Fees & Expenses: $21,404
Total: $71,404

Financial Aid: https://www.upike.edu/undergraduate/financial-aid/health-professions/kycom-scholarships/

Percent Receiving Aid: 90%

ADDITIONAL INFORMATION

Interesting tidbit: During the third and fourth years at KYCOM, students complete clinical rotations at sites in Alabama, Arkansas, Michigan, Mississippi, Ohio, Pennsylvania and Virginia.

What international experiences are available? N/A

What dual degree options exist? No dual degree options listed.

Important Updates due to COVID-19: Accept online prerequisite coursework and lab coursework. Accept pass/fail for prerequisite coursework.

Were tests required? MCAT required.

Are tests expected next year? Yes.

Percent of graduates receiving residency matches: 98-99% (2020)

What service learning opportunities exist? Student physicians provide sports physical exams to UPIKE's student-athletes. Additionally, students are encouraged to practice in underserved areas of rural America. KYCOM is a founding member of the Appalachian Osteopathic Postgraduate Training Institute Consortium (A-OPTIC): https://www.upike.edu/osteopathic-medicine/kycom-program/a-optic/

COMLEX First-Time Pass Rate (Level 1, Level 2 Cognitive Evaluation, Level 2 Performance Evaluation, Level 3)

Level 1: 85.5% (2018/19)

Level 2 CE: 92.97% (2018/19)

Level 2 PE: 92.9% (2018/19)

Level 3: 89.5% (2017/18)

ALABAMA

ARKANSAS

DELAWARE

DISTRICT OF COLUMBIA

FLORIDA

GEORGIA

KENTUCKY

LOUISIANA

MARYLAND

MISSISSIPPI

NORTH CAROLINA

OKLAHOMA

SOUTH CAROLINA

TENNESSEE

TEXAS

VIRGINIA

WEST VIRGINIA

SOUTH

ALABAMA

ARKANSAS

DELAWARE

DISTRICT OF
COLUMBIA

FLORIDA

GEORGIA

KENTUCKY

LOUISIANA

MARYLAND

MISSISSIPPI

NORTH CAROLINA

OKLAHOMA

SOUTH CAROLINA

TENNESSEE

TEXAS

VIRGINIA

WEST VIRGINIA

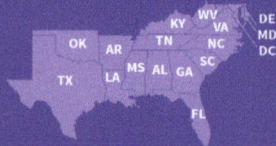

EDWARD VIA COLLEGE OF OSTEOPATHIC MEDICINE-MONROE CAMPUS (VCOM - MONROE CAMPUS)

Address: 4408 Bon Aire Dr., Monroe, LA 71203
Website: *https://www.vcom.edu/louisiana*
Contact: *https://www.vcom.edu/admissions/admissions-contact-information*
Phone: (318) 342-7131

Other campus locations: Auburn, AL; Blacksburg, VA; Spartanburg, SC

COST OF ATTENDANCE

Tuition: $46,900
Fees & Expenses: $28,282
Total: $75,182

Financial Aid: https://www.vcom.edu/virginia/current-students/tuition-and-financial-aid

Percent Receiving Aid: 91.5%

ADDITIONAL INFORMATION

Interesting tidbit: Welcoming its first class in 2020, VCOM's Louisiana campus is a partnership between VCOM and the University of Louisiana-Monroe. This new campus will address a physician shortage in Louisiana. 81% of the state has been designated a health professional shortage area by the Louisiana Department of Health.

What international experiences are available? N/A

What dual degree options exist? No dual degree options listed.

Important Updates due to COVID-19: LOR from a physician not required but encouraged.

Were tests required? MCAT required.

Are tests expected next year? Yes.

Percent of graduates receiving residency matches: N/A*

What service learning opportunities exist? N/A

COMLEX First-Time Pass Rate (Level 1, Level 2 Cognitive Evaluation, Level 2 Performance Evaluation, Level 3) - N/A*

***VCOM** – Monroe opened its campus to DO students in Fall 2020. No information/data yet.

WILLIAM CAREY UNIVERSITY COLLEGE OF OSTEOPATHIC MEDICINE (WCUCOM)

Address: 710 William Carey Parkway, WCU Box 207 Hattiesburg, MS 39401
Website: *https://www.wmcarey.edu/College/Osteopathic-Medicine*
Contact: *https://www.wmcarey.edu/page/request-information*
Phone: (601) 318-6235

Other campus locations: N/A

COST OF ATTENDANCE

Tuition: $44,000
Fees & Expenses: $27,342
Total: $71,342

Financial Aid: https://www.wmcarey.edu/page/financial-aid-apply

Percent Receiving Aid: 98%

ADDITIONAL INFORMATION

Interesting tidbit: In the third and fourth years, students spend time with clinical faculty at regional hub sites throughout the Gulf South. Students are responsible for transportation to and from assigned rotation locations without the assistance of WCUCOM.

What international experiences are available? N/A

What dual degree options exist? No dual degree options listed.

Important Updates due to COVID-19: Accept online coursework to fulfill prerequisite requirements and lab coursework but semester by semester basis. Accept prerequisite coursework Pass/Fail grades.

Were tests required? MCAT required.

Are tests expected next year? Yes.

Percent of graduates receiving residency matches: 98% (2021)

What service learning opportunities exist? N/A

COMLEX First-Time Pass Rate (Level 1, Level 2 Cognitive Evaluation, Level 2 Performance Evaluation, Level 3)

Level 1: 97.62% (2019/20)

Level 2 CE: 96.84% (2019/20)

Level 2 PE: 89.6% (2018/19)

Level 3: 93.1% (2018/19)

ALABAMA

ARKANSAS

DELAWARE

DISTRICT OF COLUMBIA

FLORIDA

GEORGIA

KENTUCKY

LOUISIANA

MARYLAND

MISSISSIPPI

NORTH CAROLINA

OKLAHOMA

SOUTH CAROLINA

TENNESSEE

TEXAS

VIRGINIA

WEST VIRGINIA

SOUTH

ALABAMA

ARKANSAS

DELAWARE

DISTRICT OF
COLUMBIA

FLORIDA

GEORGIA

KENTUCKY

LOUISIANA

MARYLAND

MISSISSIPPI

NORTH CAROLINA

OKLAHOMA

SOUTH CAROLINA

TENNESSEE

TEXAS

VIRGINIA

WEST VIRGINIA

CAMPBELL UNIVERSITY JERRY M. WALLACE SCHOOL OF OSTEOPATHIC MEDICINE (CUSOM)

Address: 4350 US 421 South, Lillington, NC 27546
Website: *https://medicine.campbell.edu/*
Contact: *https://medicine.campbell.edu/admissions/request-information/*
Phone: (855) 287-6613

Other campus locations: N/A

COST OF ATTENDANCE

Tuition: $54,600
Fees & Expenses: $24,100
Total: $78,700

Financial Aid: https://medicine.campbell.edu/admissions/tuition-financial-aid/types-of-aid/

Percent Receiving Aid: 84%

ADDITIONAL INFORMATION

Interesting tidbit: Campbell University School of Osteopathic Medicine is the first and only osteopathic medical school established in the state of North Carolina. It is located a short distance from the Research Triangle, one of the largest areas concentrating on research and technology in the world.

What international experiences are available? Medical Missions available. For more information, visit: https://medicine.campbell.edu/student-experience/medical-missions-outreach/

What dual degree options exist? JD/DO program available.

Important Updates due to COVID-19: Accept all pass/fail grades from coursework, including pre-requisite course work, taken at a regionally accredited institution during semesters impacted by COVID-19. Accept all online coursework, including lab credits, taken at a regionally accredited institution during semesters impacted by COVID-19. Invite qualified candidates to complete secondary applications, and invite qualified candidates for admission interviews before receiving MCAT scores.

Were tests required? MCAT required.

Are tests expected next year? Yes.

Percent of graduates receiving residency matches: 100% (2020)

What service learning opportunities exist? Community Care Clinic and more opportunities. For more information, visit: https://medicine.campbell.edu/about/community-engagement/

COMLEX First-Time Pass Rate (Level 1, Level 2 Cognitive Evaluation, Level 2 Performance Evaluation, Level 3)

Level 1: 96.50% (2020/21)

Level 2 CE: 100% (2020/21)

Level 2 PE: 97.40% (2019/20)

Level 3: 100% (2020)

Other: Early Acceptance Program available for Campbell freshmen students. This program grants students conditional approval into the DO program. For more information, visit: https://medicine.campbell.edu/admissions/osteopathic-medicine-admissions/early-acceptance-program/

OKLAHOMA STATE UNIVERSITY CENTER FOR HEALTH SCIENCES COLLEGE OF OSTEOPATHIC MEDICINE (OSU-COM)

Address: 1111 W. 17 Street, Tulsa, OK 74107
Website: *https://health.okstate.edu/com/index.html*
Contact: *https://applyhealth.okstate.edu/register/inquiry*
Phone: (918) 561-8324

Other campus locations: Tahlequah, OK

COST OF ATTENDANCE

In-State Tuition: $25,797
Fees & Expenses: $28,787
Total: $54,584

Out-of-State Tuition: $53,299
Fees & Expenses: $28,787
Total: $82,086

Financial Aid: https://health.okstate.edu/com/financial-aid/index.html

Percent Receiving Aid: 90%

ADDITIONAL INFORMATION

Interesting tidbit: The OSU College of Osteopathic Medicine places emphasis on admitting students from Oklahoma and those who want to practice in Oklahoma. The majority of OSU College of Osteopathic Medicine students are from Oklahoma.

What international experiences are available? Global Health Track available. For more information, visit: https://health.okstate.edu/global-health-track/index.html

What dual degree options exist? Dual degree programs available. For more information, visit: https://health.okstate.edu/com/academics/dual-degrees/index.html

Important Updates due to COVID-19: Accept online coursework to fulfill prerequisite requirements. Accept prerequisite coursework Pass/Fail grades. Accept online lab coursework.

Were tests required? MCAT and CASPer required.

Are tests expected next year? Yes.

Percent of graduates receiving residency matches: 100% (2020)

What service learning opportunities exist? Rural Health Training. For more information, visit: https://health.okstate.edu/rural-health/index.html

COMLEX First-Time Pass Rate (Level 1, Level 2 Cognitive Evaluation, Level 2 Performance Evaluation, Level 3)

Level 1: 90.27% (2019/20)

Level 2 CE: 97.22% (2019/20)

Level 2 PE: 96.9% (2019/20)

Level 3: 99.36% (2018/19)

Other: OSU-COM offers several special programs for students, including a 3+1 Program, Guaranteed Interview Program, Bridge Program, Rural Medical Track, and the Guaranteed Admissions Program. For more information on these programs, visit: https://health.okstate.edu/com/admissions/admission-options.html

ALABAMA
ARKANSAS
DELAWARE
DISTRICT OF COLUMBIA
FLORIDA
GEORGIA
KENTUCKY
LOUISIANA
MARYLAND
MISSISSIPPI
NORTH CAROLINA
OKLAHOMA
SOUTH CAROLINA
TENNESSEE
TEXAS
VIRGINIA
WEST VIRGINIA

SOUTH

ALABAMA

ARKANSAS

DELAWARE

DISTRICT OF
COLUMBIA

FLORIDA

GEORGIA

KENTUCKY

LOUISIANA

MARYLAND

MISSISSIPPI

NORTH CAROLINA

OKLAHOMA

SOUTH CAROLINA

TENNESSEE

TEXAS

VIRGINIA

WEST VIRGINIA

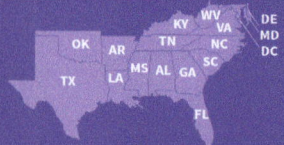

OKLAHOMA STATE UNIVERSITY CENTER FOR HEALTH SCIENCES COLLEGE OF OSTEOPATHIC MEDICINE - TAHLEQUAH (OSU-COM TAHLEQUAH)

Address: 19500 E. Ross Street, Tahlequah, OK 74464
Website: *https://health.okstate.edu/com/index.html*
Contact: *https://applyhealth.okstate.edu/register/inquiry*
Phone: Contact the Tulsa campus, (918) 561-8324

Other campus locations: Tulsa, OK

COST OF ATTENDANCE

In-State Tuition: $25,797
Fees & Expenses: $28,787
Total: $54,584

Out-of-State Tuition: $53,299
Fees & Expenses: $28,787
Total: $82,086

Financial Aid: https://health.okstate.edu/com/financial-aid/index.html

Percent Receiving Aid: 90%

ADDITIONAL INFORMATION

Interesting tidbit: OSU-COM has partnered with the Cherokee Nation to establish the "nation's first tribally-affiliated college of medicine". The entering class of 54 first-year medical students began class in Fall 2020. Medical students are and will be recruited from around Oklahoma and the United States and not be restricted to Native Americans.

What international experiences are available? Global Health Track available. For more information, visit: https://health.okstate.edu/global-health-track/index.html

What dual degree options exist? No dual degree options listed.

Important Updates due to COVID-19: Accept online coursework to fulfill prerequisite requirements. Accept prerequisite coursework Pass/Fail grades. Accept online lab coursework.

Were tests required? MCAT required.

Are tests expected next year? Yes.

Percent of graduates receiving residency matches: N/A*

What service learning opportunities exist? Rural Health Training. For more information, visit: https://health.okstate.edu/rural-health/index.html

COMLEX First-Time Pass Rate (Level 1, Level 2 Cognitive Evaluation, Level 2 Performance Evaluation, Level 3) - N/A*

*This is a new campus. Classes start Fall 2020. Hence, no COMLEX or Match data yet.

EDWARD VIA COLLEGE OF OSTEOPATHIC MEDICINE-CAROLINAS CAMPUS (VCOM - CAROLINAS CAMPUS)

Address: 350 Howard Street, Spartanburg, SC 29303
Website: *https://www.vcom.edu/carolinas*
Contact: *https://www.vcom.edu/directory*
Phone: (864) 327-9800

Other campus locations: Auburn, AL; Blacksburg, VA; Monroe, LA

COST OF ATTENDANCE

Tuition: $46,900
Fees & Expenses: $28,282
Total: $75,182

Financial Aid: https://www.vcom.edu/virginia/current-students/tuition-and-financial-aid

Percent Receiving Aid: 91.5%

ADDITIONAL INFORMATION

Interesting tidbit: The Carolinas Campus is VCOM's second campus. The Carolinas Campus is part of Spartanburg's College Town Consortium of seven colleges and universities, which offers a variety of social opportunities and benefits for students.

What international experiences are available? N/A

What dual degree options exist? Dual degree programs available. For more information, visit: https://www.vcom.edu/admissions/parallel-degree

Important Updates due to COVID-19: LOR from a physician not required but encouraged.

Were tests required? MCAT required.

Are tests expected next year? Yes.

Percent of graduates receiving residency matches: 96% (2020)

What service learning opportunities exist? Student organizations focused on community outreach.

COMLEX First-Time Pass Rate (Level 1, Level 2 Cognitive Evaluation, Level 2 Performance Evaluation, Level 3)

Level 1: 97% (2019/20)

Level 2 CE: 98% (2019/20)

Level 2 PE: 97% (2019/20)

Level 3: 96% (2018/19)

ALABAMA

ARKANSAS

DELAWARE

DISTRICT OF COLUMBIA

FLORIDA

GEORGIA

KENTUCKY

LOUISIANA

MARYLAND

MISSISSIPPI

NORTH CAROLINA

OKLAHOMA

SOUTH CAROLINA

TENNESSEE

TEXAS

VIRGINIA

WEST VIRGINIA

SOUTH

ALABAMA

ARKANSAS

DELAWARE

DISTRICT OF
COLUMBIA

FLORIDA

GEORGIA

KENTUCKY

LOUISIANA

MARYLAND

MISSISSIPPI

NORTH CAROLINA

OKLAHOMA

SOUTH CAROLINA

TENNESSEE

TEXAS

VIRGINIA

WEST VIRGINIA

LINCOLN MEMORIAL UNIVERSITY DEBUSK COLLEGE OF OSTEOPATHIC MEDICINE (LMU-DCOM)

Address: 6965 Cumberland Gap Parkway, Harrogate, TN 37752
Website: *https://www.lmunet.edu/debusk-college-of-osteopathic-medicine/index.php*
Contact: *https://www.lmunet.edu/debusk-college-of-osteopathic-medicine/do/do-dcom-at-lmu-knoxville/contact-us.php*
Phone: (423) 869-7200

Other campus locations: Knoxville, TN

COST OF ATTENDANCE

Tuition: $53,700
Fees & Expenses: $20,800
Total: $74,500

Financial Aid: https://www.lmunet.edu/debusk-college-of-osteopathic-medicine/do/financial-services/other-resources.php

Percent Receiving Aid: 79.3%

ADDITIONAL INFORMATION

Interesting tidbit: The ground-breaking for the LMU-DCOM building in May 2006 signified the beginning of Lincoln Memorial University-DeBusk College of Osteopathic Medicine (LMU-DCOM), Tennessee's newest medical school and its only osteopathic medical school.

What international experiences are available? International Studies and rotations available. For more information, visit: https://www.lmunet.edu/debusk-college-of-osteopathic-medicine/do/academics/international-studies.php

What dual degree options exist? Dual degree programs available. For more information, visit: https://www.lmunet.edu/debusk-college-of-osteopathic-medicine/do/academics/domba-program/index.php

Important Updates due to COVID-19: Accept pass/fail credits for prerequisite coursework completed during the spring and summer of 2020.

Were tests required? MCAT required.

Are tests expected next year? Yes.

Percent of graduates receiving residency matches: 98% (2020)

What service learning opportunities exist? N/A

COMLEX First-Time Pass Rate (Level 1, Level 2 Cognitive Evaluation, Level 2 Performance Evaluation, Level 3)

Level 1: 92.1% (2019/20)

Level 2 CE: 96.9% (2019/20)

Level 2 PE: N/A (2019/20)

Level 3: 95.3% (2019/20)

Other: Gross Anatomy Boot Camp available for students interested in a three-week intensive course to get a head-start on learning Gross Anatomy. For more information, visit: https://www.lmunet.edu/debusk-college-of-osteopathic-medicine/do/admissions/gross-anatomy-boot-camp.php

LINCOLN MEMORIAL UNIVERSITY DEBUSK COLLEGE OF OSTEOPATHIC MEDICINE - KNOXVILLE (LMU-DCOM KNOXVILLE)

Address: 9737 Cogdill Road, Knoxville, TN 37932
Website: *https://www.lmunet.edu/debusk-college-of-osteopathic-medicine/index.php*
Contact: *https://www.lmunet.edu/debusk-college-of-osteopathic-medicine/do/do-dcom-at-lmu-knoxville/contact-us.php*
Phone: (865) 338-5689

Other campus locations: Harrogate, TN

COST OF ATTENDANCE

Tuition: $53,700
Fees & Expenses: $24,250
Total: $77,9500

Financial Aid: https://www.lmunet.edu/debusk-college-of-osteopathic-medicine/do/financial-services/other-resources.php

Percent Receiving Aid: 79.3%

ADDITIONAL INFORMATION

Interesting tidbit: DCOM at LMU-Knoxville welcomed 125 new osteopathic medical students into its inaugural class in the fall of 2019. LMU currently operates three instructional sites in Knoxville.

What international experiences are available? International rotations available.

What dual degree options exist? No dual degree options listed.

Important Updates due to COVID-19: Accept pass/fail credits for prerequisite coursework completed during the spring and summer of 2020.

Were tests required? MCAT required.

Are tests expected next year? Yes.

Percent of graduates receiving residency matches: N/A*

What service learning opportunities exist? N/A

COMLEX First-Time Pass Rate (Level 1, Level 2 Cognitive Evaluation, Level 2 Performance Evaluation, Level 3) - N/A*

*This campus opened in 2019. No COMLEX or Match data yet.

ALABAMA

ARKANSAS

DELAWARE

DISTRICT OF COLUMBIA

FLORIDA

GEORGIA

KENTUCKY

LOUISIANA

MARYLAND

MISSISSIPPI

NORTH CAROLINA

OKLAHOMA

SOUTH CAROLINA

TENNESSEE

TEXAS

VIRGINIA

WEST VIRGINIA

SOUTH

ALABAMA

ARKANSAS

DELAWARE

DISTRICT OF
COLUMBIA

FLORIDA

GEORGIA

KENTUCKY

LOUISIANA

MARYLAND

MISSISSIPPI

NORTH CAROLINA

OKLAHOMA

SOUTH CAROLINA

TENNESSEE

TEXAS

VIRGINIA

WEST VIRGINIA

SAM HOUSTON STATE UNIVERSITY COLLEGE OF OSTEOPATHIC MEDICINE

Address: 1905 University Avenue, Huntsville, Texas 77341
Website: *https://www.shsu.edu/academics/osteopathic-medicine/*
Contact: *Contact via phone or email: comadmissions@shsu.edu*
Phone: (936) 202-5202

Other campus locations: N/A

COST OF ATTENDANCE

Tuition: $55,000
Fees & Expenses: $28,210
Total: $83,210

Financial Aid: https://www.shsu.edu/dept/financial-aid/checklists/osteopathic

Percent Receiving Aid: 80%

ADDITIONAL INFORMATION

Interesting tidbit: As a relatively young college of osteopathic medicine, SHSU-COM is currently in "Pre-Accreditation" status with COCA until the first cohort graduates in 2024. Applicants must complete a primary application with the Texas Medical & Dental Schools Application Service (TMDSAS).

What international experiences are available? N/A

What dual degree options exist? No dual degree options listed.

Important Updates due to COVID-19: Accept online coursework to fulfill prerequisite requirements. Accept prerequisite coursework Pass/Fail grades. Accept online lab coursework.

Were tests required? MCAT required.

Are tests expected next year? Yes.

Percent of graduates receiving residency matches: N/A*

What service learning opportunities exist? N/A

COMLEX First-Time Pass Rate (Level 1, Level 2 Cognitive Evaluation, Level 2 Performance Evaluation, Level 3) - N/A*

*This school matriculated its first cohort of students in fall 2020, hence no COMLEX or Match data available.

UNIVERSITY OF NORTH TEXAS HEALTH SCIENCE CENTER TEXAS COLLEGE OF OSTEOPATHIC MEDICINE (UNTHSC/TCOM)

Address: 3500 Camp Bowie Blvd., Fort Worth, TX 76107
Website: *https://www.unthsc.edu/texas-college-of-osteopathic-medicine/*
Contact: *https://www.unthsc.edu/texas-college-of-osteopathic-medicine/admissions-and-outreach/contact-us/*
Phone: (817) 735-2204

Other campus locations: N/A

COST OF ATTENDANCE

In-State Tuition: $13,078
Fees & Expenses: $41,452
Total: $54,530

Out-of-State Tuition: $28,766
Fees & Expenses: $41,452
Total: $70,218

Financial Aid: https://www.unthsc.edu/financial-aid/

Percent Receiving Aid: 70%

ADDITIONAL INFORMATION

Interesting tidbit: The Texas College of Osteopathic Medicine Class of 2019 earned the highest score in the United States on a national board exam for future osteopathic doctors. Also, The Texas College of Osteopathic Medicine was granted a 10-year Accreditation with Exceptional Outcome, the highest distinction given by the COCA.

What international experiences are available? International rotations available in Malawi, Thailand, or Russia.

What dual degree options exist? Dual degree programs available. For more information, visit: https://www.unthsc.edu/academic-affairs/dual-degree/doms-dophd-and-medical-scientist-training-programs/

Important Updates due to COVID-19: Accept courses taken during the Summer/Fall/Spring 2020 semesters graded pass/fail including required prerequisite courses (but prefer letter grades). always accepted online courses for credit completed from a regionally accredited college or university.

Were tests required? MCAT required.

Are tests expected next year? Yes.

Percent of graduates receiving residency matches: 99% (2020)

What service learning opportunities exist? TCOM offers an opportunity for students to learn about rural medicine and how to serve underserved communities. For more information on the Rural Osteopathic Medical Education of Texas (ROME), visit: https://www.unthsc.edu/texas-college-of-osteopathic-medicine/office-of-rural-medical-education/

COMLEX First-Time Pass Rate (Level 1, Level 2 Cognitive Evaluation, Level 2 Performance Evaluation, Level 3)

Level 1: 96% (2020)

Level 2 CE: 99% (2019)

Level 2 PE: 94% (2019)

Level 3: 99% (2019)

ALABAMA
ARKANSAS
DELAWARE
DISTRICT OF COLUMBIA
FLORIDA
GEORGIA
KENTUCKY
LOUISIANA
MARYLAND
MISSISSIPPI
NORTH CAROLINA
OKLAHOMA
SOUTH CAROLINA
TENNESSEE
TEXAS
VIRGINIA
WEST VIRGINIA

SOUTH

ALABAMA

ARKANSAS

DELAWARE

DISTRICT OF COLUMBIA

FLORIDA

GEORGIA

KENTUCKY

LOUISIANA

MARYLAND

MISSISSIPPI

NORTH CAROLINA

OKLAHOMA

SOUTH CAROLINA

TENNESSEE

TEXAS

VIRGINIA

WEST VIRGINIA

UNIVERSITY OF THE INCARNATE WORD SCHOOL OF OSTEOPATHIC MEDICINE (UIWSOM)

Address: 4301 Broadway, San Antonio, TX 78209
Website: *https://osteopathic-medicine.uiw.edu/*
Contact: *https://osteopathic-medicine.uiw.edu/about-us/contact-us.html*
Phone: (210) 283-6998

Other campus locations: N/A

COST OF ATTENDANCE

Tuition: $56,000
Fees & Expenses: $29,245
Total: $85,245

Financial Aid: https://osteopathic-medicine.uiw.edu/admissions/doctor-of-osteopathic-medicine/financial-assistance-and-scholarships.html

Percent Receiving Aid: 83%

ADDITIONAL INFORMATION

Interesting tidbit: UIW School of Osteopathic Medicine (UIWSOM) has been granted full accreditation from the American Osteopathic Association's Commission on Osteopathic College Accreditation (COCA) in April 2021. Even though a Texas medical school, UIWSOM does not participate in the Texas Medical and Dental School Application Service (TMDSAS).

What international experiences are available? N/A

What dual degree options exist? No dual degree options listed.

Important Updates due to COVID-19: Accept all pass/fail/satisfactory/unsatisfactory grades from regionally accredited institutions. Accept all online coursework, including laboratory credits from regionally accredited institutions. Review application without all required coursework; proof of completion will be required prior to matriculation.

Were tests required? MCAT required.

Are tests expected next year? Yes.

Percent of graduates receiving residency matches: N/A*

What service learning opportunities exist? Service opportunities available. For more information, visit: https://osteopathic-medicine.uiw.edu/student-life/service-opportunities.html

COMLEX First-Time Pass Rate (Level 1, Level 2 Cognitive Evaluation, Level 2 Performance Evaluation, Level 3)

Level 1: 94.34% (2020)

Level 2 CE: N/A

Level 2 PE: N/A

Level 3: N/A

*UIWSOM graduates its first class in May 2021. The school has not updated the outcome.

Other: Direct Admit Program available for first-time freshmen attending UIW. For more information on this program, visit: https://osteopathic-medicine.uiw.edu/admissions/direct-admit-program.html

EDWARD VIA COLLEGE OF OSTEOPATHIC MEDICINE (VCOM-VIRGINIA CAMPUS)

Address: 2265 Kraft Dr. SW, Blacksburg, VA 24060
Website: *https://www.vcom.edu/virginia*
Contact: *https://www.vcom.edu/admissions/admissions-contact-information*
Phone: (540) 231-4000

Other campus locations: Auburn, AL; Monroe, LA; Spartanburg, SC

COST OF ATTENDANCE

Tuition: $46,900
Fees & Expenses: $28,282
Total: $75,182

Financial Aid: https://www.vcom.edu/virginia/current-students/tuition-and-financial-aid

Percent Receiving Aid: 91.5%

ADDITIONAL INFORMATION

Interesting tidbit: VCOM-Virginia Campus is VCOM's first campus, born out of a collaborative partnership between VCOM and Virginia Tech. It opened in 2003 in Virginia Tech's corporate research park.

What international experiences are available? N/A

What dual degree options exist? Dual degree programs available. For more information, visit: https://www.vcom.edu/admissions/parallel-degree

Important Updates due to COVID-19: LOR from a physician not required but encouraged.

Were tests required? MCAT required.

Are tests expected next year? Yes.

Percent of graduates receiving residency matches: 96% (2020 aggregate for three campuses)

What service learning opportunities exist? Student organizations focused on community outreach.

COMLEX First-Time Pass Rate (Level 1, Level 2 Cognitive Evaluation, Level 2 Performance Evaluation, Level 3)

Level 1: 99% (2020/21)

Level 2 CE: 98% (2019/20)

Level 2 PE: 96% (2019/20)

Level 3: 99% (2018/19)

ALABAMA

ARKANSAS

DELAWARE

DISTRICT OF COLUMBIA

FLORIDA

GEORGIA

KENTUCKY

LOUISIANA

MARYLAND

MISSISSIPPI

NORTH CAROLINA

OKLAHOMA

SOUTH CAROLINA

TENNESSEE

TEXAS

VIRGINIA

WEST VIRGINIA

SOUTH

ALABAMA

ARKANSAS

DELAWARE

DISTRICT OF
COLUMBIA

FLORIDA

GEORGIA

KENTUCKY

LOUISIANA

MARYLAND

MISSISSIPPI

NORTH CAROLINA

OKLAHOMA

SOUTH CAROLINA

TENNESSEE

TEXAS

VIRGINIA

WEST VIRGINIA

LIBERTY UNIVERSITY COLLEGE OF OSTEOPATHIC MEDICINE (LUCOM)

Address: 1971 University Boulevard, Lynchburg, VA 24502
Website: *https://www.liberty.edu/lucom/*
Contact: *https://www.liberty.edu/lucom/contact/*
Phone: (434) 592-6400

Other campus locations: N/A

COST OF ATTENDANCE

Tuition: $47,000
Fees & Expenses: $27,025
Total: $74,025

Financial Aid: https://www.liberty.edu/lucom/financial-aid/

Percent Receiving Aid: 80.5%

ADDITIONAL INFORMATION

Interesting tidbit: The Liberty University College of Osteopathic Medicine (LUCOM) is the second osteopathic college in the Commonwealth of Virginia. It boasts that its education and curriculum are distinctively Christian.

What international experiences are available? International elective rotations available. For more information, visit: https://www.liberty.edu/lucom/academics/study-abroad/

What dual degree options exist? No dual degree options listed.

Important Updates due to COVID-19: Accept online coursework to fulfill prerequisite requirements. Accept prerequisite coursework Pass/Fail grades. Accept online lab coursework if there was no in-person option available due to COVID-19 restrictions.

Were tests required? MCAT required.

Are tests expected next year? Yes.

Percent of graduates receiving residency matches: 98.7% (2021)

What service learning opportunities exist? Medical Outreach programs available. For more information, visit: https://www.liberty.edu/lucom/medical-outreach/

COMLEX First-Time Pass Rate (Level 1, Level 2 Cognitive Evaluation, Level 2 Performance Evaluation, Level 3)

Level 1: 90.4% (2019/20)

Level 2 CE: 97.2% (2019/20)

Level 2 PE: 93.2% (2019/20)

Level 3: 98.2% (2018/19)

WEST VIRGINIA SCHOOL OF OSTEOPATHIC MEDICINE (WVSOM)

Address: 400 Lee Street North, Lewisburg, WV 24901
Website: *https://www.wvsom.edu/*
Contact: *https://www.wvsom.edu/Admissions/recruits-contact*
Phone: (800) 356-7836

Other campus locations: N/A

COST OF ATTENDANCE

In-State Tuition: $22,472
Fees & Expenses: $33,190
Total: $55,662

Out-of-State Tuition: $53,710
Fees & Expenses: $33,190
Total: $86,900

Financial Aid: https://www.wvsom.edu/Admissions/FA-scholarships

Percent Receiving Aid: 87%

ADDITIONAL INFORMATION

Interesting tidbit: The Statewide Campus system at the West Virginia School of Osteopathic Medicine consists of seven regions across the state where third- and fourth-year medical students fulfill their clinical rotations in participating West Virginia hospitals. The system is geared toward an enhanced curriculum that encourages students who become physicians to practice in West Virginia.

What international experiences are available? The WVSOM Center for International Medicine and Cultural Concerns (CIMCC) offers hands-on learning at international locations. For more information, visit: https://www.wvsom.edu/Programs/programs-CIMCC

What dual degree options exist? No dual degree options listed.

Important Updates due to COVID-19: Accept online coursework to fulfill prerequisites, including labs. Pass/Fail grades are acceptable, but only for Spring 2020 coursework. May interview applicants prior to receiving MCAT scores but an MCAT score may be required before we will extend a final offer to join the class.

Were tests required? MCAT required.

Are tests expected next year? Yes.

Percent of graduates receiving residency matches: 99.5% (2019)

What service learning opportunities exist? Rural Health Initiative. For more information, visit: https://www.wvsom.edu/Programs/rhi/rhi-home

COMLEX First-Time Pass Rate (Level 1, Level 2 Cognitive Evaluation, Level 2 Performance Evaluation, Level 3)

Level 1: 89.33% (2019/20)

Level 2 CE: 93.75% (2019/20)

Level 2 PE: 92.10% (2019/20)

Level 3: 97.69% (2019)

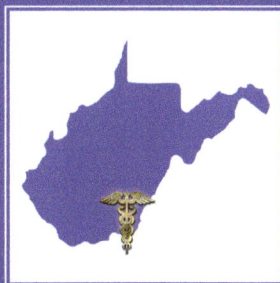

ALABAMA

ARKANSAS

DELAWARE

DISTRICT OF COLUMBIA

FLORIDA

GEORGIA

KENTUCKY

LOUISIANA

MARYLAND

MISSISSIPPI

NORTH CAROLINA

OKLAHOMA

SOUTH CAROLINA

TENNESSEE

TEXAS

VIRGINIA

WEST VIRGINIA

SOUTH

CHAPTER 5

REGION FOUR
WEST

ALASKA

ARIZONA

CALIFORNIA

COLORADO

HAWAII

IDAHO

MONTANA

NEVADA

NEW MEXICO

OREGON

UTAH

WASHINGTON

WYOMING

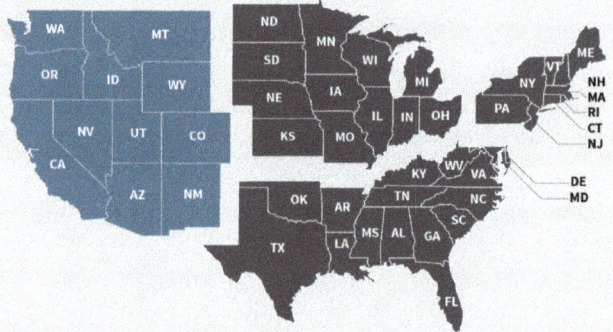

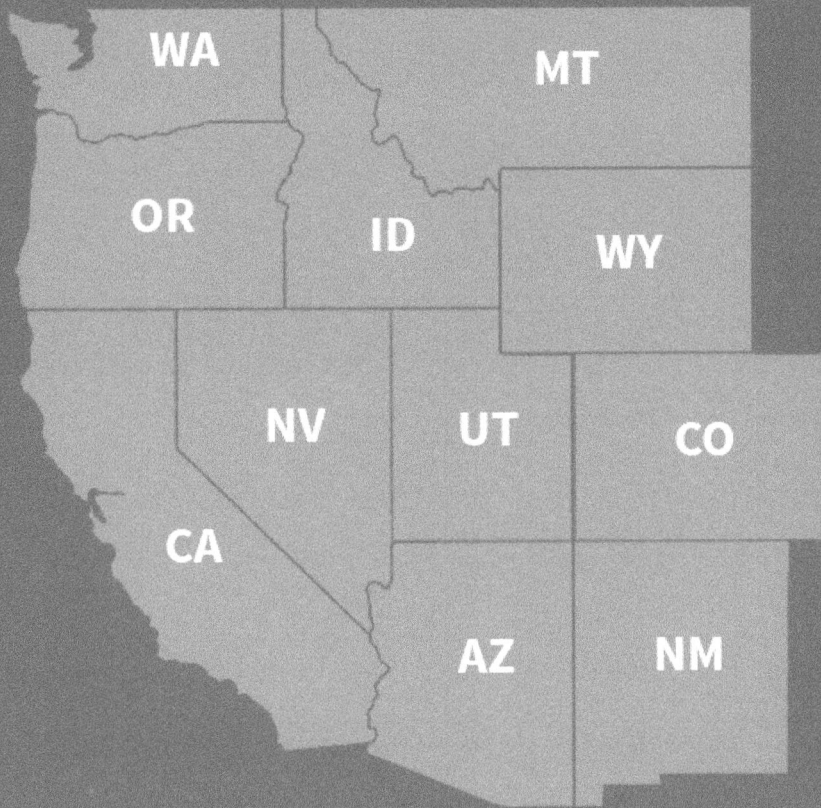

13 *Programs* | **13** *States*

1. *AZ – A.T. Still University, School of Osteopathic Medicine in Arizona (ATSU-SOMA)*
2. *AZ - Midwestern University Arizona College of Osteopathic Medicine (MWU/AZCOM)*
3. *CA - California Health Sciences University College of Osteopathic Medicine (CHSU-COM)*
4. *CA - Touro University College of Osteopathic Medicine-California (TUCOM)*
5. *CA - Western University of Health Sciences College of Osteopathic Medicine of the Pacific (WesternU/COMP)*
6. *CO - Rocky Vista University College of Osteopathic Medicine (RVUCOM)*
7. *ID - Idaho College of Osteopathic Medicine (ICOM)*
8. *NM - Burrell College of Osteopathic Medicine (BCOM)*
9. *NV - Touro University Nevada College of Osteopathic Medicine (TUNCOM)*
10. *OR - Western University of Health Sciences College of Osteopathic Medicine of the Pacific-Northwest (WesternU/COMP-Northwest)*
11. *UT - Noorda College of Osteopathic Medicine*
12. *UT - Rocky Vista University College of Osteopathic Medicine (RVUCOM-SU Campus)*
13. *WA - Pacific Northwest University of Health Sciences College of Osteopathic Medicine (PNWU-COM)*

Medical School	Ave. GPA & MCAT; Early Decision (ED): Yes/No; Int'l Students: Yes/No; Reapps: Yes/No	Admissions Statistics	Science Req. Other than Gen Chem, OChem, Physics, Bio
A.T. Still University (ATSU-SOMA) 5850 E. Still Circle, Mesa, AZ 85206	3.45 (overall) N/A (science) MCAT: 505 ED: No Int'l Student: No Reapps: N/A	**(2019)** Apps Received: 3,000 Interview Received: N/A Number Enrolled: 178 Admitted Rate: 5.9% **(2020)** Apps Received: 7,904 Interview Received: N/A Number Enrolled: 156 Admitted Rate: 2%	N/A
Midwestern University Arizona (MWU/AZCOM) 19555 N 59th Ave., Glendale, AZ 85308	3.48 (overall) 3.42 (science) MCAT: 506 ED: No Int'l Student: Yes* Reapps: Yes	**(2019)** Apps Received: 5,700 Interview Received: N/A Number Enrolled: 250 Admitted Rate: 4.38% **(2020)** Apps Received: 7,440 Interview Received: N/A Number Enrolled: 252 Admitted Rate: 3.4%	Anatomy, Physio., and Biochem. recommended
California Health Sciences University (CHSU-COM) 2500 Alluvial Avenue, Clovis, CA 93611	3.4 (overall) N/A (science) MCAT: 505 ED: No Int'l Student: No Reapps: N/A	**(2019)** N/A **(2020)** Apps Received: 3,939 Interview Received: N/A Number Enrolled: 80 Admitted Rate: 2%	CHSU-COM's first class started in 2020-2021. Thus, there is no admissions data for 2019.
Touro University College of Osteopathic Medicine-California (TUCOM) 1310 Club Drive Vallejo, CA 94592	3.5 (overall) 3.44 (science) MCAT: 507 ED: No Int'l Student: Yes Reapps: Yes	**(2019)** Apps Received: 5,000 Interview Received: 450 Number Enrolled: 135 Admitted Rate: 2.7% **(2020)** Apps Received: 6,046 Interview Received: N/A Number Enrolled: 125 Admitted Rate: 2.1%	Biochem. may substitute 4 sem. units of OChem. or Chem.

Medical School	Ave. GPA & MCAT Early Decision (ED): Yes/No Int'l Students: Yes/No Reapps: Yes/No	Admissions Statistics	Science Req. Other than Gen Chem, OChem, Physics, Bio
Western University of Health Sciences College of Osteopathic Medicine of the Pacific (WesternU/ COMP) 309 E. Second St., Pomona, CA 91766	3.72 (overall) 3.68 (science) MCAT: 509 ED: No Int'l Student: Yes Reapps: Yes	**(2019)** Apps Received: 6,023 Interview Received: 596 Number Enrolled: 220 Admitted Rate: 3.65% **(2020)** Apps Received: 7,045 Interview Received: N/A Number Enrolled: 323 Admitted Rate: 4.6%	Behav. Sciences
Rocky Vista University (RVUCOM) 8401 S. Chambers Road, Parker, CO 80134	3.55 (overall) 3.48 (science) MCAT: 508 ED: No Int'l Student: No Reapps: N/A	**(2019)** Apps Received: 5,168 Interview Received: 203 Number Enrolled: 162 Admitted Rate: 3.13% **(2020)** Apps Received: 3,924 Interview Received: N/A Number Enrolled: 293 Admitted Rate: 7.5%	Social/Behav. Sciences Biochemistry
Idaho College of Osteopathic Medicine (ICOM) 1401 E. Central Dr. Meridian, ID 83642	3.49 (overall) 3.41 (science) MCAT: 505 ED: No Int'l Student: No Reapps: N/A	**(2019)** Apps Received: 1,278 Interview Received: 600 Number Enrolled: 162 Admitted Rate: 12.7% **(2020)** Apps Received: 3,521 Interview Received: N/A Number Enrolled: 162 Admitted Rate: 4.6%	6+ Additional science hours strongly recommended. See chart.

WEST

OSTEO PROGRAMS

Medical School	Ave. GPA & MCAT / Early Decision (ED): Yes/No / Int'l Students: Yes/No / Reapps: Yes/No	Admissions Statistics	Science Req. Other than Gen Chem, OChem, Physics, Bio
Touro University Nevada College of Osteopathic Medicine (TUNCOM) 874 American Pacific Drive, Henderson, NV 89014	3.4 (overall) 3.48 (science) MCAT: 506 ED: No Int'l Student: No Reapps: N/A	**(2019)** Apps Received: 3,500 Interview Received: 550 Number Enrolled: 168 Admitted Rate: 4.8% **(2020)** Apps Received: 4,231 Interview Received: N/A Number Enrolled: 177 Admitted Rate: 4.2%	4 sem. units of Biochem. may be substituted for OChem 2 Behav. Sciences Math/Stats.
Burrell College of Osteopathic Medicine (BCOM) 3501 Arrowhead Dr., Las Cruces, NM 88001	3.66 (overall) 3.47 (science) MCAT: 501 ED: No Int'l Student: No Reapps: N/A	**(2019)** Apps Received: 5,316 Interview Received: 530 Number Enrolled: 162 Admitted Rate: 3% **(2020)** Apps Received: 4,624 Interview Received: N/A Number Enrolled: 162 Admitted Rate: 3.5%	3 credit hrs. of science course elective (See Chart)
Western University of Health Sciences College of Osteopathic Medicine of the Pacific-Northwest (WesternU/COMP-Northwest) 200 Mullins Dr., Lebanon, OR 97355	3.64 (overall) 3.59 (science) MCAT: 509 ED: No Int'l Student: No Reapps: Yes	**(2019)** Apps Received: 4,282 Interview Received: 352 Number Enrolled: 108 Admitted Rate: 2.47% **(2020)** Apps Received: 4,537 Interview Received: N/A Number Enrolled: 323 Admitted Rate: 7.1%	Behav. Sciences
Noorda College of Osteopathic Medicine** 122 East 1700 South, Building 3, Provo, Utah 84606	3.0 (minl) MCAT: 500+ (min) ED: No Int'l Student: Yes Reapps: N/A	**(2019)** N/A **(2020)** Apps Received: 1,283 Interview Received: N/A Number Enrolled: 150 Admitted Rate: 11.7%	Anatomy/Physio. w/ Lab Behav. Sciences Math/Statistics

Medical School	Ave. GPA & MCAT Early Decision (ED): Yes/No Int'l Students: Yes/No Reapps: Yes/No	Admissions Statistics	Science Req. Other than Gen Chem, OChem, Physics, Bio
Rocky Vista University (RVUCOM-SU Campus)*** 255 E. Center Street, Ivins, UT 84738	3.55 (overall) 3.48 (science) MCAT: 506 ED: No Int'l Student: No Reapps: N/A	**(2019)** Apps Received: 2,093 Interview Received: 166 Number Enrolled: 133 Admitted Rate: 6.35% **(2020)** Apps Received: 3,924 Interview Received: N/A Number Enrolled: 293 Admitted Rate: 7.5%	Social/Behav. Sciences Biochemistry
Pacific Northwest University of Health Sciences (PNWU-COM) 200 University Parkway, Suite 202, Yakima, WA 98901	3.4 (overall) 3.4 (science) MCAT: 503 ED: No Int'l Student: No Reapps: N/A	**(2019)** Apps Received: 4,461 Interview Received: 884 Number Enrolled: 144 Admitted Rate: 3.2% **(2020)** Apps Received: 5,195 Interview Received: N/A Number Enrolled: 143 Admitted Rate: 2.8%	N/A

*Intl. students must complete 30+ semester hours of coursework from college or university in the U.S.
**In July 2020, Noorda College of Osteopathic Medicine received accreditation approval from the COCA to begin recruiting students. The school plans to enroll 150 students for its first four years, with eventual expansion to a class size of 175.
***RVUCOM-SU Campus data reflects totals from all campuses.

WEST

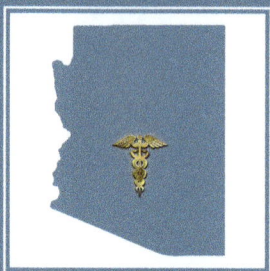

ALASKA

ARIZONA

CALIFORNIA

COLORADO

HAWAII

IDAHO

MONTANA

NEVADA

NEW MEXICO

OREGON

UTAH

WASHINGTON

WYOMING

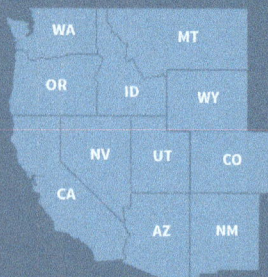

A.T. STILL UNIVERSITY, SCHOOL OF OSTEOPATHIC MEDICINE IN ARIZONA (ATSU-SOMA)

Address: 5850 E. Still Circle, Mesa, AZ 85206
Website: *https://www.atsu.edu/school-of-osteopathic-medicine-arizona*
Contact: *https://www.atsu.edu/connect/contact-atsu*
Phone: (480) 219-6000

Other campus locations: Kirksville, MO

COST OF ATTENDANCE

Tuition: $62,562
Fees & Expenses: $38,985
Total: $101,547

Financial Aid: https://www.atsu.edu/department-of-student-affairs/enrollment-services/types-of-aid

Percent Receiving Aid: 0%

ADDITIONAL INFORMATION

Interesting tidbit: The School of Osteopathic Medicine in Arizona is ATSU's newest medical school. ATSU-SOMA utilizes the Clinical Presentation Educational Model. SOMA students begin their clinical observations in Community Health Centers at the start of their second year instead of waiting until the third year as in traditional models.

What international experiences are available? N/A

What dual degree options exist? Dual degree programs available. For more information, visit: https://www.atsu.edu/school-of-osteopathic-medicine-arizona/academics/do-mph-program

Important Updates due to COVID-19: Accept online coursework to fulfill prerequisite requirements. Accept prerequisite coursework Pass/Fail grades. Accept online lab coursework.

Were tests required? MCAT required.

Are tests expected next year? Yes.

Percent of graduates receiving residency matches: 99.3% (four-year rolling average)

What service learning opportunities exist? Students encouraged to participate in volunteer programs such as Save the Family, Central Arizona Shelter System, Adelante Healthcare, and more.

COMLEX First-Time Pass Rate (Level 1, Level 2 Cognitive Evaluation, Level 2 Performance Evaluation, Level 3)

Level 1: 96% (2018/19)

Level 2 CE: 96% (2018/19)

Level 2 PE: 91% (2017/18)

Level 3: 97% (2018/19)

MIDWESTERN UNIVERSITY ARIZONA COLLEGE OF OSTEOPATHIC MEDICINE (MWU/AZCOM)

Address: 19555 N 59th Ave., Glendale, AZ 85308
Website: *https://www.midwestern.edu/academics/our-colleges/arizona-college-of-osteopathic-medicine.xml*
Contact: *https://online.midwestern.edu/public/reqinfo.cgi*
Phone: (623) 572-3215

Other campus locations: Downers Grove, IL

COST OF ATTENDANCE

Tuition: $74,516
Fees & Expenses: $27,466
Total: $101,982

Financial Aid: https://www.midwestern.edu/admissions/tuition-and-financial-aid/scholarships.xml

Percent Receiving Aid: 91%

ADDITIONAL INFORMATION

Interesting tidbit: AZCOM subscribes to a philosophy that regards the body as an integrated whole with structures and functions working interdependently. Its educational mission is to educate and train osteopathic physicians who treat their patients as unique persons with biological, psychological, and sociological needs, an approach that underscores the osteopathic commitment to patient-oriented versus disease-oriented health care.

What international experiences are available? N/A

What dual degree options exist? DO/MS in Biomedical Sciences available.

Important Updates due to COVID-19: N/A

Were tests required? MCAT required.

Are tests expected next year? Yes.

Percent of graduates receiving residency matches: 96% (2020)

What service learning opportunities exist? Clinical rotations in teaching hospitals and facilities throughout suburban and rural locations.

COMLEX First-Time Pass Rate (Level 1, Level 2 Cognitive Evaluation, Level 2 Performance Evaluation, Level 3)

Level 1: 95.28% (2019/20)

Level 2 CE: 95.4% (2019/20)

Level 2 PE: 94.9% (2019/20)

Level 3: 96.9% (2018/19)

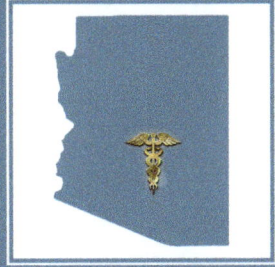

ALASKA

ARIZONA

CALIFORNIA

COLORADO

HAWAII

IDAHO

MONTANA

NEVADA

NEW MEXICO

OREGON

UTAH

WASHINGTON

WYOMING

WEST

ALASKA

ARIZONA

CALIFORNIA

COLORADO

HAWAII

IDAHO

MONTANA

NEVADA

NEW MEXICO

OREGON

UTAH

WASHINGTON

WYOMING

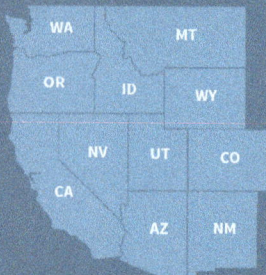

CALIFORNIA HEALTH SCIENCES UNIVERSITY COLLEGE OF OSTEOPATHIC MEDICINE (CHSU-COM)

Address: 2500 Alluvial Avenue, Clovis, CA 93611
Website: *https://osteopathic.chsu.edu/*
Contact: *https://osteopathic.chsu.edu/contact-us/*
Phone: (559) 712-4200

Other campus locations: N/A

COST OF ATTENDANCE

Tuition: $54,500
Fees & Expenses: $38,336
Total: $92,836

Financial Aid: https://osteopathic.chsu.edu/financial-aid-scholarships-tuition/

Percent Receiving Aid: 0%

ADDITIONAL INFORMATION

Interesting tidbit: The inaugural cohort of 79 medical students matriculated in July 2020. Aligned with the University mission, the CHSU-COM endeavors to recruit, train and retain physicians to serve the Central Valley of California, especially the underserved population.

What international experiences are available? Medical Missions available.

What dual degree options exist? No dual degree options listed.

Important Updates due to COVID-19: Accept a grade of PASS in a pass/no-pass grading system or CREDIT in a credit/no credit grading system, for courses taken during grading periods affected by COVID restrictions (beginning in Spring 2020).

Were tests required? MCAT required.

Are tests expected next year? Yes.

Percent of graduates receiving residency matches: N/A*

*The CHSU-COM will publish their GME match results when available after their inaugural class of osteopathic medical students participate in the residency matches during the 2023-24 academic year.

What service learning opportunities exist? N/A

COMLEX First-Time Pass Rate (Level 1, Level 2 Cognitive Evaluation, Level 2 Performance Evaluation, Level 3) **

** The inaugural class began D.O. program in July 2020. No COMLEX or Match data available yet.

TOURO UNIVERSITY COLLEGE OF OSTEOPATHIC MEDICINE-CALIFORNIA (TUCOM)

Address: 1310 Club Drive, Vallejo, CA 94592
Website: *http://com.tu.edu/*
Contact: *http://tu-4700742.hs-sites.com/tuc-interest-form*
Phone: (707) 638-5200

Other campus locations: N/A

COST OF ATTENDANCE

Tuition: $59,160
Additional Expenses: $37,922
Total: $97,082

Financial Aid: http://studentservices.tu.edu/financialaid/scholarships-do.html

Percent Receiving Aid: 81%

ADDITIONAL INFORMATION

Interesting tidbit: Percentage-wise, TUCOM is the number one medical school in the state for producing primary care physicians and for serving the disadvantaged and rural populations in California. In 2012 TUCOM-CA was awarded the HERO Award from the California Primary Care Association for being the institution that produces the most primary care clinicians in California. Also, TUCOM has earned three national recognitions for its innovative curriculum.

What international experiences are available? Global Health Program available. For more information, visit: http://com.tu.edu/globalhealth/index.html

What dual degree options exist? Dual degree programs available. For more information, visit: http://cehs.tu.edu/publichealth/dualjointdegrees/studyoptions-domph.html

Important Updates due to COVID-19: All Touro University California degree programs already accept online coursework, provided such coursework is completed at a regionally accredited institution, and Pass/Fail grading.

Were tests required? MCAT required.

Are tests expected next year? Yes.

Percent of graduates receiving residency matches: 100% (2017)

What service learning opportunities exist? Community Outreach opportunities available. For more information, visit: http://com.tu.edu/communityoutreach/

COMLEX First-Time Pass Rate (Level 1, Level 2 Cognitive Evaluation, Level 2 Performance Evaluation, Level 3)

Level 1: 96.92% (2020/21)

Level 2 CE: 96.55% (2020/21)

Level 2 PE: 92.2% (2019/20)

Level 3: 96.33% (2020)

ALASKA

ARIZONA

CALIFORNIA

COLORADO

HAWAII

IDAHO

MONTANA

NEVADA

NEW MEXICO

OREGON

UTAH

WASHINGTON

WYOMING

WEST

ALASKA

ARIZONA

CALIFORNIA

COLORADO

HAWAII

IDAHO

MONTANA

NEVADA

NEW MEXICO

OREGON

UTAH

WASHINGTON

WYOMING

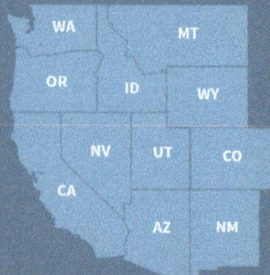

WESTERN UNIVERSITY OF HEALTH SCIENCES COLLEGE OF OSTEOPATHIC MEDICINE OF THE PACIFIC (WESTERNU/COMP)

Address: 309 E. Second St., Pomona, CA 91766
Website: *https://www.westernu.edu/osteopathic/*
Contact: *https://apply.westernu.edu/register/request-information*
Phone: (909) 623-6116

Other campus locations: Lebanon, OR

COST OF ATTENDANCE

Tuition: $59,600
Fees & Expenses: $23,551
Total: $83,151

Financial Aid: https://prospective.westernu.edu/osteopathic/do/tuition-scholarships/

Percent Receiving Aid: N/A

ADDITIONAL INFORMATION

Interesting tidbit: The College of Osteopathic Medicine of the Pacific (COMP), was established in 1977 as a direct and important response to a critical shortage of primary care physicians in the western United States. In August of 1996, COMP was restructured into a university with a new name - Western University of Health Sciences.

What international experiences are available? Global Health Track available. For more information, visit: https://www.westernu.edu/osteopathic/osteopathic-academics/longitudinal-tracks/global-health-track/

What dual degree options exist? No dual degree options listed.

Important Updates due to COVID-19: Accept pass/fail/satisfactory coursework, including prerequisite coursework. Accept all online coursework, including laboratory courses. Review your application without all required laboratory coursework. Review your application in consideration for an interview prior to receiving your MCAT exam scores.

Were tests required? MCAT required.

Are tests expected next year? Yes.

Percent of graduates receiving residency matches: 98.8% (2019)

What service learning opportunities exist? Pomona Community Health Action Team (PCHAT). For more information, visit: https://www.westernu.edu/osteopathic/outreach/pomona-community-health-action-team-pchat/

Rural Health Track: https://www.westernu.edu/osteopathic/osteopathic-academics/longitudinal-tracks/rural-health/

COMLEX First-Time Pass Rate (Level 1, Level 2 Cognitive Evaluation, Level 2 Performance Evaluation, Level 3)

Level 1: 95.1% (2019/20)

Level 2 CE: 96.4% (2019/20)

Level 2 PE: 98.5% (2018/19)

Level 3: 96.9% (2019)

ROCKY VISTA UNIVERSITY COLLEGE OF OSTEOPATHIC MEDICINE (RVUCOM)

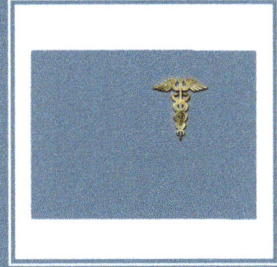

Address: 8401 S. Chambers Road, Parker, CO 80134
Website: *http://www.rvu.edu/rvu-co/com/*
Contact: *http://www.rvu.edu/contact/*
Phone: (303) 373-2008

Other campus locations: Ivins, UT

COST OF ATTENDANCE

Tuition: $60,270
Additional Expenses: $32,414
Total: $92,684

Financial Aid: http://www.rvu.edu/student-financial-services/

Percent Receiving Aid: 80%

ADDITIONAL INFORMATION

Interesting tidbit: RVU was established in 2006 as the nation's first private, for-profit health sciences university to offer a professional medical degree since 1910. RVUCOM is the founding campus.

What international experiences are available? Global Medicine Track available.

What dual degree options exist? No dual degree options listed.

Important Updates due to COVID-19: MCAT waived due to COVID.

Were tests required? MCAT not required but CASPer required.

Are tests expected next year? Yes.

Percent of graduates receiving residency matches: 100%

What service learning opportunities exist? Rural and Wilderness Medicine Track and Urban Underserved Medicine Tracks available.

COMLEX First-Time Pass Rate (Level 1, Level 2 Cognitive Evaluation, Level 2 Performance Evaluation, Level 3)

Level 1: 97.45% (2019/20)

Level 2 CE: 97.99% (2019/20)

Level 2 PE: 96.1% (2018/19)

Level 3: 97.73% (2019)

Other: Military Medicine Enrichment Pathway, Digital Health Track, and the Physician-Scientist Track are available at this campus. For more information about these tracks, visit: http://www.rvu.edu/tracks-and-special-programs/

ALASKA

ARIZONA

CALIFORNIA

COLORADO

HAWAII

IDAHO

MONTANA

NEVADA

NEW MEXICO

OREGON

UTAH

WASHINGTON

WYOMING

WEST

ALASKA

ARIZONA

CALIFORNIA

COLORADO

HAWAII

IDAHO

MONTANA

NEVADA

NEW MEXICO

OREGON

UTAH

WASHINGTON

WYOMING

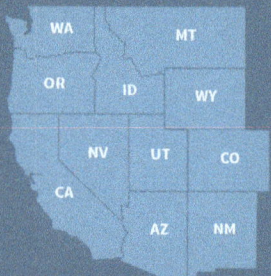

IDAHO COLLEGE OF OSTEOPATHIC MEDICINE (ICOM)

Address: 1401 E. Central Dr. Meridian, ID 83642
Website: *https://www.idahocom.org/*
Contact: *https://www.idahocom.org/contact/*
Phone: (208) 795-4266

Other campus locations: N/A

COST OF ATTENDANCE

Tuition: $54,330
Fees & Expenses: $28,014
Total: $82,344

Financial Aid: https://www.idahocom.org/admission-aid/financial-aid/

Percent Receiving Aid: 0%

ADDITIONAL INFORMATION

Interesting tidbit: ICOM's third- and fourth-year curriculum delivery occurs through the regional sites located in the states of Idaho, Montana, Wyoming, North and South Dakota and beyond. In the second year of the curriculum, students will be designated to a regional site. The Associate Dean of Clinical Education has the authority to assign a student to a rotation site and/or a regional site.

What international experiences are available? N/A

What dual degree options exist? No dual degree options listed.

Important Updates due to COVID-19: Physician LOR not required (but encouraged) due to COVID.

Were tests required? MCAT required.

Are tests expected next year? Yes.

Percent of graduates receiving residency matches: N/A*

What service learning opportunities exist? Community Outreach opportunities available. For more information, visit: https://www.idahocom.org/students/community-outreach/

COMLEX First-Time Pass Rate (Level 1, Level 2 Cognitive Evaluation, Level 2 Performance Evaluation, Level 3)

Level 1: 93.3% (2019/20)

Level 2 CE: N/A*

Level 2 PE: N/A*

Level 3: N/A*

*ICOM has not graduated their first class, therefore limited or no COMLEX or Match data.

TOURO UNIVERSITY NEVADA COLLEGE OF OSTEOPATHIC MEDICINE (TUNCOM)

Address: 874 American Pacific Drive, Henderson, NV 89014
Website: *https://tun.touro.edu/programs/osteopathic-medicine/*
Contact: *https://tun.touro.edu/about-us/contact-us/*
Phone: (702) 777-8687

Other campus locations: N/A

COST OF ATTENDANCE

Tuition: $57,800
Fees & Expenses: $35,631
Total: $94,431

Financial Aid: https://tun.touro.edu/admissions--aid/financial-aid/

Percent Receiving Aid: 89.6%

ADDITIONAL INFORMATION

Interesting tidbit: Starting third year, students will do 20 one-month clerkships over 22 months. In the fourth year, students have significant input in their schedule to maximize their internship and residency options.

What international experiences are available? N/A

What dual degree options exist? Dual degree programs available. For more information, visit: http://cehs.tu.edu/publichealth/degrees/TUNDO_MPHdegree.html

Important Updates due to COVID-19: Accept Pass/Fail grades (although not competitive). Accept online coursework.

Were tests required? MCAT and CASPer required.

Are tests expected next year? Yes.

Percent of graduates receiving residency matches: 100% (2020)

What service learning opportunities exist? Community involvement opportunities available. For more information, visit: https://tun.touro.edu/community-health--service/community-involvement/

Mobile Healthcare Outreach Initiative available. For more information, visit: https://tun.touro.edu/community-health--service/mobile-healthcare-outreach-initiative/

COMLEX First-Time Pass Rate (Level 1, Level 2 Cognitive Evaluation, Level 2 Performance Evaluation, Level 3)

Level 1: 99.2% (2019/20)

Level 2 CE: 99.2% (2019/20)

Level 2 PE: 93.8% (2019/20)

Level 3: 98.9% (2018/19)

ALASKA

ARIZONA

CALIFORNIA

COLORADO

HAWAII

IDAHO

MONTANA

NEVADA

NEW MEXICO

OREGON

UTAH

WASHINGTON

WYOMING

WEST

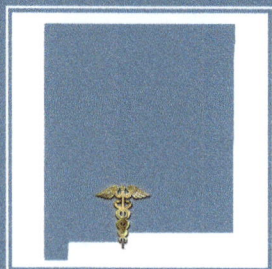

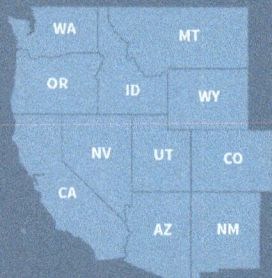

BURRELL COLLEGE OF OSTEOPATHIC MEDICINE (BCOM)

Address: 3501 Arrowhead Dr., Las Cruces, NM 88001
Website: *https://bcomnm.org/*
Contact: *https://bcomnm.org/contact/*
Phone: (575) 674-2266

Other campus locations: N/A

COST OF ATTENDANCE

Tuition: $58,335
Additional Expenses: $23,369
Total: $81,704

Financial Aid: https://bcomnm.org/students/resources/scholarship-and-loan-programs/

Percent Receiving Aid: 84%

ADDITIONAL INFORMATION

Interesting tidbit: Although Burrell College of Osteopathic Medicine is a private and free-standing college, it is very closely affiliated with New Mexico State University (NMSU). In a unique public-private partnership, the College's students have access to many university facilities and services, including NMSU's housing and meal services, at an additional cost.

What international experiences are available? N/A

What dual degree options exist? No dual degree options listed.

Important Updates due to COVID-19: Prerequisite coursework with a grade of "Pass" will be considered. Courses and laboratories completed online will be considered. Must be from accredited institutions. Physician LOR not required but preferred. Applicants may be invited to interview prior to submitting a first-time MCAT score and/or letter of recommendation from a physician or clinical experience. Applicants will not be eligible for a post-interview decision until the application is complete with all required materials submitted and minimum criteria met.

Were tests required? MCAT required.

Are tests expected next year? Yes.

Percent of graduates receiving residency matches: N/A*

What service learning opportunities exist? Translating Osteopathic Understanding into Community Health (TOUCH) Program and other service learning opportunities available. TOUCH Program: https://bcomnm.org/student-organizations/touch-program/

Service Learning: https://bcomnm.org/students/student-life/service-learning/

COMLEX First-Time Pass Rate (Level 1, Level 2 Cognitive Evaluation, Level 2 Performance Evaluation, Level 3)

Level 1: 85.03%

Level 2 CE: 93.89%

Level 2 PE: 88.81%

Level 3: N/A*

*BCOM had its first graduating class in 2020, therefore no specific data on COMLEX Level 3 or Match rate.

ALASKA

ARIZONA

CALIFORNIA

COLORADO

HAWAII

IDAHO

MONTANA

NEVADA

NEW MEXICO

OREGON

UTAH

WASHINGTON

WYOMING

WESTERN UNIVERSITY OF HEALTH SCIENCES COLLEGE OF OSTEOPATHIC MEDICINE OF THE PACIFIC-NORTHWEST (WESTERNU/COMP-NORTHWEST)

Address: 200 Mullins Dr., Lebanon, OR 97355
Website: *https://www.westernu.edu/northwest/*
Contact: *https://apply.westernu.edu/register/request-information*
Phone: (541) 259-0200

Other campus locations: Pomona, CA

COST OF ATTENDANCE

Tuition: $59,600
Fees & Expenses: $21,308
Total: $80,908

Financial Aid: https://prospective.westernu.edu/osteopathic/do/tuition-scholarships/

Percent Receiving Aid: N/A

ADDITIONAL INFORMATION

Interesting tidbit: Western University of Health Sciences' College of Osteopathic Medicine of the Pacific and COMP-Northwest have taken a multi-tiered approach to Diversity, Equity and Inclusion (DEI), evaluating and modifying curriculum, recruitment, leadership development, fundraising and research. the College's curriculum is proactively being reviewed to examine implicit bias, explore social determinants of health outcomes and empower future physicians to be effective advocates for their patients.

What international experiences are available? Global Health Track available. For more information, visit: https://www.westernu.edu/osteopathic/osteopathic-academics/longitudinal-tracks/global-health-track/

What dual degree options exist? No dual degree options listed.

Important Updates due to COVID-19: Accept all pass/fail/satisfactory coursework, including prerequisite coursework. Accept all online coursework, including laboratory courses. Review your application without all required laboratory coursework.Review your application in consideration for an interview prior to receiving your MCAT exam scores.

Were tests required? MCAT required.

Are tests expected next year? Yes.

Percent of graduates receiving residency matches: 98.8% (2019)

What service learning opportunities exist? Rural Health Track: https://www.westernu.edu/osteopathic/osteopathic-academics/longitudinal-tracks/rural-health/

COMLEX First-Time Pass Rate (Level 1, Level 2 Cognitive Evaluation, Level 2 Performance Evaluation, Level 3)

Level 1: 95.1% (2019/20)

Level 2 CE: 96.4% (2019/20)

Level 2 PE: 98.5% (2018/19)

Level 3: 96.9% (2019)

ALASKA

ARIZONA

CALIFORNIA

COLORADO

HAWAII

IDAHO

MONTANA

NEVADA

NEW MEXICO

OREGON

UTAH

WASHINGTON

WYOMING

WEST

ALASKA

ARIZONA

CALIFORNIA

COLORADO

HAWAII

IDAHO

MONTANA

NEVADA

NEW MEXICO

OREGON

UTAH

WASHINGTON

WYOMING

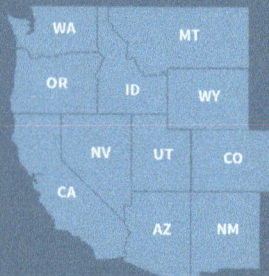

NOORDA COLLEGE OF OSTEOPATHIC MEDICINE

Address: 122 East 1700 South, Building 3, Provo, Utah 84606
Website: *https://noordacom.org/*
Contact: *info@noordacom.org*
Phone: (385) 375-8724

Other campus locations: N/A

COST OF ATTENDANCE

Tuition: $53,300
Fees & Expenses: $30,159
Total: $83,459

Financial Aid: https://www.noordacom.org/tuition/

Percent Receiving Aid: 0%

ADDITIONAL INFORMATION

Interesting tidbit: Noorda-COM, as a new medical school welcoming its inaugural class in 2021, is in pre-accreditation status. Pre-accreditation status is reviewed annually to assess the academic progress of the first-, second and third-year classes through graduation. Full accreditation is typically granted prior to when a new school graduates its first class.

What international experiences are available? N/A

What dual degree options exist? No dual degree options listed.

Important Updates due to COVID-19: Accept online coursework to fulfill prerequisite requirements. Accept prerequisite coursework Pass/Fail grades. Accept online lab coursework.

Were tests required? MCAT required.

Are tests expected next year? Yes.

Percent of graduates receiving residency matches: N/A

What service learning opportunities exist? N/A

COMLEX First-Time Pass Rate (Level 1, Level 2 Cognitive Evaluation, Level 2 Performance Evaluation, Level 3) - N/A

ROCKY VISTA UNIVERSITY COLLEGE OF OSTEOPATHIC MEDICINE (RVUCOM-SU CAMPUS)

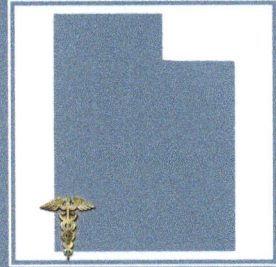

Address: 255 E. Center Street, Ivins, UT 84738
Website: *http://www.rvu.edu/rvu-su/college-of-osteopathic-medicine/*
Contact: *http://www.rvu.edu/contact/*
Phone: (435) 222-1236

Other campus locations: Parker, CO

COST OF ATTENDANCE

Tuition: $60,270
Additional Expenses: $32,414
Total: $92,6845

Financial Aid: http://www.rvu.edu/student-financial-services/

Percent Receiving Aid: 80%

ADDITIONAL INFORMATION

Interesting tidbit: The Southern Utah campus (RVU-SU) is adjacent to the Southern Utah Veterans Home, which provides students with the longitudinal care experience.

What international experiences are available? Global Medicine Track available.

What dual degree options exist? No dual degree options listed.

Important Updates due to COVID-19: MCAT waived due to COVID.

Were tests required? MCAT not required but CASPer required.

Are tests expected next year? Yes.

Percent of graduates receiving residency matches: N/A

What service learning opportunities exist? Rural and Wilderness Medicine Track

COMLEX First-Time Pass Rate (Level 1, Level 2 Cognitive Evaluation, Level 2 Performance Evaluation, Level 3)

Level 1: 97.45% (2019/20)

Level 2 CE: 97.99% (2019/20)

Level 2 PE: 96.1% (2018/19)

Level 3: 97.73% (2019)

Other: RVUCOM has an Early Acceptance Program for students attending Southern Utah University or Dixie State University who are in the Utah Rural Health Scholars Program. Provisional acceptance is given and there is no MCAT requirement. Contact admissions for more information.

Other tracks include Military Medicine Enrichment Pathway, Academic Medicine and Leadership, Digital Health, Long-Term Care, and Physician-Scientist Tracks available at this campus. For more information about these tracks, visit: http://www.rvu.edu/tracks-and-special-programs/

ALASKA

ARIZONA

CALIFORNIA

COLORADO

HAWAII

IDAHO

MONTANA

NEVADA

NEW MEXICO

OREGON

UTAH

WASHINGTON

WYOMING

WEST

ALASKA

ARIZONA

CALIFORNIA

COLORADO

HAWAII

IDAHO

MONTANA

NEVADA

NEW MEXICO

OREGON

UTAH

WASHINGTON

WYOMING

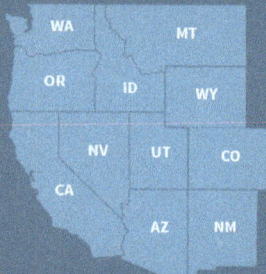

PACIFIC NORTHWEST UNIVERSITY OF HEALTH SCIENCES COLLEGE OF OSTEOPATHIC MEDICINE (PNWU-COM)

Address: 200 University Parkway, Yakima, WA 98901
Website: *https://www.pnwu.edu/*
Contact: *https://www.pnwu.edu/connect/contact-us*
Phone: (509) 452-5100

Other campus locations: N/A

COST OF ATTENDANCE

Tuition: $59,380
Additional Expenses: $19,429
Total: $78,809

Financial Aid: https://www.pnwu.edu/admissions/financial-aid/paying-school

Percent Receiving Aid: 85%

Other: SOMA Scholarship (Student Osteopathic Medical Association)

ADDITIONAL INFORMATION

Interesting tidbit: During years three and four, students engage in their clinical education in clerkships at hospitals, clinics, and physician's offices throughout the Northwest, where regional deans and regional administrators support and guide their progress toward residency.

What international experiences are available? N/A

What dual degree options exist? No dual degree options listed.

Important Updates due to COVID-19: Accept online coursework to fulfill prerequisite requirements. Accept prerequisite coursework Pass/Fail grades. Accept online lab coursework.

Were tests required? MCAT required.

Are tests expected next year? Yes.

Percent of graduates receiving residency matches: 100% (2020)

What service learning opportunities exist? N/A

COMLEX First-Time Pass Rate (Level 1, Level 2 Cognitive Evaluation, Level 2 Performance Evaluation, Level 3)

Level 1: 92.8% (2019/20)

Level 2 CE: 97.1% (2019/20)

Level 2 PE: 97.1% (2019/20)

Level 3: 95.8% (2018/19)

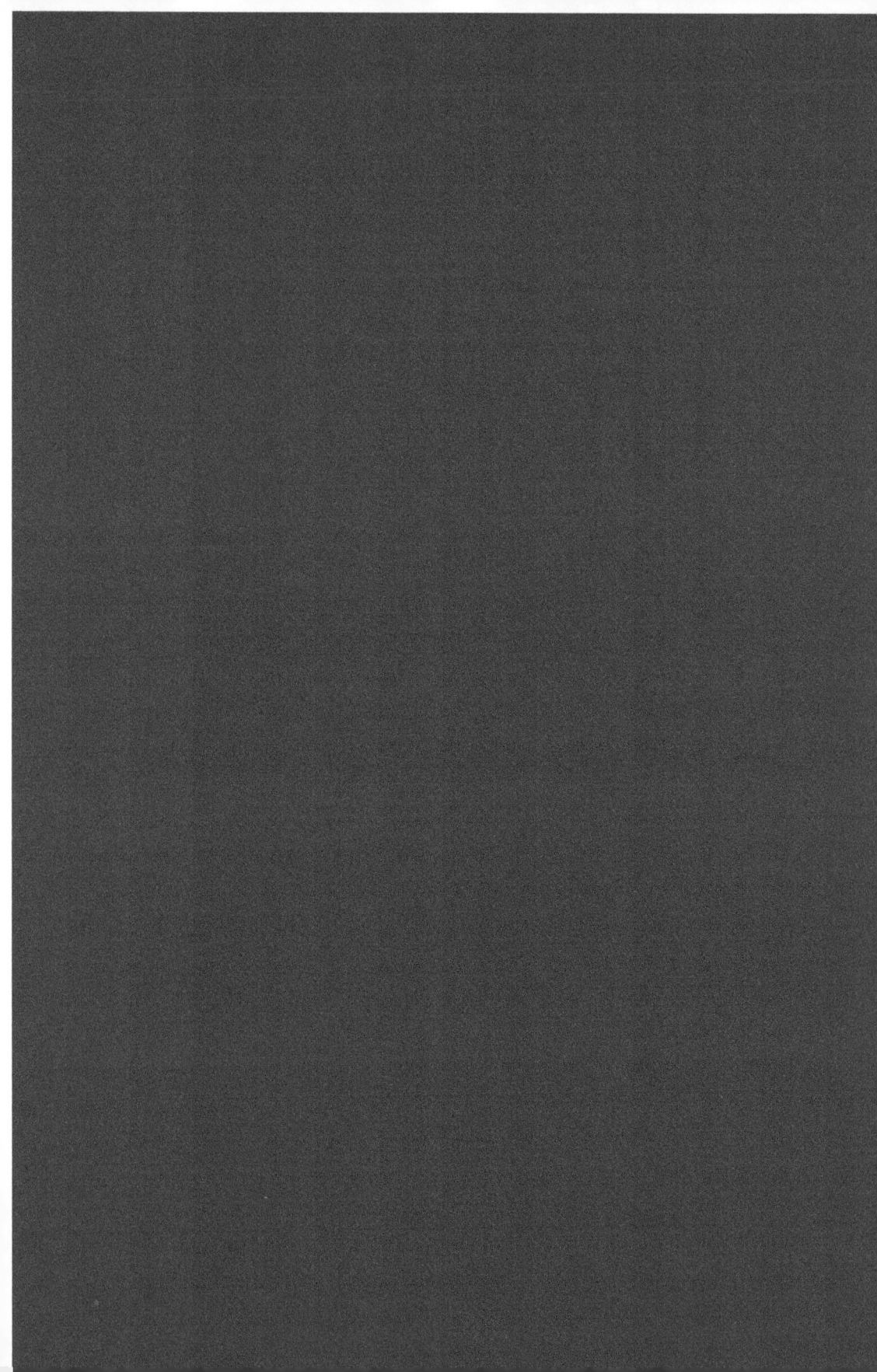

OSTEOPATHIC
MEDICAL
SCHOOL LISTS

CHAPTER 6

OSTEOPATHIC MEDICAL SCHOOLS BY CITY/STATE

DO Schools	City	State	Website
Edward Via College of Osteopathic Medicine (VCOM - Auburn Campus)	Auburn	AL	*https://www.vcom.edu/*
Alabama College of Osteopathic Medicine (ACOM)	Dothan	AL	*https://www.acom.edu/*
Arkansas College of Osteopathic Medicine (ARCOM)	Fort Smith	AR	*https://acheedu.org/arcom/*
New York Institute of Technology College of Osteopathic Medicine at Arkansas State (NYITCOM)	Jonesboro	AR	*https://www.nyit.edu/arkansas*
Midwestern University Arizona College of Osteopathic Medicine (MWU/AZCOM)	Glendale	AZ	*https://www.midwestern.edu/academics/our-colleges/arizona-college-of-osteopathic-medicine.xml*
A.T. Still University, School of Osteopathic Medicine in Arizona (ATSU-SOMA)	Mesa	AZ	*https://www.atsu.edu/school-of-osteopathic-medicine-arizona*
California Health Sciences University College of Osteopathic Medicine (CHSU-COM)	Clovis	CA	*https://osteopathic.chsu.edu/*
Western University of Health Sciences College of Osteopathic Medicine of the Pacific (WesternU/COMP)	Pomona	CA	*https://www.westernu.edu/osteopathic/*
Touro University College of Osteopathic Medicine-California (TUCOM)	Vallejo	CA	*http://com.tu.edu/*

DO Schools	City	State	Website
Rocky Vista University College of Osteopathic Medicine (RVUCOM)	Parker	CO	http://www.rvu.edu/rvu-su/college-of-osteopathic-medicine/
Lake Erie College of Osteopathic Medicine-Bradenton (LECOM-Bradenton)	Bradenton	FL	https://lecom.edu/
Nova Southeastern University Dr. Kiran C. Patel College of Osteopathic Medicine (NSU-KPCOM-Clearwater)	Clearwater	FL	https://osteopathic.nova.edu/index.html
Nova Southeastern University Dr. Kiran C. Patel College of Osteopathic Medicine (NSU-KPCOM)	Fort Lauderdale	FL	https://osteopathic.nova.edu/index.html
Philadelphia College of Osteopathic Medicine South Georgia (PCOM South Georgia)	Moultrie	GA	https://www.pcom.edu/south-georgia/
Philadelphia College of Osteopathic Medicine Georgia (PCOM Georgia)	Suwanee	GA	https://www.pcom.edu/campuses/georgia-campus/
Des Moines University College of Osteopathic Medicine (DMU-COM)	Des Moines	IA	https://www.dmu.edu/do/
Idaho College of Osteopathic Medicine (ICOM)	Meridian	ID	https://www.idahocom.org/
Midwestern University Chicago College of Osteopathic Medicine (MWU/CCOM)	Downers Grove	IL	https://www.midwestern.edu/academics/degrees-and-programs/doctor-of-osteopathic-medicine-il.xml

DO Schools	City	State	Website
Marian University College of Osteopathic Medicine (MU-COM)	Indianapolis	IN	*https://www.marian. edu/osteopathic- medical-school*
University of Pikeville Kentucky College of Osteopathic Medicine (UP-KYCOM)	Pikeville	KY	*https://www.upike. edu/osteopathic- medicine/*
Edward Via College of Osteopathic Medicine-Monroe Campus (VCOM - Monroe Campus)	Monroe	LA	*https://www.vcom. edu/louisiana*
University of New England College of Osteopathic Medicine (UNECOM)	Biddeford	ME	*https://www.une. edu/com*
Michigan State University College of Osteopathic Medicine (MSUCOM-MUC)	Clinton Twp	MI	*https://com.msu. edu/*
Michigan State University College of Osteopathic Medicine (MSUCOM-DMC)	Detroit	MI	*https://com.msu. edu/*
Michigan State University College of Osteopathic Medicine (MSUCOM)	East Lansing	MI	*https://com.msu. edu/*
Kansas City University of Medicine and Biosciences College of Osteopathic Medicine (KCU-COM)	Kansas City	MO	*http://www. kcumb.edu/ programs/college- of-osteopathic- medicine*
A. T. Still University Kirksville College of Osteopathic Medicine (ATSU-KCOM)	Kirksville	MO	*https://www. atsu.edu/ kirksville-college- of-osteopathic- medicine*

DO Schools	City	State	Website
William Carey University College of Osteopathic Medicine (WCUCOM)	Hattiesburg	MS	https://www.wmcarey.edu/College/Osteopathic-Medicine
Campbell University Jerry M. Wallace School of Osteopathic Medicine (CUSOM)	Lillington	NC	https://medicine.campbell.edu/
Rowan University School of Osteopathic Medicine (RowanSOM)	Stratford	NJ	https://som.rowan.edu/
Burrell College of Osteopathic Medicine (BCOM)	Las Cruces	NM	https://bcomnm.org/
Kansas City University of Medicine and Biosciences College of Osteopathic Medicine (KCU-COM-Joplin)	Joplin	NO	http://www.kcumb.edu/programs/college-of-osteopathic-medicine
Touro University Nevada College of Osteopathic Medicine (TUNCOM)	Henderson	NV	https://tun.touro.edu/programs/osteopathic-medicine/
Lake Erie College of Osteopathic Medicine - Elmira (LECOM-Elmira)	Elmira	NY	https://lecom.edu/
Touro College of Osteopathic Medicine (TouroCOM-Middletown)	Middletown	NY	https://tourocom.touro.edu/
Touro College of Osteopathic Medicine (TouroCOM-Harlem)	New York	NY	https://tourocom.touro.edu/
New York Institute of Technology College of Osteopathic Medicine (NYITCOM)	Old Westbury	NY	https://www.nyit.edu/medicine

DO Schools	City	State	Website
Ohio University Heritage College of Osteopathic Medicine (OU-HCOM)	Athens	OH	*https://www.ohio.edu/medicine/*
Ohio University Heritage College of Osteopathic Medicine in Dublin (OU-HCOM-Dublin)	Dublin	OH	*https://www.ohio.edu/medicine/*
Ohio University Heritage College of Osteopathic Medicine in Cleveland (OU-HCOM-Cleveland)	Warrensville Heights	OH	*https://www.ohio.edu/medicine/*
Oklahoma State University Center for Health Sciences College of Osteopathic Medicine - Tahlequah (OSU-COM Tahlequah)	Tahlequah	OK	*https://health.okstate.edu/com/index.html*
Oklahoma State University Center for Health Sciences College of Osteopathic Medicine (OSU-COM)	Tulsa	OK	*https://health.okstate.edu/com/index.html*
Western University of Health Sciences College of Osteopathic Medicine of the Pacific-Northwest (WesternU/COMP-Northwest)	Lebanon	OR	*https://www.westernu.edu/northwest/*
Lake Erie College of Osteopathic Medicine-Erie (LECOM)	Erie	PA	*https://lecom.edu/*
Lake Erie College of Osteopathic Medicine - Seton Hill (LECOM-Seton Hill)	Greensburg	PA	*https://lecom.edu/*

DO Schools	City	State	Website
Philadelphia College of Osteopathic Medicine (PCOM)	Philadelphia	PA	https://www.pcom.edu/
Edward Via College of Osteopathic Medicine-Carolinas Campus (VCOM - Carolinas Campus)	Spartanburg	SC	https://www.vcom.edu/carolinas
Lincoln Memorial University DeBusk College of Osteopathic Medicine (LMU-DCOM)	Harrogate	TN	https://www.lmunet.edu/debusk-college-of-osteopathic-medicine/index.php
Lincoln Memorial University DeBusk College of Osteopathic Medicine - Knoxville (LMU-DCOM Knoxville)	Knoxville	TN	https://www.lmunet.edu/debusk-college-of-osteopathic-medicine/index.php
University of North Texas Health Science Center Texas College of Osteopathic Medicine (UNTHSC/TCOM)	Fort Worth	TX	https://www.unthsc.edu/texas-college-of-osteopathic-medicine/
Sam Houston State University College of Osteopathic Medicine	Huntsville	TX	https://www.shsu.edu/academics/osteopathic-medicine/
University of the Incarnate Word School of Osteopathic Medicine (UIWSOM)	San Antonio	TX	https://osteopathic-medicine.uiw.edu/
Rocky Vista University College of Osteopathic Medicine (RVUCOM-SU Campus)	Ivins	UT	http://www.rvu.edu/rvu-su/college-of-osteopathic-medicine/
Noorda College of Osteopathic Medicine	Provo	UT	https://noordacom.org/

DO Schools	City	State	Website
Edward Via College of Osteopathic Medicine (VCOM-Virginia Campus)	Blacksburg	VA	https://www.vcom.edu/virginia
Liberty University College of Osteopathic Medicine (LUCOM)	Lynchburg	VA	https://www.liberty.edu/lucom/
Pacific Northwest University of Health Sciences College of Osteopathic Medicine (PNWU-COM)	Yakima	WA	https://www.pnwu.edu/
West Virginia School of Osteopathic Medicine (WVSOM)	Lewisburg	WV	https://www.wvsom.edu/

CHAPTER 7

OSTEOPATHIC MEDICAL SCHOOL PREREQUISITES

ALABAMA

School	Required	Recommended	Notes
ALABAMA COLLEGE OF OSTEOPATHIC MEDICINE (ACOM)	Bio. w/Lab, Physics w/Lab, Chem. w/Lab, OChem. w/Lab, Engl. Comp and/or Lit..	N/A	No listed information on AP credits. Contact admissions.
EDWARD VIA COLLEGE OF OSTEOPATHIC MEDICINE (VCOM - AUBURN CAMPUS)	Bio., Physics, Chem., OChem., Engl. and Comp., and 6+ Biomedical Science credit hours (see recommended).	Biomedical Science courses: Anatomy, Physio., Biochem., Immunology, Microbio., Virology, or Genetics.	No listed information on AP credits. Contact admissions.

ARIZONA

School	Required	Recommended	Notes
A.T. STILL UNIVERSITY, SCHOOL OF OSTEOPATHIC MEDICINE IN ARIZONA (ATSU-SOMA)	Bio. w/Lab, Physics w/Lab, Chem. w/Lab, OChem. w/Lab, Engl.	Genetics, Biochem., Immunology, Anatomy, Physiology, Cellular Bio. (Molecular, Physiology, etc.), and Microbio.	No listed information on AP credits. Contact admissions.
MIDWESTERN UNIVERSITY ARIZONA COLLEGE OF OSTEOPATHIC MEDICINE (MWU/ AZCOM)	Bio. w/Lab, Chem. w/Lab, OChem. w/ Lab, Physics w/Lab, Engl. Comp.	Anatomy, Physiology, and Biochem. encouraged.	AP credits accepted as long as they are listed on undergraduate transcript.

For the number of hours required for prerequisite courses, and for the most up-to-date information, please refer to the individual school websites.

*A.P. credit satisfies the requirement.

** When A.P. credit is awarded, upper-level coursework in the same subject area is required.

*** A.P. credit may satisfy the requirement on a case by case basis

112

ARKANSAS

School	Required	Recommended	Notes
ARKANSAS COLLEGE OF OSTEOPATHIC MEDICINE (ARCOM)	Biol., Biochem., Chem. w/Lab, OChem. w/Lab, Physics w/Lab, Engl. Comp and Lit., Science Electives.	Additional humanities: Literature, Philosophy, or Theology. Communication Skills: Speech, Debate, or Drama. Science Electives: Genetics, Human Physiology, Human Anatomy, Immunology, Epidemiology, etc.	AP credits not accepted.
NEW YORK INSTITUTE OF TECHNOLOGY COLLEGE OF OSTEOPATHIC MEDICINE AT ARKANSAS STATE (NYITCOM)	Engl., Bio. w/Lab, Chem. w/Lab, OChem. 1 and 2 w/ Lab (see notes), Physics w/Lab.	Behavioral Sciences, Biochem., Calculus/Statistics, Human Anatomy/ Physiology, Genetics, Microbio.	Biochemistry may be substituted for OChem. 2. No listed information on AP credits. Contact admissions.

CALIFORNIA

School	Required	Recommended	Notes
CALIFORNIA HEALTH SCIENCES UNIVERSITY COLLEGE OF OSTEOPATHIC MEDICINE (CHSU-COM)	Behav. Sciences, Bio., Chem., OChem., Physics, and Engl.	Biochem., Anatomy, Physio., Genetics, Immunology.	AP credits accepted as long as they are listed on undergraduate transcript.

For the number of hours required for prerequisite courses, and for the most up-to-date information, please refer to the individual school websites.
*A.P. credit satisfies the requirement.
** When A.P. credit is awarded, upper-level coursework in the same subject area is required.
*** A.P. credit may satisfy the requirement on a case by case basis

TOURO UNIVERSITY COLLEGE OF OSTEOPATHIC MEDICINE-CALIFORNIA (TUCOM)	Bio. w/Lab, Physics w/Lab, Chem (see Notes), College Engl., Behav. Science, Math/Computer Science.	Human Anatomy, Human Physio., Biochem.	Two Chemistry Options: 1. 8 sem. units of Chem. w/Lab, 8 sem. units of OChem. w/Lab (may sub. 4 sem. units with Biochem.) 2. 4 sem. units of Chem. w/Lab, 8 sem. units of OChem. w/Lab, 4 sem. units of Biochem. w/Lab. AP credits accepted as long as they are listed on undergraduate transcript.
WESTERN UNIVERSITY OF HEALTH SCIENCES COLLEGE OF OSTEOPATHIC MEDICINE OF THE PACIFIC (WESTERNU/COMP)	Engl., Behav. Sciences, Bio. w/Lab, OChem. w/Lab, Chem. w/Lab, Physics w/Lab.	Biochem., Genetics, Physio.	AP credits accepted as long as they are listed on undergraduate transcript.

COLORADO

School	Required	Recommended	Notes
ROCKY VISTA UNIVERSITY COLLEGE OF OSTEOPATHIC MEDICINE (RVUCOM)	Bio. w/Lab, Chem. w/Lab, OChem. w/Lab, Physics w/Lab, Engl. or Lit., Social/Behav. Sciences, Biochem.	Human Anatomy, Physio., Genetics, and Cellular Bio.	AP credits accepted as long as they are listed on undergraduate transcript.

For the number of hours required for prerequisite courses, and for the most up-to-date information, please refer to the individual school websites.

*A.P. credit satisfies the requirement.

** When A.P. credit is awarded, upper-level coursework in the same subject area is required.

*** A.P. credit may satisfy the requirement on a case by case basis

FLORIDA

School	Required	Recommended	Notes
LAKE ERIE COLLEGE OF OSTEOPATHIC MEDICINE-BRADENTON (LECOM-BRADENTON)	Bio. w/Lab, Chem. w/Lab, OChem. w/Lab, Physics w/Lab, Engl., Behavioral Sciences.	Biochem., Physiology, Microbiology and/or Anatomy.	No listed information on AP credits. Contact admissions.
NOVA SOUTHEASTERN UNIVERSITY DR. KIRAN C. PATEL COLLEGE OF OSTEOPATHIC MEDICINE (NSU-KPCOM-CLEARWATER)	Bio. w/Lab, Chem. w/Lab, OChem. w/Lab, Physics w/Lab, Engl/Humanities, Biochem.	Immunology, physio., behavioral sciences, and humanities.	AP credits accepted. Contact admissions for more information.
NOVA SOUTHEASTERN UNIVERSITY DR. KIRAN C. PATEL COLLEGE OF OSTEOPATHIC MEDICINE (NSU-KPCOM)	Bio. w/Lab, Chem. w/Lab, OChem. w/Lab, Physics w/Lab, Engl/Humanities, Biochem.	Immunology, physio., behavioral sciences, and humanities.	AP credits accepted. Contact admissions for more information.

GEORGIA

School	Required	Recommended	Notes
PHILADELPHIA COLLEGE OF OSTEOPATHIC MEDICINE GEORGIA (PCOM GEORGIA)	Bio. w/Lab, Physics w/Lab, Chem. w/Lab, OChem. w/Lab, Biochem., Engl. Comp & Lit.	N/A	AP credits accepted as long as they are listed on undergraduate transcript.
PHILADELPHIA COLLEGE OF OSTEOPATHIC MEDICINE SOUTH GEORGIA (PCOM SOUTH GEORGIA)	Bio. w/Lab, Physics w/Lab, Chem. w/Lab, OChem. w/Lab, Biochem., Engl. Comp & Lit.	N/A	AP credits accepted as long as they are listed on undergraduate transcript.

For the number of hours required for prerequisite courses, and for the most up-to-date information, please refer to the individual school websites.

*A.P. credit satisfies the requirement.

** When A.P. credit is awarded, upper-level coursework in the same subject area is required.

*** A.P. credit may satisfy the requirement on a case by case basis

IDAHO

School	Required	Recommended	Notes
IDAHO COLLEGE OF OSTEOPATHIC MEDICINE (ICOM)	Bio. w/Lab, Physics, Chem. w/Lab, OChem. w/Lab, and Engl.	6+ additional science hrs. highly recommended. Courses may include: Anatomy, Physiology, Genetics, Microbio., and Immunology.	AP credits accepted as long as they are listed on undergraduate transcript.

ILLINOIS

School	Required	Recommended	Notes
MIDWESTERN UNIVERSITY CHICAGO COLLEGE OF OSTEOPATHIC MEDICINE (MWU/CCOM)	Bio. w/Lab, Chem. w/Lab, OChem. w/Lab, Physics w/Lab, Engl. Comp.	Anatomy, Physiology, and Biochem. encouraged.	AP credits accepted as long as they are listed on undergraduate transcript.

INDIANA

School	Required	Recommended	Notes
MARIAN UNIVERSITY COLLEGE OF OSTEOPATHIC MEDICINE (MU-COM)	Bio. w/Lab, Biochem., Chem., w/Lab, OChem. w/Lab, Physics w/Lab, College Engl., Behavioral Sciences.	Molecular Bio., Genetics, Humanities, and Math/Stats.	AP credits accepted as long as they are listed on undergraduate transcript.

For the number of hours required for prerequisite courses, and for the most up-to-date information, please refer to the individual school websites.

*A.P. credit satisfies the requirement.

** When A.P. credit is awarded, upper-level coursework in the same subject area is required.

*** A.P. credit may satisfy the requirement on a case by case basis

IOWA

School	Required	Recommended	Notes
DES MOINES UNIVERSITY COLLEGE OF OSTEOPATHIC MEDICINE (DMU-COM)	Biol./Zoology w/ Lab, Chem. w/Lab, OChem. w/Lab, Biochem., Physics w/Lab (see notes), Engl./Engl. Comp/ Speech/Literature.	Cell bio., Microbio., Immunology, Physiology, and Anatomy.	AP credits not accepted. Lab not required for Biology/Zoology, Chem., OChem., or Physics, but strongly encouraged. Physics requirement: 8 semester hours, but 3 may be substituted with Statistics.

KENTUCKY

School	Required	Recommended	Notes
UNIVERSITY OF PIKEVILLE KENTUCKY COLLEGE OF OSTEOPATHIC MEDICINE (UP-KYCOM)	Engl. Comp and Lit., Chem. w/Lab, OChem. w/Lab (see Notes), Physics w/ Lab, Bio. w/Lab.	N/A	No listed information on AP credits. Contact admissions. 8 Sem. Hrs. req. for OChem., 4 of which may be substituted with Biochem.

LOUISIANA

School	Required	Recommended	Notes
EDWARD VIA COLLEGE OF OSTEOPATHIC MEDICINE-MONROE CAMPUS (VCOM - MONROE CAMPUS)	Bio., Physics, Chem., OChem., Engl. and Comp., and 6+ Biomedical Science credit hours (see recommended).	Biomedical Science courses: Anatomy, Physio., Biochem., Immunology, Microbio., Virology, or Genetics.	No listed information on AP credits. Contact admissions.

For the number of hours required for prerequisite courses, and for the most up-to-date information, please refer to the individual school websites.
*A.P. credit satisfies the requirement.
** When A.P. credit is awarded, upper-level coursework in the same subject area is required.
*** A.P. credit may satisfy the requirement on a case by case basis

MAINE

School	Required	Recommended	Notes
UNIVERSITY OF NEW ENGLAND COLLEGE OF OSTEOPATHIC MEDICINE (UNECOM)	Bio. w/Lab, Chem. w/Lab, Physics w/ Lab, OChem. w/Lab, Biochem., Upper-level coursework w/Labs, Behavioral Science, English/ Humanities.	Anatomy, Cell/ Molecular Bio., Genetics, Math/ Stats., Microbio., Physiology, Behavioral Science, and Humanities.	AP credits accepted as long as they are listed on undergraduate transcript.

MICHIGAN

School	Required	Recommended	Notes
MICHIGAN STATE UNIVERSITY COLLEGE OF OSTEOPATHIC MEDICINE (MSUCOM-DMC)	Biol., Chem.*, Engl.*, Biochem.	Strongly encourage junior/senior-level bio such as Anatomy, Physiology, Genetics, and others.	AP credits accepted as long as they are listed on undergraduate transcript.
MICHIGAN STATE UNIVERSITY COLLEGE OF OSTEOPATHIC MEDICINE (MSUCOM-MUC)	Biol., Chem.*, Engl.*, Biochem.	Strongly encourage junior/senior-level bio such as Anatomy, Physiology, Genetics, and others.	AP credits accepted as long as they are listed on undergraduate transcript.
MICHIGAN STATE UNIVERSITY COLLEGE OF OSTEOPATHIC MEDICINE (MSUCOM)	Biol., Chem.*, Engl.*, Biochem.	Strongly encourage junior/senior-level bio such as Anatomy, Physiology, Genetics, and others.	AP credits accepted as long as they are listed on undergraduate transcript.

For the number of hours required for prerequisite courses, and for the most up-to-date information, please refer to the individual school websites.
*A.P. credit satisfies the requirement.
** When A.P. credit is awarded, upper-level coursework in the same subject area is required.
*** A.P. credit may satisfy the requirement on a case by case basis

MISSISSIPPI

School	Required	Recommended	Notes
WILLIAM CAREY UNIVERSITY COLLEGE OF OSTEOPATHIC MEDICINE (WCUCOM)	Engl. Comp. and Lit., Chem. w/Lab, OChem. w/Lab, Physics w/Lab, Bio. w/Lab.	Strongly recommend Cell and molecular bio., Histology, Comparative Anatomy, Biochem., Genetics, Microbio., and Physio. Also encourage advanced Math, Psych., Social Studies, Econ., Speech, and Philosophy.	AP credits accepted. Contact admissions for more information.

MISSOURI

School	Required	Recommended	Notes
A. T. STILL UNIVERSITY KIRKSVILLE COLLEGE OF OSTEOPATHIC MEDICINE (ATSU-KCOM)	Bio. w/Lab, Physics w/Lab, Chem. w/Lab, OChem. w/Lab, Engl.	N/A	AP credits accepted. Contact admissions for more information.
KANSAS CITY UNIVERSITY OF MEDICINE AND BIOSCIENCES COLLEGE OF OSTEOPATHIC MEDICINE (KCU-COM-JOPLIN)	Bio., Biochem., Chem., Physics.	N/A	AP credits accepted as long as they are listed on undergraduate transcript.
KANSAS CITY UNIVERSITY OF MEDICINE AND BIOSCIENCES COLLEGE OF OSTEOPATHIC MEDICINE (KCU-COM)	Bio., Biochem., Chem., Physics.	N/A	AP credits accepted as long as they are listed on undergraduate transcript.

For the number of hours required for prerequisite courses, and for the most up-to-date information, please refer to the individual school websites.

*A.P. credit satisfies the requirement.

** When A.P. credit is awarded, upper-level coursework in the same subject area is required.

*** A.P. credit may satisfy the requirement on a case by case basis

NEVADA

School	Required	Recommended	Notes
TOURO UNIVERSITY NEVADA COLLEGE OF OSTEOPATHIC MEDICINE (TUNCOM)	Bio./Zoology w/ Lab, Chem. w/Lab, OChem. w/Lab (see Notes), Physics, Engl., Behav. Sciences, and Math/ Stats.	N/A	4 sem. units of Biochem. may be substituted for OChem. 2.\n\nAP credits as long as applicant provides official AP score report.

NEW JERSEY

School	Required	Recommended	Notes
ROWAN UNIVERSITY SCHOOL OF OSTEOPATHIC MEDICINE (ROWANSOM)	Bio., Chem., OChem., Physics, College-level Math, Behavioral Science, Engl. Comp.	Strongly encouraged to take six additional semester hours of science coursework, such as: Biochem., Anatomy and Physiology, Microbio.	Up to discretion of admissions committee on whether or not AP credits will satisfy prerequisites. Contact admissions for more information.

NEW MEXICO

School	Required	Recommended	Notes
BURRELL COLLEGE OF OSTEOPATHIC MEDICINE (BCOM)	Bio. w/Lab, Chem. w/Lab, OChem. w/ Lab, Physics w/ Lab, Engl., 3 credit hrs. of Science Course Elective (see recommended).	Biochem., Cell Bio., Genetics, Human Anatomy, Physio., Immunology, Microbio., Neuroscience, Behav. Science.	AP credits accepted as long as they are listed on undergraduate transcript.

NEW YORK

School	Required	Recommended	Notes
LAKE ERIE COLLEGE OF OSTEOPATHIC MEDICINE - ELMIRA (LECOM-ELMIRA)	Bio. w/Lab, Chem. w/Lab, OChem. w/ Lab, Physics w/Lab, Engl., Behavioral Sciences	Biochem., Physiology, Microbiology and/or Anatomy.	No listed information on AP credits. Contact admissions.

For the number of hours required for prerequisite courses, and for the most up-to-date information, please refer to the individual school websites.

*A.P. credit satisfies the requirement.

** When A.P. credit is awarded, upper-level coursework in the same subject area is required.

*** A.P. credit may satisfy the requirement on a case by case basis

NEW YORK INSTITUTE OF TECHNOLOGY COLLEGE OF OSTEOPATHIC MEDICINE (NYITCOM)	Engl., Bio. w/Lab, Chem. w/Lab, OChem. 1 and 2 w/Lab (see notes), Physics w/Lab.	Behavioral Sciences, Biochem., Calculus/Statistics, Human Anatomy/Physiology, Genetics, Microbio.	Biochemistry may be substituted for OChem. 2.
TOURO COLLEGE OF OSTEOPATHIC MEDICINE (TOUROCOM-HARLEM)	Biol., w/Lab*, Chem. w/Lab*, OChem. w/Lab, Physics w/Lab*, Engl.*, Math* and/or Computer Science*, Behavioral Sciences*.	4 Hours of Biochem. may count towards half of OChem. req.	AP credits accepted as long as they are listed on undergraduate transcript. AP scores must be a 4 or 5.
TOURO COLLEGE OF OSTEOPATHIC MEDICINE (TOUROCOM-MIDDLETOWN)	Biol., w/Lab*, Chem. w/Lab*, OChem. w/Lab, Physics w/Lab*, Engl.*, Math* and/or Computer Science*, Behavioral Sciences*.	4 Hours of Biochem. may count towards half of OChem. req.	AP credits accepted as long as they are listed on undergraduate transcript. AP scores must be a 4 or 5.

NORTH CAROLINA

School	Required	Recommended	Notes
CAMPBELL UNIVERSITY JERRY M. WALLACE SCHOOL OF OSTEOPATHIC MEDICINE (CUSOM)	Bio. w/Lab, Physics, Chem. w/Lab, OChem. w/Lab (see Notes), Engl.	Upper-level biomedical courses: Anatomy, Physio., Biochem., Immunology, Microbio., or Genetics. Labs included.	AP credits accepted. Contact admissions for more information. 1 Semester of OChem. may be substituted with Biochem.

OHIO

School	Required	Recommended	Notes
OHIO UNIVERSITY HERITAGE COLLEGE OF OSTEOPATHIC MEDICINE (OU-HCOM)	Engl., Behavioral Science, Biology/Zoology, Chem., OChem., Physics.	N/A	AP credits accepted. Contact admissions for more information.

For the number of hours required for prerequisite courses, and for the most up-to-date information, please refer to the individual school websites.

*A.P. credit satisfies the requirement.

** When A.P. credit is awarded, upper-level coursework in the same subject area is required.

*** A.P. credit may satisfy the requirement on a case by case basis

OHIO UNIVERSITY HERITAGE COLLEGE OF OSTEOPATHIC MEDICINE IN CLEVELAND (OU-HCOM-CLEVELAND)	Engl., Behavioral Science, Biology/Zoology, Chem., OChem., Physics.	N/A	AP credits accepted. Contact admissions for more information.
OHIO UNIVERSITY HERITAGE COLLEGE OF OSTEOPATHIC MEDICINE IN DUBLIN (OU-HCOM-DUBLIN)	Engl., Behavioral Science, Biology/Zoology, Chem., OChem., Physics.	N/A	AP credits accepted. Contact admissions for more information.

OKLAHOMA

School	Required	Recommended	Notes
OKLAHOMA STATE UNIVERSITY CENTER FOR HEALTH SCIENCES COLLEGE OF OSTEOPATHIC MEDICINE - TAHLEQUAH (OSU-COM TAHLEQUAH)	Engl., Bio. w/Lab, Physics, Chem., OChem., At least one upper div. science course (see recommended).	Upper div course may include (but is not limited to): Human Anatomy/Comparative Anatomy, Biochem., Microbio., Molecular Bio., Histology, Cell. Bio., Embryology, or Physio. Multiple (3-5) of these courses strongly encouraged.	No listed information on AP credits. Contact admissions.
OKLAHOMA STATE UNIVERSITY CENTER FOR HEALTH SCIENCES COLLEGE OF OSTEOPATHIC MEDICINE (OSU-COM)	Engl., Bio. w/Lab, Physics, Chem., OChem., At least one upper div. science course (see recommended).	Upper div course may include (but is not limited to): Human Anatomy/Comparative Anatomy, Biochem., Microbio., Molecular Bio., Histology, Cell. Bio., Embryology, or Physio. Multiple (3-5) of these courses strongly encouraged.	No listed information on AP credits. Contact admissions.

For the number of hours required for prerequisite courses, and for the most up-to-date information, please refer to the individual school websites.
*A.P. credit satisfies the requirement.
** When A.P. credit is awarded, upper-level coursework in the same subject area is required.
*** A.P. credit may satisfy the requirement on a case by case basis

OREGON

School	Required	Recommended	Notes
WESTERN UNIVERSITY OF HEALTH SCIENCES COLLEGE OF OSTEOPATHIC MEDICINE OF THE PACIFIC-NORTHWEST (WESTERNU/COMP-NORTHWEST)	Engl., Behav. Sciences, Bio. w/Lab, OChem. w/Lab, Chem. w/Lab, Physics w/Lab.	Biochem., Genetics, Physio.	AP credits accepted as long as they are listed on undergraduate transcript.

PENNSYLAVNIA

School	Required	Recommended	Notes
LAKE ERIE COLLEGE OF OSTEOPATHIC MEDICINE - SETON HILL (LECOM-SETON HILL)	Bio. w/Lab, Chem. w/Lab, OChem. w/Lab, Physics w/Lab, Engl., Behavioral Sciences.	Biochem., Physiology, Microbiology and/or Anatomy.	No listed information on AP credits. Contact admissions.
LAKE ERIE COLLEGE OF OSTEOPATHIC MEDICINE-ERIE (LECOM)	Bio. w/Lab, Chem. w/Lab, OChem. w/Lab, Physics w/Lab, Engl., Behavioral Sciences.	Biochem., Physiology, Microbiology and/or Anatomy.	No listed information on AP credits. Contact admissions.
PHILADELPHIA COLLEGE OF OSTEOPATHIC MEDICINE (PCOM)	Bio. w/Lab, Physics w/Lab, Chem. w/Lab, OChem. w/Lab, Biochem., Engl. Comp & Lit.		AP credits accepted as long as they are listed on undergraduate transcript.

SOUTH CAROLINA

School	Required	Recommended	Notes
EDWARD VIA COLLEGE OF OSTEOPATHIC MEDICINE-CAROLINAS CAMPUS (VCOM - CAROLINAS CAMPUS)	Bio., Physics, Chem., OChem., Engl. and Comp., and 6+ Biomedical Science credit hours (see recommended).	Biomedical Science courses: Anatomy, Physio., Biochem., Immunology, Microbio., Virology, or Genetics.	No listed information on AP credits. Contact admissions.

For the number of hours required for prerequisite courses, and for the most up-to-date information, please refer to the individual school websites.
*A.P. credit satisfies the requirement.
** When A.P. credit is awarded, upper-level coursework in the same subject area is required.
*** A.P. credit may satisfy the requirement on a case by case basis

TENNESSEE

School	Required	Recommended	Notes
LINCOLN MEMORIAL UNIVERSITY DEBUSK COLLEGE OF OSTEOPATHIC MEDICINE - KNOXVILLE (LMU-DCOM KNOXVILLE)	Bio. w/Lab, Chem., w/Lab, OChem. w/Lab, Physics w/Lab, and Engl.	N/A	LMU-DCOM will accept a combination of 16 hours for Chem., OChem., and Biochem. AP credits accepted as long as they are listed on undergraduate transcript.
LINCOLN MEMORIAL UNIVERSITY DEBUSK COLLEGE OF OSTEOPATHIC MEDICINE (LMU-DCOM)	Bio. w/Lab, Chem., w/Lab, OChem. w/Lab, Physics w/Lab, and Engl.	N/A	LMU-DCOM will accept a combination of 16 hours for Chem., OChem., and Biochem. AP credits accepted as long as they are listed on undergraduate transcript.

TEXAS

School	Required	Recommended	Notes
SAM HOUSTON STATE UNIVERSITY COLLEGE OF OSTEOPATHIC MEDICINE	Engl., Bio. w/Lab, Physics w/Lab, Chem. w/Lab, OChem. w/Lab (see Notes), Math (see Notes).	N/A	Biochem. may be substituted for OChem. 2. 3 credit hours of the Math req. must be Stats. AP credits accepted as long as TMDSAS accepts them as well.

For the number of hours required for prerequisite courses, and for the most up-to-date information, please refer to the individual school websites.
*A.P. credit satisfies the requirement.
** When A.P. credit is awarded, upper-level coursework in the same subject area is required.
*** A.P. credit may satisfy the requirement on a case by case basis

UNIVERSITY OF NORTH TEXAS HEALTH SCIENCE CENTER TEXAS COLLEGE OF OSTEOPATHIC MEDICINE (UNTHSC/ TCOM)	Bio. w/Lab, Chem. w/Lab, OChem. w/ Lab, Physics w/Lab, Stats., and Engl.	Human Physio. and Anatomy, Cell and Molecular Bio., and Microbio. highly recommended.	Courses for non-science majors or health career majors (Nursing, Pharmacy, or Allied Health) are not accepted towards prerequisites. No listed information on AP credits. Contact admissions.
UNIVERSITY OF THE INCARNATE WORD SCHOOL OF OSTEOPATHIC MEDICINE (UIWSOM)	Bio. w/Lab, Chem., w/Lab, OChem. w/ Lab, Physics w/Lab, and Engl.	Advanced Sciences: Human Anatomy, Physio., Biochem., Genetics. Cell Bio., Neuroscience, Microbio., Behav. Science, and Immunology. 6+ sem. hrs. of Philosophy or Humanities coursework. 6+ sem. hrs. of Math/Stats.	AP credits accepted as long as they are listed on undergraduate transcript. Highly recommended to take upper-level science coursework if AP credits satisfy any science prerequisites.

UTAH

School	Required	Recommended	Notes
NOORDA COLLEGE OF OSTEOPATHIC MEDICINE	Bio./Zoology w/ Lab, Chem. w/Lab, OChem. w/Lab, Biochem., Physics, Anatomy/Physio. w/Lab, Engl. Comp. and/or Lit., Behav. Sciences, and Math/ Stats.	Immunology, Histology, Embryology, Sociology, Philosophy, and Medical Terminology.	No listed information on AP credits. Contact admissions.
ROCKY VISTA UNIVERSITY COLLEGE OF OSTEOPATHIC MEDICINE (RVUCOM-SU CAMPUS)	Bio. w/Lab, Chem. w/Lab, OChem. w/ Lab, Physics w/Lab, Engl. or Lit., Social/ Behav. Sciences, Biochem.	Human Anatomy, Physio., Genetics, and Cellular Bio.	AP credits accepted as long as they are listed on undergraduate transcript.

For the number of hours required for prerequisite courses, and for the most up-to-date information, please refer to the individual school websites.

*A.P. credit satisfies the requirement.

** When A.P. credit is awarded, upper-level coursework in the same subject area is required.

*** A.P. credit may satisfy the requirement on a case by case basis

VIRGINIA

School	Required	Recommended	Notes
EDWARD VIA COLLEGE OF OSTEOPATHIC MEDICINE (VCOM-VIRGINIA CAMPUS)	Bio., Physics, Chem., OChem., Engl. and Comp., and 6+ Biomedical Science credit hours (see recommended).	Biomedical Science courses: Anatomy, Physio., Biochem., Immunology, Microbio., Virology, or Genetics.	AP credits accepted as long as they are listed on undergraduate transcript.
LIBERTY UNIVERSITY COLLEGE OF OSTEOPATHIC MEDICINE (LUCOM)	Biochem. or Cellular Bio. (see recommended), Bio. w/Lab, Engl., Chem w/Lab, OChem. w/Lab, Physics w/Lab, and 4 additional science hours (see recommended).	Biochem. or Cellular Bio.: completion of both highly recommended. Additional science hours: Genetics, Human Anatomy, Immunology, or Epidemiology. Other recommended coursework: Literature, Philosophy, Theology, Speech, Debate, Drama, and Stats.	AP credits accepted as long as they are listed on undergraduate transcript.

WASHINGTON

School	Required	Recommended	Notes
PACIFIC NORTHWEST UNIVERSITY OF HEALTH SCIENCES COLLEGE OF OSTEOPATHIC MEDICINE (PNWU-COM)	Engl. Comp and Lit., Chem., OChem., Physics, Bio.	Biochem., Molecular Bio., Genetics, Behav. Sciences, Humanities.	Required science courses likely include lab. Contact admissions for more information. AP credits accepted as long as they are listed on undergraduate transcript.

For the number of hours required for prerequisite courses, and for the most up-to-date information, please refer to the individual school websites.

*A.P. credit satisfies the requirement.

** When A.P. credit is awarded, upper-level coursework in the same subject area is required.

*** A.P. credit may satisfy the requirement on a case by case basis

WEST VIRGINIA

School	Required	Recommended	Notes
WEST VIRGINIA SCHOOL OF OSTEOPATHIC MEDICINE (WVSOM)	Engl., Behav. Sciences, Biology/ Zoology w/2 hrs of Lab, Chem., Biochem., and Physics. 4 hrs of lab may be applied to any combination of Bio., Chem., or Physics.	Anatomy, Embryology, Cell Bio., Histology, Medical Microbio., Modern Genetics, Physio., Immunology, Psych., Sociology.	AP credits accepted. Contact admissions for more information.

For the number of hours required for prerequisite courses, and for the most up-to-date information, please refer to the individual school websites.
*A.P. credit satisfies the requirement.
** When A.P. credit is awarded, upper-level coursework in the same subject area is required.
*** A.P. credit may satisfy the requirement on a case by case basis

CHAPTER 8

OSTEOPATHIC MEDICAL SCHOOLS BY AVERAGE MCAT SCORE

DO Schools	MCAT
Philadelphia College of Osteopathic Medicine South Georgia (PCOM South Georgia)	500
University of Pikeville Kentucky College of Osteopathic Medicine (UP-KYCOM)	500
William Carey University College of Osteopathic Medicine (WCUCOM)	500
Oklahoma State University Center for Health Sciences College of Osteopathic Medicine - Tahlequah (OSU-COM Tahlequah)	500
Oklahoma State University Center for Health Sciences College of Osteopathic Medicine (OSU-COM)	500
Noorda College of Osteopathic Medicine	500
Edward Via College of Osteopathic Medicine (VCOM - Auburn Campus)	501
Edward Via College of Osteopathic Medicine-Monroe Campus (VCOM - Monroe Campus)	501
Edward Via College of Osteopathic Medicine-Carolinas Campus (VCOM - Carolinas Campus)	501
Lincoln Memorial University DeBusk College of Osteopathic Medicine (LMU-DCOM)	501
Edward Via College of Osteopathic Medicine (VCOM-Virginia Campus)	501
West Virginia School of Osteopathic Medicine (WVSOM)	501
Burrell College of Osteopathic Medicine (BCOM)	501
Arkansas College of Osteopathic Medicine (ARCOM)	502
Lake Erie College of Osteopathic Medicine-Erie (LECOM)	503
Lake Erie College of Osteopathic Medicine - Seton Hill (LECOM-Seton Hill)	503
Lake Erie College of Osteopathic Medicine-Bradenton (LECOM-Bradenton)	503
Philadelphia College of Osteopathic Medicine Georgia (PCOM Georgia)	503
University of the Incarnate Word School of Osteopathic Medicine (UIWSOM)	503
Pacific Northwest University of Health Sciences College of Osteopathic Medicine (PNWU-COM)	503
University of New England College of Osteopathic Medicine (UNECOM)	504
Philadelphia College of Osteopathic Medicine (PCOM)	504
Marian University College of Osteopathic Medicine (MU-COM)	504
A. T. Still University Kirksville College of Osteopathic Medicine (ATSU-KCOM)	504
Ohio University Heritage College of Osteopathic Medicine (OU-HCOM)	504
Ohio University Heritage College of Osteopathic Medicine in Dublin (OU-HCOM-Dublin)	504
Ohio University Heritage College of Osteopathic Medicine in Cleveland (OU-HCOM-Cleveland)	504
Alabama College of Osteopathic Medicine (ACOM)	504
Sam Houston State University College of Osteopathic Medicine	504

DO Schools	MCAT
Liberty University College of Osteopathic Medicine (LUCOM)	504
Rowan University School of Osteopathic Medicine (RowanSOM)	505
Touro College of Osteopathic Medicine (TouroCOM-Middletown)	505
Touro College of Osteopathic Medicine (TouroCOM-Harlem)	505
New York Institute of Technology College of Osteopathic Medicine (NYITCOM)	505
New York Institute of Technology College of Osteopathic Medicine at Arkansas State (NYITCOM)	505
Nova Southeastern University Dr. Kiran C. Patel College of Osteopathic Medicine (NSU-KPCOM-Clearwater)	505
Nova Southeastern University Dr. Kiran C. Patel College of Osteopathic Medicine (NSU-KPCOM)	505
A.T. Still University, School of Osteopathic Medicine in Arizona (ATSU-SOMA)	505
California Health Sciences University College of Osteopathic Medicine (CHSU-COM)	505
Idaho College of Osteopathic Medicine (ICOM)	505
Michigan State University College of Osteopathic Medicine (MSUCOM-MUC)	506
Michigan State University College of Osteopathic Medicine (MSUCOM-DMC)	506
Michigan State University College of Osteopathic Medicine (MSUCOM)	506
Kansas City University of Medicine and Biosciences College of Osteopathic Medicine (KCU-COM-Joplin)	506
Midwestern University Arizona College of Osteopathic Medicine (MWU/AZCOM)	506
Touro University Nevada College of Osteopathic Medicine (TUNCOM)	506
Rocky Vista University College of Osteopathic Medicine (RVUCOM-SU Campus)	506
Des Moines University College of Osteopathic Medicine (DMU-COM)	507
Kansas City University of Medicine and Biosciences College of Osteopathic Medicine (KCU-COM)	507
Campbell University Jerry M. Wallace School of Osteopathic Medicine (CUSOM)	507
Lincoln Memorial University DeBusk College of Osteopathic Medicine - Knoxville (LMU-DCOM Knoxville)	507
University of North Texas Health Science Center Texas College of Osteopathic Medicine (UNTHSC/TCOM)	507
Touro University College of Osteopathic Medicine-California (TUCOM)	507
Midwestern University Chicago College of Osteopathic Medicine (MWU/CCOM)	508
Rocky Vista University College of Osteopathic Medicine (RVUCOM)	508
Western University of Health Sciences College of Osteopathic Medicine of the Pacific (WesternU/COMP)	509

DO Schools	MCAT
Western University of Health Sciences College of Osteopathic Medicine of the Pacific-Northwest (WesternU/COMP-Northwest)	509
Lake Erie College of Osteopathic Medicine - Elmira (LECOM-Elmira)	N/A

CHAPTER 9

OSTEOPATHIC MEDICAL SCHOOLS BY COST OF ATTENDANCE

DO Schools	Tuition (In-State)	Tuition (Out-of-State)	COA (Out-of-State)
Lake Erie College of Osteopathic Medicine - Seton Hill (LECOM-Seton Hill)	$37,000.00	$37,000.00	$66,653.00
Lake Erie College of Osteopathic Medicine - Elmira (LECOM-Elmira)	$39,700.00	$39,700.00	$69,428.00
University of North Texas Health Science Center Texas College of Osteopathic Medicine (UNTHSC/TCOM)	$13,078.00	$28,766.00	$70,218.00
Lake Erie College of Osteopathic Medicine-Erie (LECOM)	$37,000.00	$37,000.00	$71,048.00
William Carey University College of Osteopathic Medicine (WCUCOM)	$44,000.00	$44,000.00	$71,342.00
University of Pikeville Kentucky College of Osteopathic Medicine (UP-KYCOM)	$50,000.00	$50,000.00	$71,404.00
Lake Erie College of Osteopathic Medicine-Bradenton (LECOM-Bradenton)	$35,830.00	$37,640.00	$71,598.00
Liberty University College of Osteopathic Medicine (LUCOM)	$47,000.00	$47,000.00	$74,025.00
Lincoln Memorial University DeBusk College of Osteopathic Medicine (LMU-DCOM)	$53,700.00	$53,700.00	$74,500.00
Edward Via College of Osteopathic Medicine (VCOM - Auburn Campus)	$46,900.00	$46,900.00	$75,182.00
Edward Via College of Osteopathic Medicine-Monroe Campus (VCOM - Monroe Campus)	$46,900.00	$46,900.00	$75,182.00
Edward Via College of Osteopathic Medicine-Carolinas Campus (VCOM - Carolinas Campus)	$46,900.00	$46,900.00	$75,182.00
Edward Via College of Osteopathic Medicine (VCOM-Virginia Campus)	$46,900.00	$46,900.00	$75,182.00
Kansas City University of Medicine and Biosciences College of Osteopathic Medicine (KCU-COM-Joplin)	$49,888.00	$49,888.00	$76,195.00
Kansas City University of Medicine and Biosciences College of Osteopathic Medicine (KCU-COM)	$49,888.00	$49,888.00	$76,195.00
Arkansas College of Osteopathic Medicine (ARCOM)	$43,000.00	$43,000.00	$76,326.00

DO Schools	Tuition (In-State)	Tuition (Out-of-State)	COA (Out-of-State)
Marian University College of Osteopathic Medicine (MU-COM)	$55,300.00	$55,300.00	$76,981.00
Lincoln Memorial University DeBusk College of Osteopathic Medicine - Knoxville (LMU-DCOM Knoxville)	$53,700.00	$53,700.00	$77,950.00
Campbell University Jerry M. Wallace School of Osteopathic Medicine (CUSOM)	$54,600.00	$54,600.00	$78,700.00
Pacific Northwest University of Health Sciences College of Osteopathic Medicine (PNWU-COM)	$59,380.00	$59,380.00	$78,809.00
Des Moines University College of Osteopathic Medicine (DMU-COM)	$53,720.00	$53,720.00	$79,093.00
Philadelphia College of Osteopathic Medicine (PCOM)	$54,336.00	$54,336.00	$79,638.00
Philadelphia College of Osteopathic Medicine South Georgia (PCOM South Georgia)	$54,336.00	$54,336.00	$79,638.00
Philadelphia College of Osteopathic Medicine Georgia (PCOM Georgia)	$54,336.00	$54,336.00	$79,638.00
Western University of Health Sciences College of Osteopathic Medicine of the Pacific-Northwest (WesternU/COMP-Northwest)	$59,600.00	$59,600.00	$80,908.00
Burrell College of Osteopathic Medicine (BCOM)	$58,335.00	$58,335.00	$81,704.00
Oklahoma State University Center for Health Sciences College of Osteopathic Medicine - Tahlequah (OSU-COM Tahlequah)	$25,796.60	$53,298.56	$82,086.00
Oklahoma State University Center for Health Sciences College of Osteopathic Medicine (OSU-COM)	$25,796.60	$53,298.56	$82,086.00
Idaho College of Osteopathic Medicine (ICOM)	$54,330.00	$54,330.00	$82,344.00
Alabama College of Osteopathic Medicine (ACOM)	$55,440.00	$55,440.00	$83,120.00
Western University of Health Sciences College of Osteopathic Medicine of the Pacific (WesternU/COMP)	$59,600.00	$59,600.00	$83,151.00

DO Schools	Tuition (In-State)	Tuition (Out-of-State)	COA (Out-of-State)
Sam Houston State University College of Osteopathic Medicine	$55,000.00	$55,000.00	$83,210.00
Noorda College of Osteopathic Medicine	$53,300.00	$53,300.00	$83,459.00
University of the Incarnate Word School of Osteopathic Medicine (UIWSOM)	$56,000.00	$56,000.00	$85,245.00
Ohio University Heritage College of Osteopathic Medicine (OU-HCOM)	$37,068.00	$52,864.00	$85,659.00
Ohio University Heritage College of Osteopathic Medicine in Dublin (OU-HCOM-Dublin)	$37,068.00	$52,864.00	$85,659.00
Ohio University Heritage College of Osteopathic Medicine in Cleveland (OU-HCOM-Cleveland)	$37,068.00	$52,864.00	$85,659.00
West Virginia School of Osteopathic Medicine (WVSOM)	$22,472.00	$53,710.00	$86,900.00
A. T. Still University Kirksville College of Osteopathic Medicine (ATSU-KCOM)	$59,368.00	$59,368.00	$87,207.00
University of New England College of Osteopathic Medicine (UNECOM)	$60,040.00	$60,040.00	$89,880.00
Rocky Vista University College of Osteopathic Medicine (RVUCOM)	$60,270.00	$60,270.00	$92,684.00
Rocky Vista University College of Osteopathic Medicine (RVUCOM-SU Campus)	$60,270.00	$60,270.00	$92,684.00
California Health Sciences University College of Osteopathic Medicine (CHSU-COM)	$54,500.00	$54,500.00	$92,836.00
Touro University Nevada College of Osteopathic Medicine (TUNCOM)	$57,800.00	$57,800.00	$93,431.00
New York Institute of Technology College of Osteopathic Medicine (NYITCOM)	$60,450.00	$60,450.00	$95,783.00
New York Institute of Technology College of Osteopathic Medicine at Arkansas State (NYITCOM)	$60,450.00	$60,450.00	$95,783.00
Touro University College of Osteopathic Medicine-California (TUCOM)	$59,160.00	$59,160.00	$97,082.00
Michigan State University College of Osteopathic Medicine (MSUCOM-MUC)	$46,968.00	$65,323.00	$100,107.00

DO Schools	Tuition (In-State)	Tuition (Out-of-State)	COA (Out-of-State)
Michigan State University College of Osteopathic Medicine (MSUCOM-DMC)	$46,968.00	$65,323.00	$100,107.00
Michigan State University College of Osteopathic Medicine (MSUCOM)	$46,968.00	$65,323.00	$100,107.00
A.T. Still University, School of Osteopathic Medicine in Arizona (ATSU-SOMA)	$62,562.00	$62,562.00	$101,547.00
Midwestern University Arizona College of Osteopathic Medicine (MWU/AZCOM)	$74,516.00	$74,516.00	$101,982.00
Touro College of Osteopathic Medicine (TouroCOM-Middletown)	$59,780.00	$59,780.00	$103,578.00
Midwestern University Chicago College of Osteopathic Medicine (MWU/CCOM)	$73,348.00	$73,348.00	$105,895.00
Touro College of Osteopathic Medicine (TouroCOM-Harlem)	$59,780.00	$59,780.00	$106,452.00
Nova Southeastern University Dr. Kiran C. Patel College of Osteopathic Medicine (NSU-KPCOM-Clearwater)	$55,784.00	$63,638.00	$109,850.00
Nova Southeastern University Dr. Kiran C. Patel College of Osteopathic Medicine (NSU-KPCOM)	$55,784.00	$63,638.00	$109,850.00
Rowan University School of Osteopathic Medicine (RowanSOM)	$41,339.00	$66,324.00	$117,682.25

CHAPTER 10

OSTEOPATHIC MEDICAL SCHOOLS BY NUMBER OF INCOMING STUDENTS

Osteo School	# Enrolled in 2020
Sam Houston State University College of Osteopathic Medicine	75
California Health Sciences University College of Osteopathic Medicine (CHSU-COM)	80
Touro University College of Osteopathic Medicine-California (TUCOM)	125
University of Pikeville Kentucky College of Osteopathic Medicine (UP-KYCOM)	132
Philadelphia College of Osteopathic Medicine Georgia (PCOM Georgia)	135
Philadelphia College of Osteopathic Medicine South Georgia (PCOM South Georgia)	135
Pacific Northwest University of Health Sciences College of Osteopathic Medicine (PNWU-COM)	143
Noorda College of Osteopathic Medicine	150
Edward Via College of Osteopathic Medicine-Monroe Campus (VCOM - Monroe Campus)	154
A.T. Still University, School of Osteopathic Medicine in Arizona (ATSU-SOMA)	156
Marian University College of Osteopathic Medicine (MU-COM)	158
William Carey University College of Osteopathic Medicine (WCUCOM)	158
Liberty University College of Osteopathic Medicine (LUCOM)	159
Arkansas College of Osteopathic Medicine (ARCOM)	162
Burrell College of Osteopathic Medicine (BCOM)	162
Campbell University Jerry M. Wallace School of Osteopathic Medicine (CUSOM)	162
Edward Via College of Osteopathic Medicine (VCOM - Auburn Campus)	162
Idaho College of Osteopathic Medicine (ICOM)	162
University of the Incarnate Word School of Osteopathic Medicine (UIWSOM)	162
A. T. Still University Kirksville College of Osteopathic Medicine (ATSU-KCOM)	168
Edward Via College of Osteopathic Medicine-Carolinas Campus (VCOM - Carolinas Campus)	171
Oklahoma State University Center for Health Sciences College of Osteopathic Medicine - Tahlequah (OSU-COM Tahlequah)	171
Oklahoma State University Center for Health Sciences College of Osteopathic Medicine (OSU-COM)	171
Touro University Nevada College of Osteopathic Medicine (TUNCOM)	177

Osteo School	# Enrolled in 2020
University of New England College of Osteopathic Medicine (UNECOM)	178
Edward Via College of Osteopathic Medicine (VCOM-Virginia Campus)	185
Lake Erie College of Osteopathic Medicine-Bradenton (LECOM-Bradenton)	196
Midwestern University Chicago College of Osteopathic Medicine (MWU/CCOM)	205
Alabama College of Osteopathic Medicine (ACOM)	206
West Virginia School of Osteopathic Medicine (WVSOM)	207
Rowan University School of Osteopathic Medicine (RowanSOM)	219
Des Moines University College of Osteopathic Medicine (DMU-COM)	221
University of North Texas Health Science Center Texas College of Osteopathic Medicine (UNTHSC/TCOM)	237
Midwestern University Arizona College of Osteopathic Medicine (MWU/AZCOM)	252
Ohio University Heritage College of Osteopathic Medicine (OU-HCOM)	252
Ohio University Heritage College of Osteopathic Medicine in Cleveland (OU-HCOM-Cleveland)	252
Ohio University Heritage College of Osteopathic Medicine in Dublin (OU-HCOM-Dublin)	252
Philadelphia College of Osteopathic Medicine (PCOM)	270
Touro College of Osteopathic Medicine (TouroCOM-Harlem)	270
Touro College of Osteopathic Medicine (TouroCOM-Middletown)	270
Rocky Vista University College of Osteopathic Medicine (RVUCOM-SU Campus)	293
Rocky Vista University College of Osteopathic Medicine (RVUCOM)	293
Michigan State University College of Osteopathic Medicine (MSUCOM-DMC)	294
Michigan State University College of Osteopathic Medicine (MSUCOM-MUC)	294
Michigan State University College of Osteopathic Medicine (MSUCOM)	294
Western University of Health Sciences College of Osteopathic Medicine of the Pacific (WesternU/COMP)	323
Western University of Health Sciences College of Osteopathic Medicine of the Pacific-Northwest (WesternU/COMP-Northwest)	323
Lake Erie College of Osteopathic Medicine - Seton Hill (LECOM-Seton Hill)	381

Osteo School	# Enrolled in 2020
Lake Erie College of Osteopathic Medicine-Erie (LECOM)	381
Lincoln Memorial University DeBusk College of Osteopathic Medicine - Knoxville (LMU-DCOM Knoxville)	393
Lincoln Memorial University DeBusk College of Osteopathic Medicine (LMU-DCOM)	393
Nova Southeastern University Dr. Kiran C. Patel College of Osteopathic Medicine (NSU-KPCOM-Clearwater)	410
Nova Southeastern University Dr. Kiran C. Patel College of Osteopathic Medicine (NSU-KPCOM)	410
Kansas City University of Medicine and Biosciences College of Osteopathic Medicine (KCU-COM-Joplin)	432
Kansas City University of Medicine and Biosciences College of Osteopathic Medicine (KCU-COM)	432
New York Institute of Technology College of Osteopathic Medicine (NYITCOM)	438
New York Institute of Technology College of Osteopathic Medicine at Arkansas State (NYITCOM)	438
Lake Erie College of Osteopathic Medicine - Elmira (LECOM-Elmira)	N/A

CHAPTER 11

MEDICAL SCHOOLS BY CITY/STATE

MD Schools	City	State	Website
University of Alabama School of Medicine	Birmingham	AL	*https://www.uab.edu/medicine/home/*
University of South Alabama College of Medicine	Mobile	AL	*https://www.southalabama.edu/colleges/com/*
University of Arkansas for Medical Sciences College of Medicine	Little Rock	AR	*https://medicine.uams.edu/*
The University of Arizona College of Medicine – Phoenix	Phoenix	AZ	*https://phoenixmed.arizona.edu/*
The University of Arizona College of Medicine – Tucson	Tucson	AZ	*https://medicine.arizona.edu/*
California University of Science and Medicine – School of Medicine	Colton	CA	*https://www.cusm.org/*
California Northstate University College of Medicine	Elk Grove	CA	*https://medicine.cnsu.edu/*
University of California, Irvine School of Medicine	Irvine	CA	*https://www.som.uci.edu/*
University of California, San Diego School of Medicine	La Jolla	CA	*https://medschool.ucsd.edu/Pages/default.aspx*
Loma Linda University School of Medicine	Loma Linda	CA	*https://medicine.llu.edu/*
David Geffen School of Medicine at UCLA	Los Angeles	CA	*https://medschool.ucla.edu/*
Keck School of Medicine of the University of Southern California	Los Angeles	CA	*https://keck.usc.edu/*
Kaiser Permanente School of Medicine	Pasadena	CA	*https://medschool.kp.org/*
University of California, Riverside School of Medicine	Riverside	CA	*https://medschool.ucr.edu/*

MD Schools	City	State	Website
University of California, Davis School of Medicine	Sacramento	CA	*https://health. ucdavis.edu/ medschool/*
University of California, San Francisco School of Medicine	San Francisco	CA	*https://medschool. ucsf.edu/*
Stanford University School of Medicine	Stanford	CA	*http://med.stanford. edu/*
University of Colorado School of Medicine	Aurora	CO	*https://medschool. cuanschutz.edu/*
University of Connecticut School of Medicine	Farmington	CT	*https://medicine. uconn.edu/*
Frank H. Netter MD School of Medicine at Quinnipiac University	Hamden	CT	*https://www.qu.edu/ schools/medicine. html*
Yale School of Medicine	New Haven	CT	*https://medicine. yale.edu/*
Georgetown University School of Medicine	Washington	DC	*https://som. georgetown.edu/*
Howard University College of Medicine	Washington	DC	*https://medicine. howard.edu/*
The George Washington University School of Medicine and Health Sciences	Washington	DC	*https://smhs.gwu. edu/*
Charles E. Schmidt College of Medicine at Florida Atlantic University	Boca Raton	FL	*http://med.fau.edu/*
Nova Southeastern University Dr. Kiran C. Patel College of Allopathic Medicine	Davie	FL	*https://md.nova.edu/ index.html*
University of Florida College of Medicine	Gainesville	FL	*https://med.ufl.edu/*

MD Schools	City	State	Website
Florida International University Herbert Wertheim College of Medicine	Miami	FL	*https://medicine.fiu.edu/*
University of Miami Leonard M. Miller School of Medicine	Miami	FL	*https://med.miami.edu/*
University of Central Florida College of Medicine	Orlando	FL	*https://med.ucf.edu/*
The Florida State University College of Medicine	Tallahassee	FL	*https://med.fsu.edu/*
USF Health Morsani College of Medicine	Tampa	FL	*https://health.usf.edu/medicine*
Emory University School of Medicine	Atlanta	GA	*https://www.med.emory.edu/*
Morehouse School of Medicine	Atlanta	GA	*https://www.msm.edu/*
Medical College of Georgia at Augusta University	Augusta	GA	*https://www.augusta.edu/mcg/*
Mercer University School of Medicine	Macon	GA	*https://medicine.mercer.edu/*
John A. Burns School of Medicine University of Hawaii at Manoa	Honolulu	HI	*https://jabsom.hawaii.edu/*
University of Iowa Roy J. and Lucille A. Carver College of Medicine	Iowa City	IA	*https://medicine.uiowa.edu/*
Carle Illinois College of Medicine	Champaign	IL	*https://medicine.illinois.edu/*
Northwestern University Feinberg School of Medicine	Chicago	IL	*https://www.feinberg.northwestern.edu/*
Rush Medical College of Rush University Medical Center	Chicago	IL	*https://www.rushu.rush.edu/rush-medical-college*

MD Schools	City	State	Website
University of Chicago Division of the Biological Sciences, The Pritzker School of Medicine	Chicago	IL	https://pritzker.uchicago.edu/
University of Illinois College of Medicine	Chicago	IL	https://medicine.uic.edu/
Loyola University Chicago Stritch School of Medicine	Maywood	IL	https://ssom.luc.edu/
Chicago Medical School at Rosalind Franklin University of Medicine and Science	North Chicago	IL	https://www.rosalindfranklin.edu/academics/chicago-medical-school/
Southern Illinois University School of Medicine	Springfield	IL	https://www.siumed.edu/
Indiana University School of Medicine	Indianapolis	IN	https://medicine.iu.edu/
University of Kansas School of Medicine	Kansas City	KS	http://www.kumc.edu/school-of-medicine.html
University of Kentucky College of Medicine	Lexington	KY	https://med.uky.edu/
University of Louisville School of Medicine	Louisville	KY	http://louisville.edu/medicine
LSU Health Sciences Center School of Medicine in New Orleans	New Orleans	LA	https://www.medschool.lsuhsc.edu/
Tulane University School of Medicine	New Orleans	LA	https://medicine.tulane.edu/
Louisiana State University School of Medicine in Shreveport	Shreveport	LA	https://www.lsuhs.edu/our-schools/school-of-medicine
Boston University School of Medicine	Boston	MA	https://www.bumc.bu.edu/busm/
Harvard Medical School	Boston	MA	https://hms.harvard.edu/

MD Schools	City	State	Website
Tufts University School of Medicine	Boston	MA	*https://medicine.tufts.edu/*
University of Massachusetts Medical School	North Worcester	MA	*https://www.umassmed.edu/*
Johns Hopkins University School of Medicine	Baltimore	MD	*https://www.hopkinsmedicine.org/som/*
University of Maryland School of Medicine	Baltimore	MD	*https://www.medschool.umaryland.edu/*
Uniformed Services University of the Health Sciences, F. Edward Hébert School of Medicine	Bethesda	MD	*https://www.usuhs.edu/medschool*
University of Michigan Medical School	Ann Arbor	MI	*https://medicine.umich.edu/medschool/home*
Wayne State University School of Medicine	Detroit	MI	*https://www.med.wayne.edu/*
Michigan State University College of Human Medicine	East Lansing	MI	*http://humanmedicine.msu.edu/*
Western Michigan University Homer Stryker M.D. School of Medicine	Kalamazoo	MI	*https://med.wmich.edu/*
Central Michigan University College of Medicine	Mt Pleasant	MI	*https://www.cmich.edu/colleges/med/Pages/default.aspx*
Oakland University William Beaumont School of Medicine	Rochester	MI	*https://oakland.edu/medicine/*
University of Minnesota Medical School	Minneapolis	MN	*https://med.umn.edu/*
Mayo Clinic Alix School of Medicine	Rochester	MN	*https://college.mayo.edu/academics/school-of-medicine/*
University of Missouri-Columbia School of Medicine	Columbia	MO	*https://medicine.missouri.edu/*

MD Schools	City	State	Website
University of Missouri-Kansas City School of Medicine	Kansas City	MO	https://med.umkc.edu/
Saint Louis University School of Medicine	St. Louis	MO	https://www.slu.edu/medicine/index.php
Washington University in St. Louis School of Medicine	St. Louis	MO	https://medicine.wustl.edu/
University of Mississippi School of Medicine	Jackson	MS	https://www.umc.edu/som/SOM_Home.html
University of North Carolina School of Medicine	Chapel Hill	NC	https://www.med.unc.edu/
Duke University School of Medicine	Durham	NC	https://medschool.duke.edu/
The Brody School of Medicine at East Carolina University	Greenville	NC	https://medicine.ecu.edu/
Wake Forest School of Medicine	Winston-Salem	NC	https://school.wakehealth.edu/
University of North Dakota School of Medicine and Health Sciences	Grand Forks	ND	https://med.und.edu/
Creighton University School of Medicine	Omaha	NE	https://medschool.creighton.edu/
University of Nebraska College of Medicine	Omaha	NE	https://www.unmc.edu/com/
Geisel School of Medicine at Dartmouth	Hanover	NH	https://geiselmed.dartmouth.edu/
Cooper Medical School of Rowan University	Camden	NJ	https://cmsru.rowan.edu/
Rutgers, Robert Wood Johnson Medical School	New Brunswick	NJ	http://rwjms.rutgers.edu/
Rutgers New Jersey Medical School	Newark	NJ	http://njms.rutgers.edu/

MD Schools	City	State	Website
Hackensack-Meridian School of Medicine at Seton Hall University	Nutley	NJ	*https://www.shu.edu/medicine/*
University of New Mexico School of Medicine	Albuquerque	NM	*https://hsc.unm.edu/school-of-medicine/*
University of Nevada, Las Vegas School of Medicine	Las Vegas	NV	*https://www.unlv.edu/medicine*
University of Nevada, Reno School of Medicine	Reno	NV	*https://med.unr.edu/*
Albany Medical College	Albany	NY	*https://www.amc.edu/Academic/index.cfm*
Albert Einstein College of Medicine	Bronx	NY	*https://www.einstein.yu.edu/*
State University of New York Downstate Medical Center College of Medicine	Brooklyn	NY	*https://www.downstate.edu/college-of-medicine/*
Jacobs School of Medicine and Biomedical Sciences at the University at Buffalo	Buffalo	NY	*http://medicine.buffalo.edu/*
New York University Long Island School of Medicine	Mineola	NY	*https://medli.nyu.edu/*
Columbia University Vagelos College of Physicians and Surgeons	New York	NY	*https://www.ps.columbia.edu/*
CUNY School of Medicine	New York	NY	*https://www.ccny.cuny.edu/csom*
Donald and Barbara Zucker School of Medicine at Hofstra/Northwell	New York	NY	*https://medicine.hofstra.edu/*
Icahn School of Medicine at Mount Sinai	New York	NY	*https://icahn.mssm.edu/*

MD Schools	City	State	Website
New York University Grossman School of Medicine	New York	NY	https://med.nyu.edu/our-community/about-us
Weill Cornell Medicine	New York	NY	https://weill.cornell.edu/
University of Rochester School of Medicine and Dentistry	Rochester	NY	https://www.urmc.rochester.edu/smd.aspx
Renaissance School of Medicine at Stony Brook University	Stony Brook	NY	https://renaissance.stonybrookmedicine.edu/
State University of New York Upstate Medical University College of Medicine	Syracuse	NY	https://www.upstate.edu/com/
New York Medical College	Valhalla	NY	https://www.nymc.edu/
University of Cincinnati College of Medicine	Cincinnati	OH	https://www.med.uc.edu/
Case Western Reserve University School of Medicine	Cleveland	OH	https://case.edu/medicine/
The Ohio State University College of Medicine	Columbus	OH	https://medicine.osu.edu/
Boonshoft School of Medicine Wright State University	Dayton	OH	https://medicine.wright.edu/
Northeast Ohio Medical University College of Medicine	Rootstown	OH	https://www.neomed.edu/
The University of Toledo College of Medicine and Life Sciences	Toledo	OH	https://www.utoledo.edu/med/
University of Oklahoma College of Medicine	Oklahoma City	OK	https://medicine.ouhsc.edu/
Oregon Health & Science University School of Medicine	Portland	OR	https://www.ohsu.edu/school-of-medicine

MD Schools	City	State	Website
Penn State College of Medicine	Hershey	PA	*https://med.psu.edu/*
Drexel University College of Medicine	Philadelphia	PA	*https://drexel.edu/ medicine/*
Lewis Katz School of Medicine at Temple University	Philadelphia	PA	*https://medicine. temple.edu/*
Sidney Kimmel Medical College at Thomas Jefferson University	Philadelphia	PA	*https://www. jefferson.edu/ university/skmc.html*
The Raymond and Ruth Perelman School of Medicine at the University of Pennsylvania	Philadelphia	PA	*https://www.med. upenn.edu/*
University of Pittsburgh School of Medicine	Pittsburgh	PA	*https://www. medschool.pitt.edu/*
Geisinger Commonwealth School of Medicine	Scranton	PA	*https://www. geisinger.edu/ education*
Universidad Central del Caribe School of Medicine	Bayamon	PR	*http://www.uccaribe. edu/medicine/*
San Juan Bautista School of Medicine	Caguas	PR	*https://www. sanjuanbautista. edu/*
Ponce Health Sciences University School of Medicine	Ponce	PR	*https://www.psm. edu/school-of- medicine/*
University of Puerto Rico School of Medicine	San Juan	PR	*https://md.rcm.upr. edu/md-program/*
The Warren Alpert Medical School of Brown University	Providence	RI	*https://medical. brown.edu/*
Medical University of South Carolina College of Medicine	Charleston	SC	*https://medicine. musc.edu/*
University of South Carolina School of Medicine, Columbia	Columbia	SC	*https://www.sc.edu/ study/colleges_ schools/medicine/ index.php*

MD Schools	City	State	Website
University of South Carolina School of Medicine, Greenville	Greenville	SC	https://www.sc.edu/ study/colleges_ schools/medicine_ greenville/index.php
University of South Dakota Sanford School of Medicine	Sioux Falls	SD	https://www.usd. edu/medicine
East Tennessee State University James H. Quillen College of Medicine	Johnson City	TN	https://www.etsu. edu/com/
University of Tennessee Health Science Center College of Medicine	Memphis	TN	https://www.uthsc. edu/medicine/
Meharry Medical College School of Medicine	Nashville	TN	https://home.mmc. edu/
Vanderbilt University School of Medicine	Nashville	TN	https://medschool. vanderbilt.edu/
The University of Texas at Austin Dell Medical School	Austin	TX	https://dellmed. utexas.edu/
Texas A&M University Health Science Center College of Medicine	Bryan	TX	https://medicine. tamu.edu/
The University of Texas Southwestern Medical School	Dallas	TX	https://www. utsouthwestern.edu/ education/medical- school/
The University of Texas Rio Grande Valley School of Medicine	Edinburg	TX	https://www.utrgv. edu/school-of- medicine/
Paul L. Foster School of Medicine Texas Tech University Health Sciences Center	El Paso	TX	https://elpaso.ttuhsc. edu/som/
TCU and UNTHSC School of Medicine	Fort Worth	TX	https://mdschool.tcu. edu/

MD Schools	City	State	Website
The University of Texas Medical Branch at Galveston School of Medicine	Galveston	TX	*https://som.utmb.edu/*
Baylor College of Medicine	Houston	TX	*https://www.bcm.edu/*
McGovern Medical School at The University of Texas Health Science Center at Houston	Houston	TX	*https://med.uth.edu/*
University of Houston College of Medicine	Houston	TX	*https://www.uh.edu/medicine/*
Texas Tech University Health Sciences Center School of Medicine	Lubbock	TX	*https://www.ttuhsc.edu/medicine/default.aspx*
The University of Texas Health Science Center at San Antonio Joe R. and Teresa Lozano Long School of Medicine	San Antonio	TX	*http://som.uthscsa.edu/*
University of Utah School of Medicine	Salt Lake City	UT	*https://medicine.utah.edu/*
University of Virginia School of Medicine	Charlottesville	VA	*https://med.virginia.edu/*
Eastern Virginia Medical School	Norfolk	VA	*https://www.evms.edu/*
Virginia Commonwealth University School of Medicine	Richmond	VA	*https://medschool.vcu.edu/*
Virginia Tech Carilion School of Medicine	Roanoke	VA	*https://medicine.vtc.vt.edu/*
The Robert Larner, M.D. College of Medicine at the University of Vermont	Burlington	VT	*http://www.med.uvm.edu/*
University of Washington School of Medicine	Seattle	WA	*https://www.uwmedicine.org/school-of-medicine*

MD Schools	City	State	Website
Washington State University Elson S. Floyd College of Medicine	Spokane	WA	*https://medicine.wsu.edu/*
University of Wisconsin School of Medicine and Public Health	Madison	WI	*https://www.med.wisc.edu/*
Medical College of Wisconsin	Milwaukee	WI	*https://www.mcw.edu/*
Marshall University Joan C. Edwards School of Medicine	Huntington	WV	https://jcesom.marshall.edu/
West Virginia University School of Medicine	Morgantown	WV	https://medicine.hsc.wvu.edu/

CHAPTER 12

DENTAL SCHOOLS BY CITY/STATE

Dental Schools	City	State	Website
University of Alabama at Birmingham School of Dentistry	Birmingham	AL	https://www.uab.edu/dentistry/home/
Midwestern University College of Dental Medicine-Arizona	Glendale	AZ	https://www.midwestern.edu/academics/our-colleges/college-of-dental-medicine%E2%80%93arizona.xml
Arizona School of Dentistry & Oral Health	Mesa	AZ	https://www.atsu.edu/arizona-school-of-dentistry-and-oral-health
California North State College of Dental Medicine	Elk Grove	CA	http://dentalmedicine.cnsu.edu/
Loma Linda University School of Dentistry	Loma Linda	CA	https://dentistry.llu.edu/
Herman Ostrow School of Dentistry of USC	Los Angeles	CA	https://dentistry.usc.edu/
University of California, Los Angeles, School of Dentistry	Los Angeles	CA	https://www.dentistry.ucla.edu/
Western University of Health Sciences College of Dental Medicine	Pomona	CA	https://www.westernu.edu/dentistry/
University of California, San Francisco, School of Dentistry	San Francisco	CA	https://dentistry.ucsf.edu/
University of the Pacific Arthur A. Dugoni School of Dentistry	San Francisco	CA	https://www.dental.pacific.edu/
University of Colorado School of Dental Medicine	Aurora	CO	http://www.ucdenver.edu/academics/colleges/dentalmedicine/Pages/DentalMedicine.aspx
University of Connecticut School of Dental Medicine	Farmington	CT	https://dentalmedicine.uconn.edu/
Howard University College of Dentistry	Washington	DC	http://healthsciences.howard.edu/education/colleges/dentistry
Lake Erie College of Osteopathic Medicine School of Dental Medicine	Bradenton	FL	https://lecom.edu/academics/school-of-dental-medicine/
Nova Southeastern University College of Dental Medicine	Davie	FL	https://dental.nova.edu/index.html

Dental Schools	City	State	Website
University of Florida College of Dentistry	Gainesville	FL	https://dental.ufl.edu/
Dental College of Georgia at Augusta University	Augusta	GA	https://www.augusta.edu/dentalmedicine/
The University of Iowa College of Dentistry & Dental Clinics	Iowa City	IA	https://www.dentistry.uiowa.edu/
Southern Illinois University School of Dental Medicine	Alton	IL	http://www.siue.edu/dental/
University of Illinois at Chicago College of Dentistry	Chicago	IL	https://dentistry.uic.edu/
Midwestern University College of Dental Medicine-Illinois	Downers Grove	IL	https://www.midwestern.edu/academics/our-colleges/college-of-dental-medicine%E2%80%93illinois.xml
Indiana University School of Dentistry	Indianapolis	IN	https://dentistry.iu.edu/
University of Kentucky College of Dentistry	Lexington	KY	https://dentistry.uky.edu/
University of Louisville School of Dentistry	Louisville	KY	https://louisville.edu/dentistry
Louisiana State University Health New Orleans School of Dentistry	New Orleans	LA	https://www.lsusd.lsuhsc.edu/
Boston University Henry M. Goldman School of Dental Medicine	Boston	MA	http://www.bu.edu/dental/
Harvard School of Dental Medicine	Boston	MA	https://hsdm.harvard.edu/
Tufts University School of Dental Medicine	Boston	MA	https://dental.tufts.edu/
University of Maryland School of Dentistry	Baltimore	MD	https://www.dental.umaryland.edu/
University of New England College of Dental Medicine	Portland	ME	https://www.une.edu/dentalmedicine
University of Michigan School of Dentistry	Ann Arbor	MI	https://www.dent.umich.edu/
University of Detroit Mercy School of Dentistry	Detroit	MI	https://dental.udmercy.edu/
University of Minnesota School of Dentistry	Minneapolis	MN	https://www.dentistry.umn.edu/

Dental Schools	City	State	Website
University of Missouri-Kansas City School of Dentistry	Kansas City	MO	https://dentistry.umkc.edu/
Missouri School of Dentistry & Oral Health	Kirksville	MO	https://www.atsu.edu/missouri-school-of-dentistry-and-oral-health
University of Mississippi Medical Center School of Dentistry	Jackson	MS	https://www.umc.edu/sod/SOD_Home.html
University of North Carolina at Chapel Hill Adams School of Dentistry	Chapel Hill	NC	https://www.dentistry.unc.edu/
East Carolina University School of Dental Medicine	Greenville	NC	https://www.ecu.edu/cs-dhs/dental/
University of Nebraska Medical Center College of Dentistry	Lincoln	NE	https://www.unmc.edu/dentistry/
Creighton University School of Dentistry	Omaha	NE	https://dentistry.creighton.edu/
Rutgers, The State University of New Jersey, School of Dental Medicine	Newark	NJ	http://sdm.rutgers.edu/
University of Nevada, Las Vegas, School of Dental Medicine	Las Vegas	NV	https://www.unlv.edu/dental
University at Buffalo School of Dental Medicine	Buffalo	NY	http://dental.buffalo.edu/
Touro College of Dental Medicine at New York Medical College	Hawthorne	NY	https://dental.touro.edu/
Columbia University College of Dental Medicine	New York	NY	https://www.dental.columbia.edu/
NYU College of Dentistry	New York	NY	https://dental.nyu.edu/
Stony Brook University School of Dental Medicine	Stony Brook	NY	https://dentistry.stonybrookmedicine.edu/
Case Western Reserve University School of Dental Medicine	Cleveland	OH	https://case.edu/dental/
The Ohio State University College of Dentistry	Columbus	OH	https://dentistry.osu.edu/
University of Oklahoma College of Dentistry	Oklahoma City	OK	https://dentistry.ouhsc.edu/

Dental Schools	City	State	Website
Oregon Health & Science University School of Dentistry	Portland	OR	https://www.ohsu.edu/school-of-dentistry
The Maurice H. Kornberg School of Dentistry, Temple University	Philadelphia	PA	https://dentistry.temple.edu/
University of Pennsylvania School of Dental Medicine	Philadelphia	PA	https://www.dental.upenn.edu/
University of Pittsburgh School of Dental Medicine	Pittsburgh	PA	https://www.dental.pitt.edu/
University of Puerto Rico School of Dental Medicine	San Juan	PR	https://dental.rcm.upr.edu/
Medical University of South Carolina James B. Edwards College of Dental Medicine	Charleston	SC	https://dentistry.musc.edu/
University of Tennessee Health Science Center College of Dentistry	Memphis	TN	https://www.uthsc.edu/dentistry/
Meharry Medical College School of Dentistry	Nashville	TN	https://home.mmc.edu/school-of-dentistry/
Texas A&M College of Dentistry	Dallas	TX	https://dentistry.tamu.edu/
Texas Tech University Health Sciences Center El Paso Woody L. Hunt School of Dental Medicine	El Paso	TX	https://elpaso.ttuhsc.edu/sdm/
The University of Texas School of Dentistry at Houston	Houston	TX	https://dentistry.uth.edu/
UT Health San Antonio School of Dentistry	San Antonio	TX	https://www.uthscsa.edu/academics/dental
University of Utah School of Dentistry	Salt Lake City	UT	https://dentistry.utah.edu/
Roseman University of Health Sciences College of Dental Medicine – South Jordan, Utah	South Jordan	UT	https://dental.roseman.edu/
Virginia Commonwealth University School of Dentistry	Richmond	VA	https://dentistry.vcu.edu/
University of Washington School of Dentistry	Seattle	WA	https://dental.washington.edu/

Dental Schools	City	State	Website
Marquette University School of Dentistry	Milwaukee	WI	https://www.marquette.edu/dentistry/
West Virginia University School of Dentistry	Morgantown	WV	https://dentistry.wvu.edu/

CHAPTER 13

PHYSICIAN ASSISTANT SCHOOLS BY CITY/STATE

PA Schools	City	State	Website
University of Washington - MEDEX Northwest, Anchorage	Anchorage	AK	https://depts.washington.edu/medex/pa-program/
University of Alabama at Birmingham	Birmingham	AL	http://www.uab.edu/shp/cds/physician-assistant
Samford University	Homewood	AL	https://www.samford.edu/healthprofessions/master-of-science-in-physician-assistant-studies
University of South Alabama	Mobile	AL	https://www.southalabama.edu/colleges/alliedhealth/pa/
Faulkner University	Montgomery	AL	https://www.faulkner.edu/graduate/graduate-degrees/physican-assistant-studies-ms-pas/
University of Arkansas	Little Rock	AR	http://healthprofessions.uams.edu/programs/physicianassistant/
Harding University	Searcy	AR	http://www.harding.edu/PAprogram/
Midwestern University - Glendale	Glendale	AZ	https://www.midwestern.edu/academics/degrees-and-programs/master-of-medical-sciences-in-physician-assistant-studies-az.xml
A.T. Still University - Arizona School of Health Sciences	Mesa	AZ	https://www.atsu.edu/physician-assistant-degree
Northern Arizona University	Phoenix	AZ	http://www.nau.edu/pa
University of Southern California	Alhambra	CA	https://keck.usc.edu/physician-assistant-program/
Marshall B. Ketchum University	Fullerton	CA	https://www.ketchum.edu/pa-studies
Chapman University	Irvine	CA	https://www.chapman.edu/crean/academic-programs/graduate-programs/physician-assistant/index.aspx
University of La Verne	La Verne	CA	https://artsci.laverne.edu/physician-assistant/

PA Schools	City	State	Website
Loma Linda University	Loma Linda	CA	http://www.llu.edu/allied-health/sahp/pa
Charles R. Drew University	Los Angeles	CA	https://www.cdrewu.edu/cosh/PA
Samuel Merritt University	Oakland	CA	http://www.samuelmerritt.edu/physician_assistant
Western University of Health Sciences	Pomona	CA	http://prospective.westernu.edu/physician-assistant/welcome-14/
California Baptist University	Riverside	CA	https://calbaptist.edu/programs/master-of-science-physician-assistant-studies/
University of California, Davis	Sacramento	CA	https://health.ucdavis.edu/nursing/admissions/programs/mhs-pa.html
University of the Pacific	Sacramento	CA	http://pacific.edu/PAprogram
California State University, Monterey Bay	Salinas	CA	http://csumb.edu/mspa
Point Loma Nazarene University	San Diego	CA	https://www.pointloma.edu/graduate-studies/programs/physician-assistant-ms-m#applicationinformation
Dominican University of California	San Rafael	CA	https://www.dominican.edu/directory/physician-assistant-studies
Stanford University	Stanford	CA	https://med.stanford.edu/pa
Touro University California	Vallejo	CA	http://cehs.tu.edu/paprogram/
Southern California University of Health Sciences	Whittier	CA	https://www.scuhs.edu/academics/csih/master-of-science-physician-assistant-program/
Red Rocks Community College	Arvada	CO	https://www.rrcc.edu/physician-assistant
University of Colorado	Aurora	CO	http://www.ucdenver.edu/academics/colleges/medicalschool/education/degree_programs/PAProgram/Pages/Home.aspx

PA Schools	City	State	Website
Colorado Mesa University	Grand Junction	CO	https://www.coloradomesa.edu/kinesiology/graduate/pa-program/index.html
Rocky Vista University	Parker	CO	https://www.rvu.edu/admissions/mpas/
Yale University	New Haven	CT	http://www.paprogram.yale.edu/
University of Bridgeport	Bridgeport	CT	http://www.bridgeport.edu/academics/schools-colleges/physician-assistant-institute/physician-assistant-ms
Sacred Heart University	Fairfield	CT	https://www.sacredheart.edu/majors--programs/physician-assistant-studies---mpas/
Quinnipiac University	Hamden	CT	http://www.quinnipiac.edu/gradphysicianasst
University of Saint Joseph	West Hartford	CT	https://www.usj.edu/academics/academic-schools/sppas/physician-assistant-studies/admissions/
George Washington University	Washington	DC	https://smhs.gwu.edu/physician-assistant/
Keiser University	Fort Lauderdale	FL	https://www.keiseruniversity.edu/master-of-science-in-physician-assistant/
Nova Southeastern University - Fort Lauderdale	Fort Lauderdale	FL	http://www.nova.edu/chcs/pa/fortlauderdale/index.html
Nova Southeastern University - Orlando	Fort Lauderdale	FL	https://healthsciences.nova.edu/pa/orlando/index.html
Florida Gulf Coast University	Fort Myers	FL	https://www2.fgcu.edu/mariebcollege/HS/MPAS/index.html
Nova Southeastern University - Fort Myers	Fort Myers	FL	https://healthsciences.nova.edu/pa/fort-myers/index.html
University of Florida	Gainesville	FL	https://pap.med.ufl.edu/
Nova Southeastern University - Jacksonville	Jacksonville	FL	https://healthsciences.nova.edu/pa/jacksonville/index.html

PA Schools	City	State	Website
Barry University - Miami	Miami	FL	http://www.barry.edu/physician-assistant/
Barry University - St. Petersburg	Miami	FL	http://www.barry.edu/physician-assistant/
Florida International University Herbert Wertheim College of Medicine	Miami	FL	https://medicine.fiu.edu/academics/degrees-and-programs/master-in-physician-studies/index.html
Miami Dade College	Miami	FL	http://www.mdc.edu/physicianassistantas/
AdventHealth University	Orlando	FL	https://www.ahu.edu/academics/ms-physician-assistant
South University, West Palm Beach	Royal Palm Beach	FL	https://www.southuniversity.edu/west-palm-beach/physician-assistant-ms
Gannon University - Ruskin	Ruskin	FL	https://www.gannon.edu/academic-offerings/health-professions-and-sciences/graduate/master-of-physician-assistant-science/admission-requirements/
Florida State University	Tallahassee	FL	https://med.fsu.edu/index.cfm?page=pa.home
South University, Tampa	Tampa	FL	http://www.southuniversity.edu/tampa/areas-of-study/physician-assistant/physician-assistant-master-of-science-ms
University of South Florida	Tampa	FL	https://health.usf.edu/medicine/pa/
University of Tampa	Tampa	FL	https://www.ut.edu/graduate-degrees/physician-assistant-medicine-program
Emory University	Atlanta	GA	http://med.emory.edu/pa/
Mercer University	Atlanta	GA	http://chp.mercer.edu/academics-departments/physician-assistant-studies/
Morehouse School of Medicine	Atlanta	GA	http://www.msm.edu//physicianassistantprogram/index.php

PA Schools	City	State	Website
South College - Atlanta	Atlanta	GA	https://www.south.edu/programs/master-health-science-physician-assistant-studies/atlanta/
Augusta University	Augusta	GA	https://www.augusta.edu/alliedhealth/pa/
Brenau University	Gainesville	GA	https://www.brenau.edu/healthsciences/physician-assistant-studies/
South University, Savannah	Savannah	GA	https://www.southuniversity.edu/savannah/areas-of-study/physician-assistant/physician-assistant-master-of-science-ms
PCOM - Georgia	Suwanee	GA	https://www.pcom.edu/academics/programs-and-degrees/physician-assistant-studies/georgia.html
University of Washington - MEDEX Northwest, Kona	Kealakekua	HI	https://depts.washington.edu/medex/pa-program/
St. Ambrose University	Davenport	IA	http://www.sau.edu/master-of-physician-assistant-studies
Des Moines University	Des Moines	IA	https://www.dmu.edu/pa/
University of Dubuque	Dubuque	IA	http://www.dbq.edu/Academics/OfficeofAcademicAffairs/GraduatePrograms/MasterofScienceinPhysician-AssistantStudies/
University of Iowa	Iowa City	IA	http://www.medicine.uiowa.edu/pa/
Northwestern College	Orange City	IA	https://www.nwciowa.edu/graduate/physician-assistant
Idaho State University - Caldwell	Caldwell	ID	https://www.isu.edu/pa/
Idaho State University - Meridian	Meridian	ID	https://www.isu.edu/pa/
Idaho State University - Pocatello	Meridian	ID	https://www.isu.edu/pa/
Southern Illinois University	Carbondale	IL	https://www.siumed.edu/paprogram

PA Schools	City	State	Website
Northwestern University	Chicago	IL	http://www.feinberg.northwestern.edu/sites/pa/
Rush University	Chicago	IL	http://www.rushu.rush.edu/pa-program
Midwestern University - Downers Grove	Downers Grove	IL	https://www.midwestern.edu/admissions/apply/master-of-medical-sciences-in-physician-assistant-studies-in-downers-grove.xml
Rosalind Franklin University of Medicine	North Chicago	IL	https://www.rosalindfranklin.edu/academics/college-of-health-professions/degree-programs/physician-assistant-practice-ms/
Dominican University of Illinois	River Forest	IL	https://www.dom.edu/admission/graduate/health-sciences-programs/mmspas
Trine University	Angola	IN	http://www.trine.edu/academics/majors-and-minors/graduate/master-physician-assistant-studies/index.aspx
University of Evansville	Evansville	IN	https://www.evansville.edu/majors/physicianassistant/
University of Saint Francis	Fort Wayne	IN	http://pa.sf.edu/
Franklin College	Franklin	IN	https://franklincollege.edu/academics/graduate-programs/master-science-physician-assistant/
Butler University	Indianapolis	IN	http://www.butler.edu/physician-assistant/
Indiana University School of Health and Human Sciences	Indianapolis	IN	https://shhs.iupui.edu/admissions/graduate-professional/master-physician-assistant-studies.html
Indiana State University	Terre Haute	IN	https://www.indstate.edu/health/program/pa
Valparaiso University	Valparaiso	IN	https://www.valpo.edu/physician-assistant-program/programs/admission/

PA Schools	City	State	Website
Wichita State University	Wichita	KS	http://www.wichita.edu/thisis/home/?u=pa
University of Kentucky - Lexington	Lexington	KY	http://www.uky.edu/chs/academic-programs/physician-assistant-studies
Sullivan University	Louisville	KY	https://www.sullivan.edu/programs/master-of-science-in-physician-assistant
University of Kentucky - Morehead	Morehead	KY	https://www.uky.edu/chs/academic-programs/physician-assistant-studies
University of the Cumberlands	Williamsburg	KY	http://gradweb.ucumberlands.edu/medicine/mpas/overview
University of the Cumberlands, Northern Kentucky Campus	Williamsburg	KY	https://www.ucumberlands.edu/academics/graduate/programs/master-science-physician-assistant-studies
Franciscan Missionaries of Our Lady University	Baton Rouge	LA	https://www.franu.edu/academics/academic-programs/physician-assistant-studies
Lousiana State University - New Orleans	New Orleans	LA	http://alliedhealth.lsuhsc.edu/pa/
Xavier University of Louisiana	New Orleans	LA	https://www.xula.edu/physician-assistant-program-about
Louisiana State University Health Sciences Center Shreveport	Shreveport	LA	https://lsuhscshreveportedu.finalsite.com/departments/allied-health-professions-departments/physician-assistant
Boston University School of Medicine	Boston	MA	http://bu.edu/paprogram
MCPHS - Boston	Boston	MA	https://www.mcphs.edu/academics/school-of-physician-assistant-studies/physician-assistant/physician-assistant-studies-mpas

PA Schools	City	State	Website
MGH Institute of Health Professions	Boston	MA	http://www.mghihp.edu/academics/school-of-health-and-rehabilitation-sciences/physician-assistant-studies/default.aspx
Northeastern University	Boston	MA	https://bouve.northeastern.edu/physician-assistant/ms/
Tufts University	Boston	MA	https://medicine.tufts.edu/education/physician-assistant
Bay Path University	East Longmeadow	MA	https://www.baypath.edu/academics/graduate-programs/physician-assistant-studies-ms/
Springfield College	Springfield	MA	https://springfield.edu/programs/physician-assistant-studies
Westfield State University	Westfield	MA	https://www.westfield.ma.edu/academics/master-of-science-in-physician-assistant-studies/
MCPHS - Worcester	Worcester	MA	https://www.mcphs.edu/academics/school-of-physician-assistant-studies/physician-assistant/physican-assistant-studies-mpas-accelerated
University of Maryland Baltimore/Ann Arundel Community College	Arnold	MD	https://graduate.umaryland.edu/mshs-pa-umb/
Towson University CCBC - Essex	Baltimore	MD	https://www.towson.edu/chp/departments/health-sciences/grad/physician-assistant/
Frostburg State University	Hagerstown	MD	https://www.frostburg.edu/academics/majorminors/graduate/ms-physician-assistant/index.php
University of Maryland Eastern Shore	Princess Anne	MD	http://www.umes.edu/pa
University of New England	Portland	ME	http://www.une.edu/wchp/pa

PA Schools	City	State	Website
Concordia University Ann Arbor	Ann Arbor	MI	https://www.cuaa.edu/academics/programs/physician-assistant-masters/index.html#overview
University of Detroit Mercy	Detroit	MI	http://healthprofessions.udmercy.edu/academics/pa/grad.php
Wayne State Unversity	Detroit	MI	http://www.pa.cphs.wayne.edu/
University of Michigan - Flint	Flint	MI	https://www.umflint.edu/physician-assistant-ms/
Grand Valley State University - Grand Rapids	Grand Rapids	MI	http://www.gvsu.edu/pas
Western Michigan University	Kalamazoo	MI	http://www.wmich.edu/pa
Central Michigan University	Mount Pleasant	MI	https://www.cmich.edu/colleges/CHP/hp_academics/srms/physician_assistant/Pages/PA-Program-at-CMU.aspx
Grand Valley State University - Traverse City	Traverse City	MI	https://www.gvsu.edu/pas/traverse-city-campus-89.htm
Eastern Michigan University	Ypsilanti	MI	http://www.emich.edu/pa
College of St. Scholastica	Duluth	MN	http://www.css.edu/graduate/masters-doctoral-and-professional-programs/areas-of-study/ms-physician-assistant.html
Augsburg University	Minneapolis	MN	http://www.augsburg.edu/pa/
Mayo Clinic School of Health Sciences	Rochester	MN	https://college.mayo.edu/academics/health-sciences-education/physician-assistant-program-minnesota/
Saint Catherine University	Saint Paul	MN	https://www.stkate.edu/academic-programs/gc/physician-assistant-studies-mpas

PA Schools	City	State	Website
Bethel University	St. Paul	MN	https://www.bethel.edu/graduate/academics/physician-assistant/
Stephens College	Columbia	MO	https://www.stephens.edu/academics/graduate-programs/master-in-physician-assistant-studies/
University of Missouri-Kansas City	Kansas City	MO	http://med.umkc.edu/pa/
Saint Louis University	Saint Louis	MO	https://www.slu.edu/doisy/degrees/graduate/physician-assistant-mms.php
Missouri State University	Springfield	MO	http://www.missouristate.edu/pas
Mississippi College	Clinton	MS	http://www.mc.edu/academics/departments/pa/
Mississippi State University - Meridian	Meridian	MS	https://www.meridian.msstate.edu/academics/physician-assistant/
Rocky Mountain College	Billings	MT	http://pa.rocky.edu/
Gardner-Webb University	Boiling Springs	NC	https://gardner-webb.edu/academic-programs-and-resources/colleges-and-schools/health-sciences/schools-and-departments/physician-assistant-studies/index
Wake Forest University - Boone	Boone	NC	http://www.wakehealth.edu/Physician-Assistant-Program/
Campbell University	Buies Creek	NC	https://cphs.campbell.edu/academic-programs/physician-assistant/master-physician-assistant-practice/
UNC-Chapel Hill	Chapel Hill	NC	http://www.med.unc.edu/ahs/unc-pa
Duke University	Durham	NC	http://pa.duke.edu/
Elon University	Elon	NC	https://www.elon.edu/u/academics/health-sciences/physician-assistant/
Methodist University	Fayetteville	NC	http://www.methodist.edu/paprogram
East Carolina University	Greenville	NC	http://www.ecu.edu/pa

PA Schools	City	State	Website
Wingate University - Hendersonville	Hendersonville	NC	https://www.wingate.edu/academics/hendersonville/physician-assistant
High Point University	High Point	NC	http://www.highpoint.edu/physicianassistant/
Pfeiffer University	Misenheimer	NC	https://www.pfeiffer.edu/mspas
Wingate University	Wingate	NC	http://pa.wingate.edu/
Wake Forest University - Winston Salem	Winston-Salem	NC	http://www.wakehealth.edu/Physician-Assistant-Program/
University of North Dakota	Grand Forks	ND	http://med.und.edu/physician-assistant/index.cfm
University of Nebraska Medical Center - Kearney	Kearney	NE	https://www.unmc.edu/alliedhealth/education/pa/
Union College	Lincoln	NE	http://www.ucollege.edu/pa
College of Saint Mary	Omaha	NE	http://www.csm.edu/academics/health-human-services/master-science-degree-physician-assistant-studies
Creighton University	Omaha	NE	https://medschool.creighton.edu/program/physician-assistant-mpas
University of Nebraska Medical Center - Omaha	Omaha	NE	https://www.unmc.edu/alliedhealth/education/pa/
MCPHS - Manchester	Manchester	NH	https://www.mcphs.edu/academics/school-of-physician-assistant-studies/physician-assistant/physican-assistant-studies-mpas-accelerated
Franklin Pierce University	West Lebanon	NH	http://www.franklinpierce.edu/academics/gradstudies/programs_of_study/mpas/index.htm
Saint Elizabeth University	Morristown	NJ	https://cse.smartcatalogiq.com/en/2019-2020/academic-catalog/academic-programs/physician-assistant/ms-in-physician-assistant

PA Schools	City	State	Website
Seton Hall University	Nutley	NJ	https://www.shu.edu/academics/ms-physician-assistant.cfm
Kean University	Union	NJ	https://www.kean.edu/academics/programs/physician-assistant-studies-ms
Thomas Jefferson University - New Jersey	Voorhees	NJ	https://www.jefferson.edu/university/health-professions/departments/physician-assistant-studies/degrees-programs/graduate/ms-new-jersery.html
Monmouth University	West Long Branch	NJ	https://www.monmouth.edu/graduate/ms-physician-assistant/
Rutgers University	West Piscataway	NJ	https://shp.rutgers.edu/physician-assistant/master-of-science-physician-assistant-program/
University of New Mexico	Albuquerque	NM	http://goto.unm.edu/pa
University of St. Francis	Albuquerque	NM	http://www.stfrancis.edu/academics/physician-assistant-studies
Touro University Nevada	Henderson	NV	https://tun.touro.edu/programs/physician-assistant-studies/
University of Nevada, Reno	Reno	NV	https://med.unr.edu/physician-assistant
Albany Medical College	Albany	NY	https://www.amc.edu/academic/PhysicianAssistant/index.cfm
Daemen College	Amherst	NY	https://www.daemen.edu/academics/areas-study/physician-assistant/physician-assistant-studies-ms
Mercy College	Bronx	NY	https://www.mercy.edu/degrees-programs/ms-physician-assistant

PA Schools	City	State	Website
Long Island University	Brooklyn	NY	https://www.liu.edu/ Brooklyn/Academics/ Schools/School-of-Health-Professions/Dept/Physician-Assistant/MS-PAS
SUNY Downstate Medical Center	Brooklyn	NY	https://sls.downstate.edu/ admissions/chrp/pa/index. html
Canisius College	Buffalo	NY	https://www.canisius.edu/ academics/programs/ physician-assistant
D'Youville College	Buffalo	NY	http://www.dyc.edu/ academics/pa/
Touro College - Long Island	Central Islip	NY	https://shs.touro.edu/ programs/physician-assistant/physician-assistant-long-island/
Touro College - NUMC	East Meadow	NY	https://shs.touro.edu/ programs/physician-assistant/physician-assistant-long-island/
Hofstra University	Hempstead	NY	https://www.hofstra. edu/academics/colleges/ nursing-physician-assistant/ physician-assistant/
Ithaca College	Ithaca	NY	https://www.ithaca. edu/academics/school-health-sciences-and-human-performance/ graduate-programs/ physician-assistant-studies
CUNY York College	Jamaica	NY	http://www.york.cuny.edu/ academics/departments/ health-professions/ physician-assistant
Pace University - Lenox Hill Hospital, NYC	New York	NY	http://www.pace.edu/ college-health-professions/ explore-programs/physician-assistant-program
The CUNY School of Medicine	New York	NY	https://www.ccny.cuny.edu/ csom/
Touro College Manhattan	New York	NY	https://shs.touro.edu/ programs/physician-assistant/physician-assistant-manhattan/

PA Schools	City	State	Website
Weil Cornell Graduate School of Medical Sciences	New York	NY	https://gradschool.weill.cornell.edu/programs/health-sciences-physician-assistants
Yeshiva University, Katz School of Science and Health	New York	NY	https://www.yu.edu/katz/programs/graduate/physician-assistant
New York Institute of Technology	Old Westbury	NY	http://www.nyit.edu/pa
Pace University - Pleasantville	Pleasantville	NY	https://www.pace.edu/college-health-professions/graduate-degree-programs/physician-assistant-program-pleasantville
Clarkson University	Potsdam	NY	http://www.clarkson.edu/pa
Marist College	Poughkeepsie	NY	http://www.marist.edu/science/physassist/
St. John's University	Queens	NY	https://www.stjohns.edu/academics/programs/physician-assistant-master-science
Rochester Institute of Technology	Rochester	NY	http://www.rit.edu/healthsciences/graduate-programs/physician-assistant
Stony Brook University Southhampton	Southampton	NY	https://healthtechnology.stonybrookmedicine.edu/programs/pa/elpa
St. Bonaventure University	St. Bonaventure	NY	https://www.sbu.edu/academics/physician-assistant-studies
Wagner College	Staten Island	NY	http://wagner.edu/physician-assistant/
Stony Brook University Health Science Center	Stony Brook	NY	https://healthtechnology.stonybrookmedicine.edu/programs/pa/elpa
Le Moyne College	Syracuse	NY	https://www.lemoyne.edu/pa
SUNY Upstate Medical Center	Syracuse	NY	http://www.upstate.edu/chp/programs/pa/index.php
University of Mount Union	Alliance	OH	https://www.mountunion.edu/physician-assistant-studies

PA Schools	City	State	Website
Ashland University	Ashland	OH	https://www.ashland.edu/conhs/majors/master-science-physician-assistant-studies
Baldwin Wallace University	Berea	OH	https://www.bw.edu/graduate/physician-assistant/
Mount St. Joseph University	Cincinnati	OH	http://www.msj.edu/PA
Case Western Reserve University	Cleveland	OH	http://case.edu/medicine/physician-assistant/
Ohio Dominican University	Columbus	OH	http://www.ohiodominican.edu/academics/graduate/physician-assistant-program
University of Dayton	Dayton	OH	https://udayton.edu/education/departments_and_programs/pa/index.php
Ohio University	Dublin	OH	https://www.ohio.edu/chsp/rcs/pa/
University of Findlay	Findlay	OH	https://www.findlay.edu/healthprofessions/physicianassistant-ma/
Kettering College	Kettering	OH	http://kc.edu/academics/physician-assistant/
Marietta College	Marietta	OH	https://www.marietta.edu/pa-program
Lake Erie College	Painesville	OH	http://www.lec.edu/pa
Mercy College of Ohio	Toledo	OH	https://mercycollege.edu/academics/programs/graduate/physician-assistant-studies
University of Toledo	Toledo	OH	http://www.utoledo.edu/med/grad/pa/
Northeastern State University	Muskogee	OK	https://academics.nsuok.edu/healthprofessions/Degree-Programs/Graduate/Physician-Assistant-Studie
Oklahoma City University	Oklahoma City	OK	https://www.okcu.edu/physician-assistant/home
University of Oklahoma - Oklahoma City	Oklahoma City	OK	https://medicine.ouhsc.edu/Prospective-Students/Degree-Programs/Physician-Associate-Program

PA Schools	City	State	Website
Oklahoma State University Center for Health Sciences	Tulsa	OK	https://medicine.okstate.edu/pa/index.html
University of Oklahoma - Tulsa	Tulsa	OK	http://www.ou.edu/tulsa/community_medicine/scm-pa-program
Pacific University	Hillsboro	OR	http://www.pacificu.edu/pa
George Fox University	Newberg	OR	https://www.georgefox.edu/pa/index.html
Oregon Health & Science University	Portland	OR	https://www.ohsu.edu/school-of-medicine/physician-assistant
DeSales University	Center Valley	PA	https://www.desales.edu/academics/graduate-studies/master-of-science-in-physician-assistant-studies-(mspas)
Misericordia University	Dallas	PA	https://www.misericordia.edu/page.cfm?p=655
Salus University	Elkins Park	PA	http://www.salus.edu/Colleges/Health-Sciences/Physician-Assistant.aspx
Gannon University - Erie, PA	Erie	PA	http://www.gannon.edu/academic-departments/physician-assistant-department/
Mercyhurst University	Erie	PA	https://www.mercyhurst.edu/academics/physician-assistant-studies-program
Arcadia University	Glenside	PA	https://www.arcadia.edu/academics/programs/physician-assistant
Seton Hill University	Greensburg	PA	https://www.setonhill.edu/academics/graduate-programs/physician-assistant-ms/
Thiel College	Greenville	PA	https://www.thiel.edu/graduate-degrees/physician-assistant
Penn State University	Hershey	PA	https://med.psu.edu/physician-assistant
Lock Haven University	Lock Haven	PA	https://paportal.lhup.edu/PA/

PA Schools	City	State	Website
Saint Francis University	Loretto	PA	https://www.francis.edu/Physician-Assistant-Science/
Drexel University	Philadelphia	PA	http://drexel.edu/cnhp/academics/departments/Physician-Assistant/
Philadelphia College of Osteopathic Medicine (PCOM)	Philadelphia	PA	https://www.pcom.edu/academics/programs-and-degrees/physician-assistant-studies/
Temple University Lewis Katz School of Medicine	Philadelphia	PA	https://medicine.temple.edu/education/physician-assistant-program
Thomas Jefferson University - City Center	Philadelphia	PA	https://www.jefferson.edu/university/health-professions/departments/physician-assistant-studies/degrees-programs/graduate/ms-center-city.html
Thomas Jefferson University - East Falls	Philadelphia	PA	https://www.jefferson.edu/university/health-professions/departments/physician-assistant-studies/degrees-programs/graduate/ms-east-falls/applying.html
University of the Sciences	Philadelphia	PA	https://www.usciences.edu/samson-college-of-health-sciences/physician-assistant-studies/index.html
Chatham University	Pittsburgh	PA	http://www.chatham.edu/mpas/
Duquesne University	Pittsburgh	PA	http://www.duq.edu/academics/schools/health-sciences/academic-programs/physician-assistant
University of Pittsburgh	Pittsburgh	PA	https://www.shrs.pitt.edu/PAProgram
Marywood University	Scranton	PA	http://www.marywood.edu/pa-program
Slippery Rock University	Slippery Rock	PA	http://www.sru.edu/academics/graduate-programs/physician-assistant-studies-master-of-science

PA Schools	City	State	Website
West Chester University	West Chester	PA	https://www.wcupa.edu/healthSciences/physicianAssistant/default.aspx?gclid=EAIaIQobCh-MInYy7kYO36wIVAeWzCh-2qzAkbEAAYASAAEgItF-vD_BwE
King's College	Wilkes-Barre	PA	https://www.kings.edu/academics/undergraduate_majors/physicianassistant
Pennsylvania College of Technology	Williamsport	PA	https://www.pct.edu/academics/nhs/physician-assistant/physician-assistant-studies
San Juan Bautista School of Medicine	Caguas	PR	https://www.sanjuanbautista.edu/education/programs/pa-program.html
Johnson & Wales University	Providence	RI	http://www.jwu.edu/PA
Bryant University	Smithfield	RI	http://gradschool.bryant.edu/health-sciences.htm
Charleston Southern University	Charleston	SC	http://www.csuniv.edu/pa
Medical University of South Carolina	Charleston	SC	https://education.musc.edu/students/enrollment/bulletin/colleges-and-degrees/health-professions/ms-in-physician-assistant
Presbyterian College	Clinton	SC	https://www.presby.edu/academics/graduate-professional/physician-assistant-program/
University of South Carolina SOM	Columbia	SC	http://www.southalabama.edu/alliedhealth/pa
North Greenville University	Greer	SC	http://www.ngu.edu/pa-medicine.php
University of South Dakota	Vemillion	SD	http://www.usd.edu/pa
Lincoln Memorial University	Harrogate	TN	https://www.lmunet.edu/school-of-medical-sciences/pa-harrogate/index.php

PA Schools	City	State	Website
Lincoln Memorial University - Knoxville	Knoxville	TN	https://www.lmunet.edu/school-of-medical-sciences/pa-knoxville/index.php
South College - Knoxville	Knoxville	TN	https://www.south.edu/programs/master-health-science-physician-assistant-studies/knoxville/
Christian Brothers University	Memphis	TN	https://www.cbu.edu/pa
University of Tennessee Health Science Center	Memphis	TN	http://www.uthsc.edu/allied/pa
Milligan University	Milligan	TN	http://www.milligan.edu/pa
Lipscomb University	Nashville	TN	https://www.lipscomb.edu
South College - Nashville	Nashville	TN	https://www.south.edu/programs/master-health-science-physician-assistant-studies/nashville/
Trevecca Nazarene University	Nashville	TN	https://www.trevecca.edu/programs/physician-assistant
Bethel University (TN)	Paris	TN	https://www.bethelu.edu/academics/degrees-and-programs/physician-assistant-studies
Hardin-Simmons University	Abilene	TX	https://www.hsutx.edu/pa
University of Mary Hardin-Baylor	Belton	TX	https://go.umhb.edu/graduate/physician-assistant/home
University of Texas Southwestern Medical Center	Dallas	TX	http://www.utsouthwestern.edu/pa
University of Texas Rio Grande Valley	Edinburgh	TX	https://www.utrgv.edu/pa/
U.S. Army Medical Center of Excellence IPAP	Fort Sam Houston	TX	https://medcoe.army.mil/ipap
University of North Texas HS Center Fort Worth	Fort Worth	TX	https://www.unthsc.edu/school-of-health-professions/physician-assistant-studies/

PA Schools	City	State	Website
University of Texas Medical Branch at Galveston	Galveston	TX	http://shp.utmb.edu/PhysicianAssistantStudies/
Baylor College of Medicine	Houston	TX	https://www.bcm.edu/education/school-of-health-professions/physician-assistant-program
University of Texas Health Science Center - Laredo	Laredo	TX	https://www.uthscsa.edu/academics/health-professions/programs/physician-assistant-studies-ms/laredo-pa-extension-program
Texas Tech University Health Sciences Center	Midland	TX	https://www.ttuhsc.edu/health-professions/master-physician-assistant-studies/
University of Texas Health Science Center - San Antonio	San Antonio	TX	http://www.uthscsa.edu/shp/pa/
University of Utah	Salt Lake City	UT	https://medicine.utah.edu/dfpm/physician-assistant-studies/program/
Rocky Mountain University of Health Professions	South Provo	UT	https://rm.edu/academics/master-of-physician-assistant-studies/
South University, Richmond	Glen Allen	VA	https://www.southuniversity.edu/richmond/physician-assistant-ms
James Madison University	Harrisonburg	VA	http://www.healthsci.jmu.edu/PA/
Shenandoah University - Loudoun	Leesburg	VA	https://www.su.edu/physician-assistant/masters-of-science-in-physician-assistant-studies/
University of Lynchburg	Lynchburg	VA	http://www.lynchburg.edu/graduate/physician-assistant-medicine/
Emory & Henry College	Marion	VA	http://www.ehc.edu/academics/programs/school-health-sciences/shs-programs/school-health-sciences-graduate-programs/physician-assistant-pa/

PA Schools	City	State	Website
Eastern Virginia Medical School (early assurance, too)	Norfolk	VA	http://www.evms.edu/education/masters_programs/physician_assistant_program/
Mary Baldwin University	Roanoke	VA	https://go.marybaldwin.edu/health_sciences/pas/
Radford University Carilion	Roanoke	VA	https://www.radford.edu/content/grad/home/academics/graduate-programs/pa.html
Shenandoah Universityn - Winchester	Winchester	VA	https://www.su.edu/physician-assistant/masters-of-science-in-physician-assistant-studies/
University of Washington - MEDEX Northwest, Seattle	Seattle	WA	https://depts.washington.edu/medex/pa-program/
University of Washington - MEDEX Northwest, Spokane	Spokane	WA	https://depts.washington.edu/medex/pa-program/
University of Washington - MEDEX Northwest, Tacoma	Tacoma	WA	https://depts.washington.edu/medex/pa-program/
University of Wisconsin - La Crosse	La Crosse	WI	https://www.uwlax.edu/grad/physician-assistant-studies/
University of Wisconsin-Madison	Madison	WI	https://www.med.wisc.edu/education/physician-assistant-pa-program/
Concordia University - Wisconsin	Mequon	WI	https://www.cuw.edu/academics/programs/physician-assistant-masters/
Marquette University	Milwaukee	WI	http://www.marquette.edu/physician-assistant
Caroll University	Waukesha	WI	http://www.carrollu.edu/gradprograms/physasst/admission.asp
University of Charleston	Charleston	WV	http://www.ucwv.edu/pa/
Marshall University Joan C. Edwards School of Medicine	Huntington	WV	https://jcesom.marshall.edu/students/physician-assistant-program/
West Virginia University	Morgantown	WV	https://medicine.hsc.wvu.edu/physician-assistant-studies/

PA Schools	City	State	Website
Alderson-Broaddus University	Philippi	WV	http://ab.edu/academics/master-of-science-in-physician-assistant-studies/
West Liberty University	West Liberty	WV	http://www.westliberty.edu/physician-assistant/

CHAPTER 14

PHARMACY SCHOOLS BY CITY/STATE

Pharmacy Schools	City	State	Website
Auburn University Harrison School of Pharmacy	Auburn	AL	https://pharmacy.auburn.edu/
Samford University McWhorter School of Pharmacy	Birmingham	AL	https://www.samford.edu/pharmacy/
University of Arkansas for Medical Sciences College of Pharmacy	Little Rock	AR	https://pharmacy.uams.edu/
Harding University College of Pharmacy	Searcy	AR	https://www.harding.edu/academics/colleges-departments/pharmacy
Midwestern University College of Pharmacy-Glendale	Glendale	AZ	https://www.midwestern.edu/academics/our-colleges/college-of-pharmacy%E2%80%93glendale.xml
University of Arizona College of Pharmacy	Tucson	AZ	https://www.pharmacy.arizona.edu/
Keck Graduate Institute (KGI) School of Pharmacy and Health Sciences	Claremont	CA	https://www.kgi.edu/academics/school-of-pharmacy-and-health-sciences/overview/
California Health Sciences University College of Pharmacy	Clovis	CA	https://pharmacy.chsu.edu/
California Northstate University College of Pharmacy	Elk Grove	CA	https://pharmacy.cnsu.edu/
Marshall B. Ketchum University College of Pharmacy	Fullerton	CA	https://www.ketchum.edu/pharmacy
Chapman University School of Pharmacy	Irvine	CA	https://www.chapman.edu/pharmacy/index.aspx
University of California, San Diego Skaggs School of Pharmacy & Pharmaceutical Sciences	La Jolla	CA	https://pharmacy.ucsd.edu/
Loma Linda University School of Pharmacy	Loma Linda	CA	https://pharmacy.llu.edu/
West Coast University School of Pharmacy	Los Angeles	CA	https://westcoastuniversity.edu/programs/doctor-pharmacy.html
University of Southern California School of Pharmacy	Los Angeles	CA	https://pharmacyschool.usc.edu/
Western University of Health Sciences College of Pharmacy	Pomona	CA	https://www.westernu.edu/pharmacy/
University of California, San Francisco School of Pharmacy	San Francisco	CA	https://pharmacy.ucsf.edu/

Pharmacy Schools	City	State	Website
American University of Health Sciences School of Pharmacy	Signal Hill	CA	https://www.auhs.edu/academics/pharmacy/
University of the Pacific Thomas J. Long School of Pharmacy	Stockton	CA	https://www.pacific.edu/academics/schools-and-colleges/thomas-j-long-school-of-pharmacy.html
Touro University - California College of Pharmacy	Vallejo	CA	http://cop.tu.edu/
University of Colorado Anschutz Medical Campus Skaggs School of Pharmacy and Pharmaceutical Sciences	Aurora	CO	http://www.ucdenver.edu/academics/colleges/pharmacy/Pages/SchoolofPharmacy.aspx
Regis University Rueckert-Hartman College for Health Professions School of Pharmacy	Denver	CO	https://www.regis.edu/academics/colleges-and-schools/rueckert-hartman/pharmacy/index
University of Connecticut School of Pharmacy	Storrs	CT	https://pharmacy.uconn.edu/
University of Saint Joseph School of Pharmacy and Physician Assistant Studies	West Hartford	CT	https://www.usj.edu/academics/academic-schools/sppas/
Howard University College of Pharmacy	Washington	DC	http://pharmacy.howard.edu/
Nova Southeastern University College of Pharmacy	Fort Lauderdale	FL	https://pharmacy.nova.edu/index.html
University of Florida College of Pharmacy	Gainesville	FL	https://pharmacy.ufl.edu/
Larkin University College of Pharmacy	Miami	FL	https://ularkin.org/pharmacy/
Florida Agricultural & Mechanical University College of Pharmacy and Pharmaceutical Sciences	Tallahassee	FL	https://pharmacy.famu.edu/
University of South Florida Health Taneja College of Pharmacy	Tampa	FL	https://health.usf.edu/pharmacy
Palm Beach Atlantic University Lloyd L. Gregory School of Pharmacy	West Palm Beach	FL	https://www.pba.edu/academics/schools/gregory-pharmacy/index.html
University of Georgia College of Pharmacy	Athens	GA	https://rx.uga.edu/
Mercer University College of Pharmacy	Atlanta	GA	https://pharmacy.mercer.edu/

Pharmacy Schools	City	State	Website
South University School of Pharmacy	Savannah	GA	https://www.southuniversity.edu/degree-programs/pharmacy
Philadelphia College of Osteopathic Medicine - Georgia School of Pharmacy	Suwanee	GA	https://www.pcom.edu/academics/programs-and-degrees/doctor-of-pharmacy/
University of Hawaii at Hilo Daniel K. Inouye College of Pharmacy	Hilo	HI	https://pharmacy.uhh.hawaii.edu/
Drake University College of Pharmacy and Health Sciences	Des Moines	IA	https://www.drake.edu/cphs/
University of Iowa College of Pharmacy	Iowa City	IA	https://pharmacy.uiowa.edu/
Idaho State University College of Pharmacy	Pocatello	ID	https://www.isu.edu/pharmacy/
University of Illinois at Chicago College of Pharmacy	Chicago	IL	https://pharmacy.uic.edu/
Chicago State University College of Pharmacy	Chicago	IL	https://www.csu.edu/collegeofpharmacy/
Southern Illinois University Edwardsville School of Pharmacy	Edwardsville	IL	https://www.siue.edu/pharmacy/
Midwestern University Chicago College of Pharmacy	Downer's Grove	IL	https://www.midwestern.edu/academics/degrees-and-programs/doctor-of-pharmacy-il.xml
Rosalind Franklin University of Medicine and Science College of Pharmacy	North Chicago	IL	https://www.rosalindfranklin.edu/academics/college-of-pharmacy/
Roosevelt University College of Pharmacy	Schaumburg	IL	https://www.roosevelt.edu/colleges/pharmacy
Butler University College of Pharmacy and Health Sciences	Indianapolis	IN	https://www.butler.edu/cophs
Manchester University College of Pharmacy, Natural and Health Sciences	North Manchester	IN	https://www.manchester.edu/academics/colleges/college-of-pharmacy-natural-health-sciences
Purdue University College of Pharmacy	West Lafayette	IN	https://www.pharmacy.purdue.edu/
University of Kansas School of Pharmacy	Lawrence	KS	https://pharmacy.ku.edu/

Pharmacy Schools	City	State	Website
University of Kentucky College of Pharmacy	Lexington	KY	https://pharmacy.uky.edu/
Sullivan University College of Pharmacy	Louisville	KY	https://www.sullivan.edu/colleges/college-of-pharmacy-and-health-sciences
University of Louisiana at Monroe College of Pharmacy	Monroe	LA	https://www.ulm.edu/pharmacy/
Xavier University of Louisiana College of Pharmacy	New Orleans	LA	https://www.xula.edu/collegeofpharmacy
MCPHS University School of Pharmacy - Boston	Boston	MA	https://www.mcphs.edu/
Northeastern University Bouvé College of Health Sciences School of Pharmacy	Boston	MA	https://bouve.northeastern.edu/pharmacy/
Western New England University College of Pharmacy	Springfield	MA	https://www1.wne.edu/pharmacy-and-health-sciences/
MCPHS University School of Pharmacy - Worcester	Worcester	MA	https://www.mcphs.edu/
University of Maryland School of Pharmacy	Baltimore	MD	https://www.pharmacy.umaryland.edu/
Notre Dame of Maryland University School of Pharmacy	Baltimore	MD	https://www.ndm.edu/colleges-schools/school-pharmacy
University of Maryland Eastern Shore School of Pharmacy and Health Professions	Princess Anne	MD	https://www.umes.edu/pharmacy/
Husson University School of Pharmacy	Bangor	ME	https://www.husson.edu/pharmacy/
University of New England College of Pharmacy	Portland	ME	https://www.une.edu/pharmacy
University of Michigan College of Pharmacy	Ann Arbor	MI	https://pharmacy.umich.edu/
Ferris State University College of Pharmacy	Big Rapids	MI	https://www.ferris.edu/pharmacy/
Wayne State University Eugene Applebaum College of Pharmacy and Health Sciences	Detroit	MI	https://cphs.wayne.edu/
University of Minnesota College of Pharmacy	Duluth	MN	https://www.pharmacy.umn.edu/
University of Missouri-Kansas City School of Pharmacy	Kansas City	MO	https://pharmacy.umkc.edu/

Pharmacy Schools	City	State	Website
St. Louis College of Pharmacy	St. Louis	MO	https://www.uhsp.edu/
William Carey University School of Pharmacy	Biloxi	MS	https://www.wmcarey.edu/School/Pharmacy
University of Mississippi School of Pharmacy	University	MS	https://pharmacy.olemiss.edu/
University of Montana College of Health Professions and Biomedical Sciences Skaggs School of Pharmacy	Missoula	MT	http://health.umt.edu/pharmacy/
Campbell University College of Pharmacy and Health Sciences	Buies Creek	NC	https://cphs.campbell.edu/
University of North Carolina Eshelman School of Pharmacy	Chapel Hill	NC	https://pharmacy.unc.edu/
High Point University Fred Wilson School of Pharmacy	High Point	NC	http://www.highpoint.edu/pharmacy/
Wingate University School of Pharmacy	Wingate	NC	https://www.wingate.edu/academics/graduate/pharmacy
North Dakota State University College of Health Professions School of Pharmacy	Fargo	ND	https://www.ndsu.edu/pharmacy/
University of Nebraska Medical Center College of Pharmacy	Omaha	NE	https://www.unmc.edu/pharmacy/
Creighton University School of Pharmacy and Health Professions	Omaha	NE	https://spahp.creighton.edu/
Fairleigh Dickinson University School of Pharmacy	Florham Park	NJ	https://view2.fdu.edu/academics/pharmacy/
Rutgers, the State University of New Jersey Ernest Mario School of Pharmacy	Piscataway	NJ	https://pharmacy.rutgers.edu/
University of New Mexico College of Pharmacy	Albuquerque	NM	https://hsc.unm.edu/college-of-pharmacy/
Roseman University of Health Sciences College of Pharmacy	Henderson	NV	https://pharmacy.roseman.edu/
Albany College of Pharmacy and Health Sciences School of Pharmacy and Pharmaceutical Sciences	Albany	NY	https://www.acphs.edu/
Long Island University Arnold and Marie Schwartz College of Pharmacy and Health Sciences	Brooklyn	NY	https://liu.edu/Pharmacy

Pharmacy Schools	City	State	Website
D'Youville College School of Pharmacy	Buffalo	NY	http://www.dyc.edu/academics/schools-and-departments/pharmacy/
University at Buffalo The State University of New York School of Pharmacy & Pharmaceutical Sciences	Buffalo	NY	http://pharmacy.buffalo.edu/
Binghamton University State University of New York School of Pharmacy and Pharmaceutical Sciences	Johnson City	NY	https://www.binghamton.edu/pharmacy-and-pharmaceutical-sciences/
Touro New York College of Pharmacy	New York	NY	https://tcop.touro.edu/
University of California, Irvine*	Irvine	CA	https://pharmsci.uci.edu/pharm-d/
St. John's University College of Pharmacy and Health Sciences	Queens	NY	https://www.stjohns.edu/academics/programs/doctor-pharmacy
St. John Fisher College Wegmans School of Pharmacy	Rochester	NY	https://www.sjfc.edu/schools/school-of-pharmacy/
Ohio Northern University Raabe College of Pharmacy	Ada	OH	https://www.onu.edu/college-pharmacy
Cedarville University School of Pharmacy	Cedarville	OH	https://www.cedarville.edu/Academic-Schools-and-Departments/Pharmacy.aspx
University of Cincinnati James L. Winkle College of Pharmacy	Cincinnati	OH	https://pharmacy.uc.edu/
Ohio State University College of Pharmacy	Columbus	OH	https://pharmacy.osu.edu/
University of Findlay College of Pharmacy	Findlay	OH	https://www.findlay.edu/pharmacy/
Northeast Ohio Medical University College of Pharmacy	Rootstown	OH	https://www.neomed.edu/pharmacy/
University of Toledo College of Pharmacy and Pharmaceutical Sciences	Toledo	OH	https://www.utoledo.edu/pharmacy/
University of Oklahoma College of Pharmacy	Oklahoma City	OK	https://pharmacy.ouhsc.edu/
Southwestern Oklahoma State University College of Pharmacy	Weatherford	OK	https://www.swosu.edu/academics/pharmacy/index.aspx

Pharmacy Schools	City	State	Website
Oregon State University College of Pharmacy	Corvallis	OR	https://pharmacy.oregonstate.edu/
Pacific University School of Pharmacy	Hillsboro	OR	https://www.pacificu.edu/academics/colleges/college-health-professions/school-pharmacy
Lake Erie College of Osteopathic Medicine School of Pharmacy	Erie	PA	https://lecom.edu/academics/school-of-pharmacy/
Temple University School of Pharmacy	Philadelphia	PA	https://pharmacy.temple.edu/
Thomas Jefferson University Jefferson College of Pharmacy	Philadelphia	PA	https://www.jefferson.edu/university/pharmacy.html
University of the Sciences Philadelphia College of Pharmacy	Philadelphia	PA	https://www.usciences.edu/philadelphia-college-of-pharmacy/
Duquesne University School of Pharmacy	Pittsburgh	PA	https://www.duq.edu/academics/schools/pharmacy
University of Pittsburgh School of Pharmacy	Pittsburgh	PA	https://www.pharmacy.pitt.edu/
Wilkes University Nesbitt School of Pharmacy	Wilkes-Barre	PA	https://www.wilkes.edu/academics/colleges/nesbitt-school-of-pharmacy/index.aspx
University of Puerto Rico Medical Sciences Campus School of Pharmacy	San Juan	PR	https://farmacia.rcm.upr.edu/academic-programs/doctor-of-pharmacy-program/
University of Rhode Island College of Pharmacy	Kingston	RI	https://web.uri.edu/pharmacy/
Medical University of South Carolina College of Pharmacy	Charleston	SC	https://pharmacy.musc.edu/
Presbyterian College School of Pharmacy	Clinton	SC	https://pharmacy.presby.edu/
University of South Carolina College of Pharmacy	Columbia	SC	https://www.sc.edu/study/colleges_schools/pharmacy/index.php
South Dakota State University College of Pharmacy and Allied Health Professions	Brookings	SD	https://www.sdstate.edu/pharmacy-allied-health-professions
Union University College of Pharmacy	Jackson	TN	https://www.uu.edu/programs/pharmacy/

Pharmacy Schools	City	State	Website
East Tennessee State University Bill Gatton College of Pharmacy	Johnson City	TN	https://www.etsu.edu/pharmacy/
South College School of Pharmacy	Knoxville	TN	https://www.south.edu/programs/doctor-pharmacy/
University of Tennessee Health Science Center College of Pharmacy	Memphis	TN	https://www.uthsc.edu/pharmacy/
Lipscomb University College of Pharmacy and Health Sciences	Nashville	TN	https://www.lipscomb.edu/pharmacy
Belmont University College of Pharmacy	Nashville	TN	http://www.belmont.edu/pharmacy/index.html
University of Texas at Austin College of Pharmacy	Austin	TX	https://pharmacy.utexas.edu/
University of Texas at El Paso School of Pharmacy	El Paso	TX	https://www.utep.edu/pharmacy/
University of North Texas Health Science Center UNT System College of Pharmacy	Fort Worth	TX	https://www.unthsc.edu/college-of-pharmacy/
University of Houston College of Pharmacy	Houston	TX	https://www.uh.edu/pharmacy/
Texas Southern University College of Pharmacy and Health Sciences	Houston	TX	http://www.tsu.edu/academics/colleges-and-schools/college-of-pharmacy-and-health-sciences/
Texas A & M University Health Science Center Irma Lerma Rangel College of Pharmacy	Kingsville	TX	https://pharmacy.tamu.edu/
Texas Tech University Health Sciences Center Jerry H. Hodge School of Pharmacy	Lubbock	TX	https://www.ttuhsc.edu/pharmacy/default.aspx
University of the Incarnate Word Feik School of Pharmacy	San Antonio	TX	https://pharmacy.uiw.edu/
University of Texas at Tyler Ben and Maytee Fisch College of Pharmacy	Tyler	TX	https://www.uttyler.edu/pharmacy/
University of Utah College of Pharmacy	Salt Lake City	UT	https://pharmacy.utah.edu/
Hampton University School of Pharmacy	Hampton	VA	http://wp.hamptonu.edu/pharmacy/
Appalachian College of Pharmacy	Oakwood	VA	https://www.acp.edu/

Pharmacy Schools	City	State	Website
Virginia Commonwealth University at the Medical College of Virginia Campus School of Pharmacy	Richmond	VA	https://pharmacy.vcu.edu/
Shenandoah University Bernard J. Dunn School of Pharmacy	Winchester	VA	https://www.su.edu/pharmacy/
University of Washington School of Pharmacy	Seattle	WA	https://sop.washington.edu/
Washington State University College of Pharmacy and Pharmaceutical Sciences	Spokane	WA	https://pharmacy.wsu.edu/
University of Wisconsin-Madison School of Pharmacy	Madison	WI	https://pharmacy.wisc.edu/
Concordia University Wisconsin School of Pharmacy	Mequon	WI	https://www.cuw.edu/academics/schools/pharmacy/index.html
Medical College of Wisconsin School of Pharmacy	Milwaukee	WI	https://www.mcw.edu/education/pharmacy-school
University of Charleston School of Pharmacy	Charleston	WV	https://www.ucwv.edu/academics/schools/school-of-pharmacy/
Marshall University School of Pharmacy	Huntington	WV	https://www.marshall.edu/pharmacy/
West Virginia University School of Pharmacy	Morgantown	WV	https://pharmacy.wvu.edu/
University of Wyoming School of Pharmacy	Laramie	WY	http://www.uwyo.edu/pharmacy/

CHAPTER 15

VETERINARY MEDICAL SCHOOLS BY CITY/STATE

Vet Schools	City	State	Website
Auburn University College of Veterinary Medicine	Auburn	AL	https://www.vetmed.auburn.edu/
Tuskegee University School of Veterinary Medicine	Tuskegee	AL	https://www.tuskegee.edu/programs-courses/colleges-schools/cvm
Midwestern University College of Veterinary Medicine	Glendale	AZ	https://www.midwestern.edu/academics/our-colleges/college-of-veterinary-medicine.xml
University of Arizona College of Veterinary Medicine	Oro Valley	AZ	https://vetmed.arizona.edu/
University of California, Davis School of Veterinary Medicine	Davis	CA	https://www.vetmed.ucdavis.edu/
Western University of Health Sciences College of Veterinary Medicine	Pomona	CA	https://www.westernu.edu/veterinary/
Colorado State University College of Veterinary Medicine and Biomedical Sciences	Fort Collins	CO	https://vetmedbiosci.colostate.edu/dvm/
University of Florida College of Veterinary Medicine	Gainesville	FL	https://education.vetmed.ufl.edu/
University of Georgia College of Veterinary Medicine	Athens	GA	https://vet.uga.edu/
Iowa State University College of Veterinary Medicine	Ames	IA	https://vetmed.iastate.edu/
University of Illinois College of Veterinary Medicine	Urbana	IL	https://vetmed.illinois.edu/
Purdue University College of Veterinary Medicine	West Lafayette	IN	https://www.purdue.edu/vet/
Kansas State University College of Veterinary Medicine	Manhattan	KS	https://www.vet.k-state.edu/
Louisiana State University School of Veterinary Medicine	Baton Rouge	LA	https://www.lsu.edu/vetmed/
Tufts University School of Veterinary Medicine	North Grafton	MA	https://vet.tufts.edu/
Michigan State University College of Veterinary Medicine	East Lansing	MI	https://cvm.msu.edu/
University of Minnesota College of Veterinary Medicine	St. Paul	MN	https://vetmed.umn.edu/
University of Missouri - Columbia College of Veterinary Medicine	Columbia	MO	https://cvm.missouri.edu/

Vet Schools	City	State	Website
Mississippi State University College of Veterinary Medicine	Mississippi State	MS	https://www.vetmed.msstate.edu/
North Carolina State University College of Veterinary Medicine	Raleigh	NC	https://cvm.ncsu.edu/
Cornell University College of Veterinary Medicine	Ithica	NY	https://www.vet.cornell.edu/
Long Island University School of Veterinary Medicine	Brookville	NY	https://liu.edu/vetmed
Ohio State University College of Veterinary Medicine	Columbus	OH	https://vet.osu.edu/
Oklahoma State University College of Veterinary Medicine	Stillwater	OK	https://vetmed.okstate.edu/
Oregon State University College of Veterinary Medicine	Corvallis	OR	https://vetmed.oregonstate.edu/
University of Pennsylvania School of Veterinary Medicine	Philadelphia	PA	https://www.vet.upenn.edu/
Lincoln Memorial University College of Veterinary Medicine	Harrogate	TN	https://www.lmunet.edu/college-of-veterinary-medicine/index.php
University of Tennessee College of Veterinary Medicine	Knoxville	TN	https://vetmed.tennessee.edu/
Texas A&M University College of Veterinary Medicine & Biomedical Sciences	College Station	TX	https://vetmed.tamu.edu/
Texas Tech University School of Veterinary Medicine	Amarillo	TX	https://www.depts.ttu.edu/vetschool/
Virginia Tech Virginia-Maryland College of Veterinary Medicine	Blacksburg	VA	http://www.vetmed.vt.edu/
Washington State University College of Veterinary Medicine	Pullman	WA	https://www.vetmed.wsu.edu/
University of Wisconsin-Madison School of Veterinary Medicine	Madison	WI	https://www.vetmed.wisc.edu/

COMPREHENSIVE HEALTH CARE SERIES

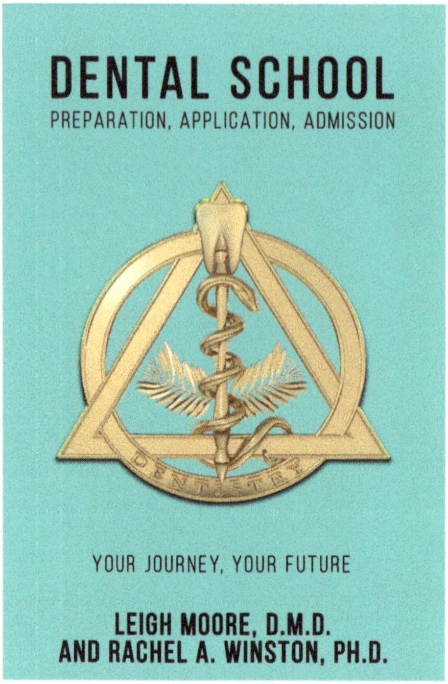

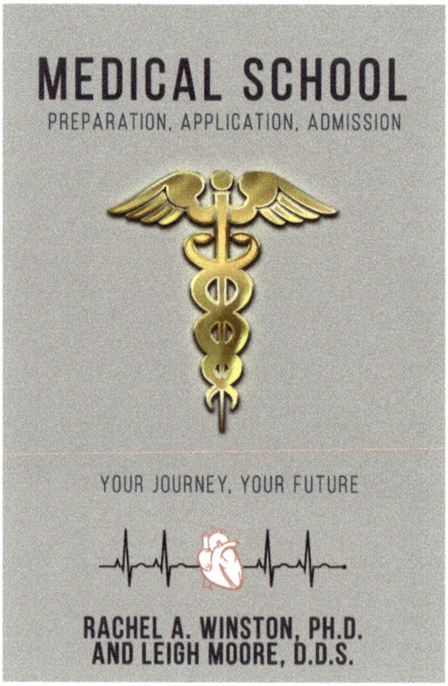

DENTAL SCHOOL
PREPARATION, APPLICATION, ADMISSION

YOUR JOURNEY, YOUR FUTURE

**LEIGH MOORE, D.M.D.
AND RACHEL A. WINSTON, PH.D.**

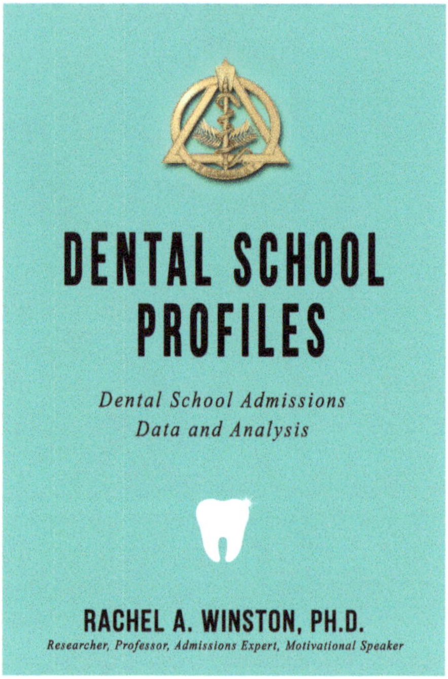

DENTAL SCHOOL PROFILES

*Dental School Admissions
Data and Analysis*

RACHEL A. WINSTON, PH.D.
Researcher, Professor, Admissions Expert, Motivational Speaker

MEDICAL SCHOOL
PREPARATION, APPLICATION, ADMISSION

YOUR JOURNEY, YOUR FUTURE

**RACHEL A. WINSTON, PH.D.
AND LEIGH MOORE, D.D.S.**

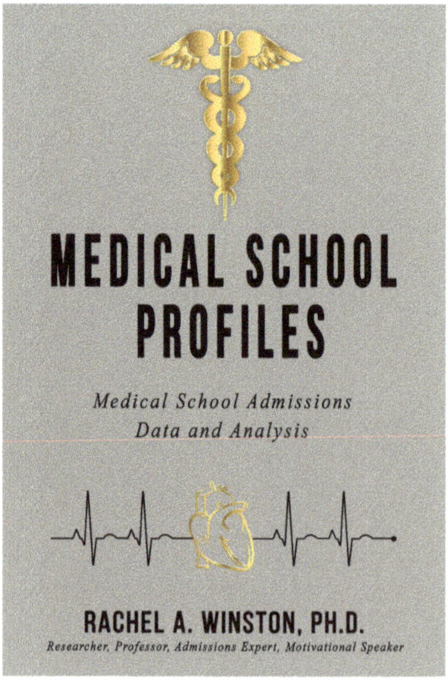

MEDICAL SCHOOL PROFILES

*Medical School Admissions
Data and Analysis*

RACHEL A. WINSTON, PH.D.
Researcher, Professor, Admissions Expert, Motivational Speaker

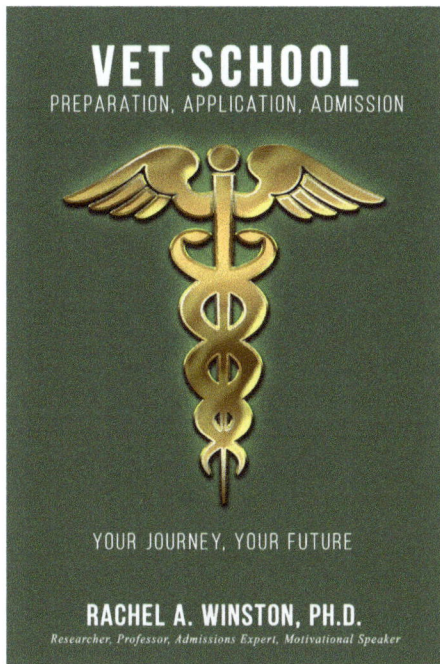

VET SCHOOL
PREPARATION, APPLICATION, ADMISSION

YOUR JOURNEY, YOUR FUTURE

RACHEL A. WINSTON, PH.D.
Researcher, Professor, Admissions Expert, Motivational Speaker

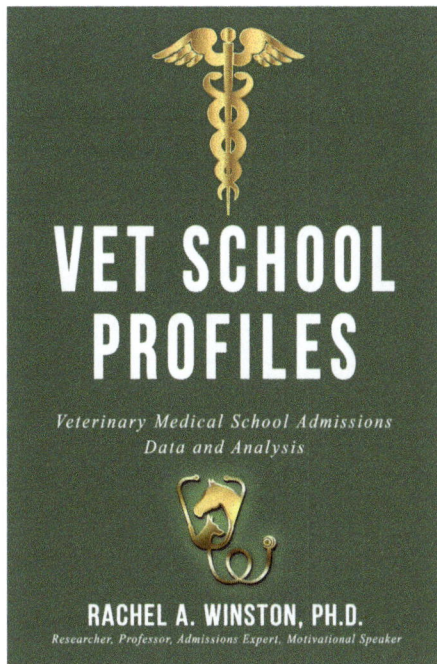

VET SCHOOL PROFILES

Veterinary Medical School Admissions Data and Analysis

RACHEL A. WINSTON, PH.D.
Researcher, Professor, Admissions Expert, Motivational Speaker

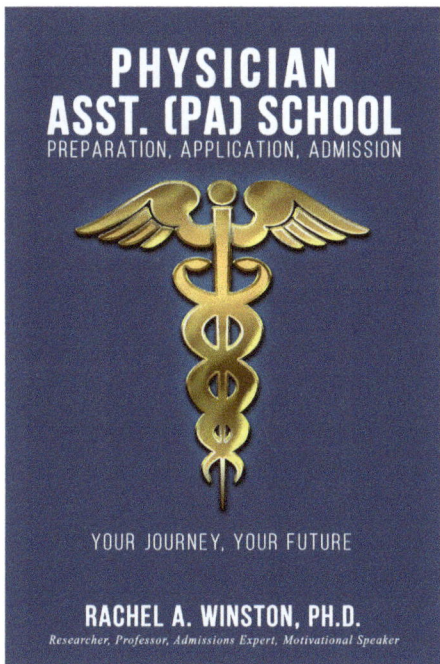

PHYSICIAN ASST. (PA) SCHOOL
PREPARATION, APPLICATION, ADMISSION

YOUR JOURNEY, YOUR FUTURE

RACHEL A. WINSTON, PH.D.
Researcher, Professor, Admissions Expert, Motivational Speaker

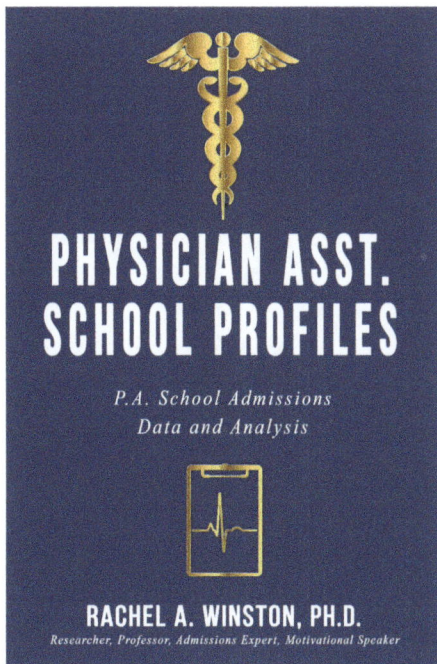

PHYSICIAN ASST. SCHOOL PROFILES

P.A. School Admissions Data and Analysis

RACHEL A. WINSTON, PH.D.
Researcher, Professor, Admissions Expert, Motivational Speaker

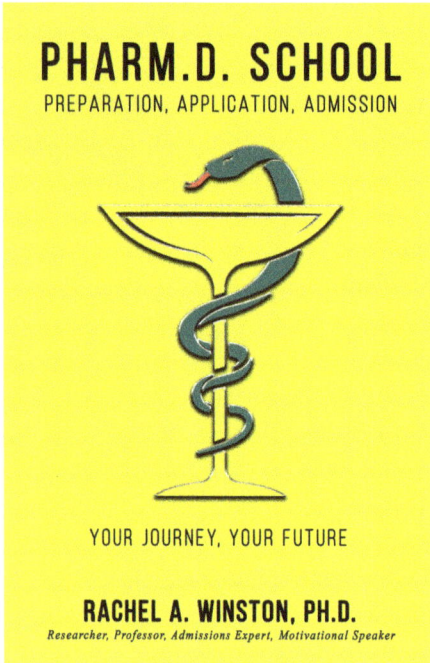

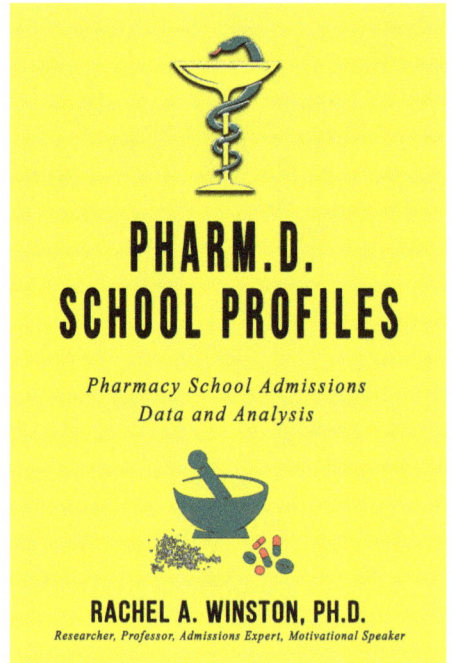

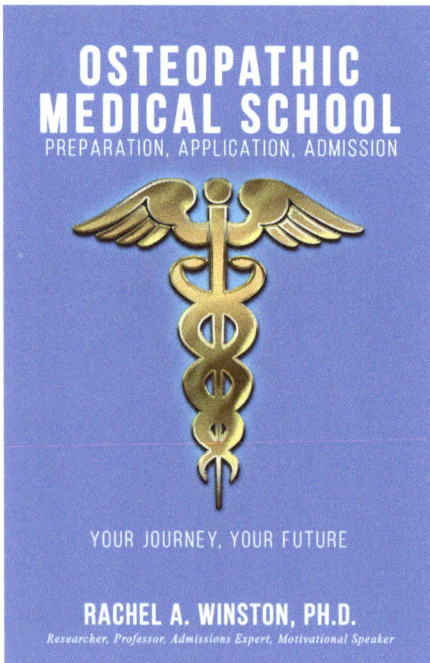

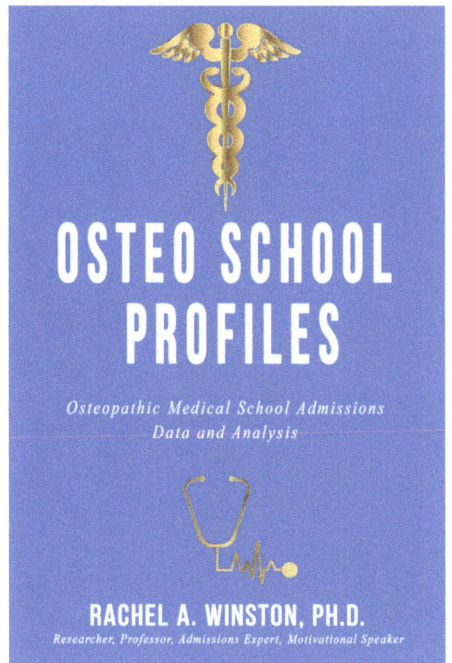

This comprehensive healthcare series is designed in full color to aid the growing number of applicants seeking clear, comprehensive materials. As a college admissions expert and former UCLA College Counseling Certificate Program faculty member, Dr. Winston is dedicated to helping students obtain the information they need.

FOR MORE INFORMATION

bsmdguide.com
medschoolexpert.com

Purchase books at Lizard-publishing.com

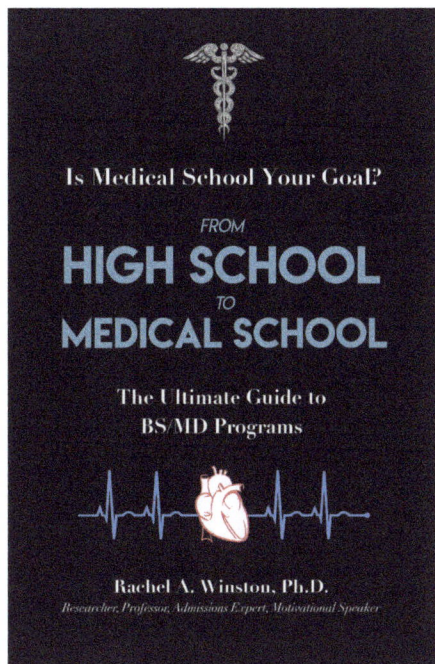

Is Medical School Your Goal?

FROM

HIGH SCHOOL
TO
MEDICAL SCHOOL

The Ultimate Guide to
BS/MD Programs

Rachel A. Winston, Ph.D.
Researcher, Professor, Admissions Expert, Motivational Speaker

SERVICES OFFERED BY LIZARD EDUCATION:

- College Counseling
- Admissions News/Resources
- Essay Support and Editing
- Interview Preparation
- Road Trips to Visit Colleges
- Career Planning/Majors/Resumes
- BS/MD, BS/DO, BS/JD, BS/DDS
- Medical School
- Graduate School (Masters & Doctorate)
- Film Studio and Editing

- Portfolio Assistance/SlideRoom
- Athletics Recruiting/Highlight Films
- International Admissions/Visa/TOEFL
- Financial Aid and Scholarships
- UCs, Ivy Leagues, and Colleges Nationwide
- Book Publishing
- Engineering, Robotics, STEM
- Art Portfolios

Email: collegeguide@yahoo.com
Website: collegelizard.com

LIZARD

INDEX

www.ingramcontent.com/pod-product-compliance
Lightning Source LLC
Chambersburg PA
CBHW052018030426

42335CB00026B/3185